D1707781

PARIS DREA

PARIS DREAMING

What the City of Light taught me about life, love & lipstick

KATRINA LAWRENCE

HarperCollins*Publishers*

Lines from *Sabrina* included with kind permission of Paramount Pictures.

HarperCollins*Publishers*

First published in Australia in 2017
by HarperCollins*Publishers* Australia Pty Limited
ABN 36 009 913 517
harpercollins.com.au

HarperCollins*Publishers*
Level 13, 201 Elizabeth Street, Sydney NSW 2000, Australia
Unit D1, 63 Apollo Drive, Rosedale, Auckland 0632, New Zealand
A 53, Sector 57, Noida, UP, India
1 London Bridge Street, London SE1 9GF, United Kingdom
2 Bloor Street East, 20th floor, Toronto, Ontario M4W 1A8, Canada
195 Broadway, New York NY 10007, USA

National Library of Australia Cataloguing-in-Publication data:

Creator: Lawrence, Katrina, author.
Title: Paris dreaming / Katrina Lawrence.
ISBN: 978 1 4607 5360 6 (hardback)
ISBN: 978 1 4607 0808 8 (ebook)
Notes: Includes bibliographical references.
Subjects: Paris (France) – Description and travel.
Paris (France) – Guidebooks.

Cover and internal design by Hazel Lam, HarperCollins Design Studio
Cover and internal illustrations © Clementine Campardou 2017
All other images by shutterstock.com
Author photo © Carla Coulson
Typeset in Adobe Garamond Pro by Kirby Jones
Printed and bound in Australia by McPhersons Printing Group
The papers used by HarperCollins in the manufacture of this book are a natural, recyclable product made from wood grown in sustainable plantation forests. The fibre source and manufacturing processes meet recognised international environmental standards, and carry certification.

To my parents,
for giving me the world,
but especially Paris.

And to my husband and sons,
for sharing the journey.

Paris isn't for changing planes … It's … It's for changing your outlook.
For throwing open the windows and letting in …
letting in la vie en rose.

Sabrina Fairchild (played by Audrey Hepburn), *Sabrina*

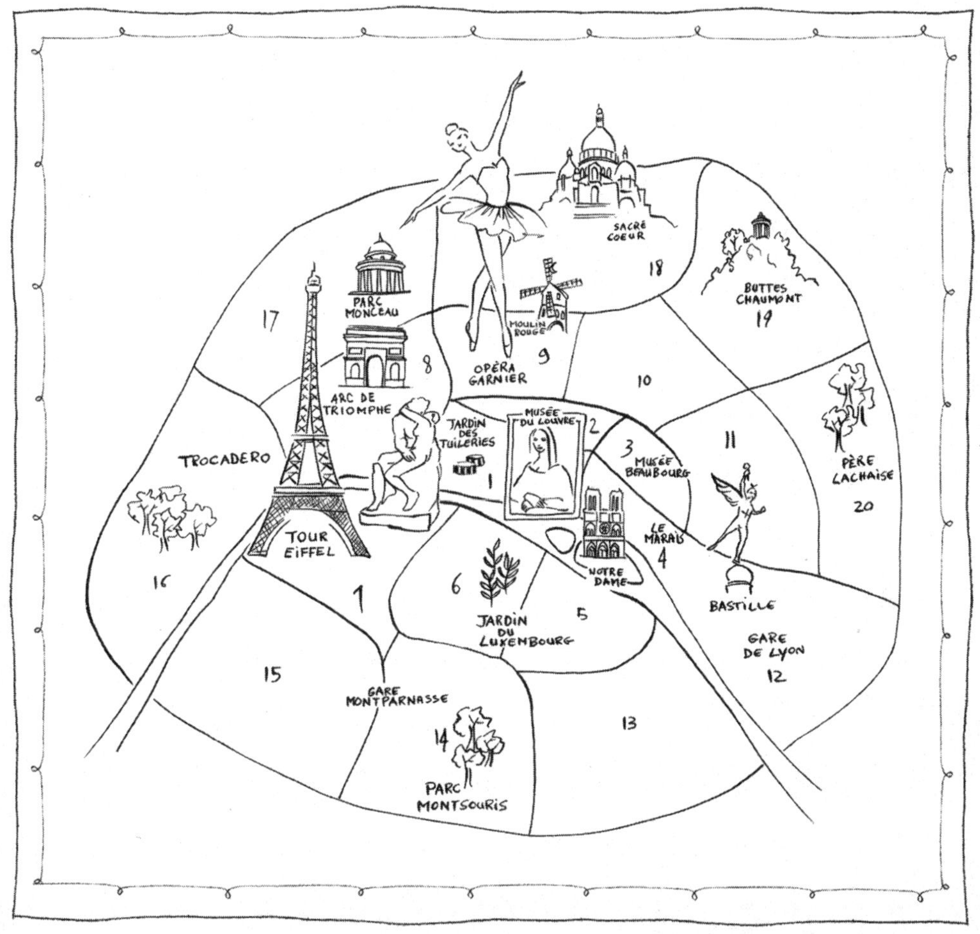

CONTENTS

The author, aged five, in Paris. (*Brian Lawrence*)

PROLOGUE

PARISIENNE

[paʀizjɛn] *nf* girl or woman of Paris

Have you ever gone somewhere for the first time, yet felt like you've been there before? And had the notion not so much that a place belongs to you, but rather you belong to it? You turn a corner into a street on which you've never, ever set foot, but suddenly you feel more at home, more at ease, than you do anywhere else in the world.

The expression déjà vu — literally: 'already seen' — was coined by a French parapsychologist in the late nineteenth century, and many figured it was proof of past life until psychoanalyst Sigmund Freud came along and put it all down to repressed desires. Déjà vu is usually a fleeting sensation, a quick flick of the sixth-sense switch that makes your skin tingle and sets off a faint ringing of *Twilight Zone*-esque music in your mind.

I was twenty-one and studying in Paris for a few months when I experienced a different type of déjà vu. I came across a cobbled lane that took me through a kind of portal, into a parallel universe where this city suddenly, wonderfully felt like home. I wish I could say that I looked down at those cobblestones to see, perched upon them, a dainty duo of mint satin slippers adorned with diamond buckles, rather than my scuffed pair of chunky cherry Doc Martens. *Hélas*, I can't confess to glittering visions of a past life as a seventeenth-century *comtesse*. But there was most definitely a sense that I had somehow lived this place before, or was meant to live it. It wasn't an ephemeral or eerie feeling, more a heightened awareness and appreciation of this beautiful city. Perhaps Freud was right. I just really, desperately wanted to fulfil the fantasy of being a Parisienne.

I walked and walked that entire day, led not by a map but a more intuitive navigation system. I ended up on the hill of Montmartre, standing in front of the beacon that is the church of Sacré-Coeur, its cream Roman–Byzantine domes made from stone that whitens with time. I looked over the City of Light spread before me, its luminous limestone buildings and its whimsically slanted zinc roofs glinting in the setting sunshine. It was winter, yet Paris was basking in the glow of the magic hour, that brilliant time of day when the sun bursts forth for one last hurrah and soaks everything beneath it in syrupy gold.

And that's when I experienced what was to become a common occurrence: what I call my Paris Syndrome. I find myself so overwhelmed by the city around me, I actually have to shut my eyes to it. Its dazzling beauty is literally blinding. My breath catches and my heart palpitates to the point where I am physically light-headed. Impressionist painter Claude Monet had the perfect description for his beloved city, '*cet étourdissant Paris*'. Giddy-fying. I know just what he meant.

I've always been a sucker for beautiful things. I did become a beauty editor, after all, and admiring aesthetics is a prerequisite of the job. My work has taken me many times to Paris, the undisputed global beauty capital — the city of light-reflecting foundation and lipstick.

I mean, of course, Paris and beauty: they just go together. Like a stripy top and a baguette, Serge Gainsbourg and Jane Birkin, Nutella and crêpes. The beauty industry could only blossom in a city that truly, madly, deeply appreciates beautiful things. How could perfumers not concoct the world's most delicious *parfums* when their nostrils are continually tempted by the city's culinary delights or markets piled high with peonies and roses? How could makeup artists and hair stylists not be inspired to create works of art when they can just pop into the Louvre for some classic inspiration?

Curiously, I haven't yet got around to actually living in my spiritual home. Truth is, I cherish Paris as my getaway plan. Some people retreat to a health spa to recharge their physical and emotional batteries. I take myself to Paris to reset my spirits and renew my sense of purpose in life.

Paris, a place that is as much myth as reality, is indeed a city for the world's dreamers, for yearning outsiders who inhabit the city in their hearts, and blur their own idealised vision of Paris with the real thing, looking longingly at it through a rose-tinted filter. And there's nothing wrong with that: Parisian is a state of mind as much as place. Every woman has an inner Parisienne just waiting to wiggle out: how else to explain the shelves heaving with books on the secrets of dressing the Parisian part?

'I think it's all a big hoax,' scoffs a friend of mine, a former Parisienne who lives down the road from me in Bondi Beach. 'Sure, I guess Parisian women by and large dress elegantly, but in a really simple and sometimes boring way.'

I once asked her what I tend to incredulously ask every Parisian who has moved to Australia: 'But why?' Her answer was along the lines of all the others: 'I feel a freedom here that I didn't in France.'

The grass is always greener, as they say … which is even an expression in French. Although, I must note, the manicured lawns of Paris are literally greener than the sundried gardens of Australia.

'No, seriously,' my expatriate friend insisted. 'I couldn't even pour my own wine at a dinner party. I had to wait for a man to do it. I mean, that's just ludicrous. You might wish to be Parisian. I am so happy I'm now Australian.'

The French, I've found, largely see Australia as an enviably casual and carefree place. They have been conditioned by centuries of etiquette, while non-Indigenous Australians have come from all corners of the globe, in a relatively short period of time, and social traditions are still in flux. We are young and free, as the song goes.

Australia was settled by the British in 1788, the year before the French Revolution began — a violent, blood-soaked time when France fought to forge a new identity as the land of liberty, equality and fraternity. To the French, Australia must have seemed like a blank slate, a fresh start.

Australia was actually almost French. Back in the eighteenth century, the French referred to the unknown expanse of land down south, partially mapped by the Dutch, as France Australe (Southern France) and set their sights and sails upon making that dream a reality. Enter Louis-Antoine de Bougainville who, in 1766, cast off on his frigate, *La Boudeuse* (which means 'sulky girl', a curious choice of name for a ship about to lug a crew of gnarly men across treacherous seas). On a stop in Rio de Janeiro, the expedition's botanist delighted at the colourful flowering vine there, and did his career no harm by naming it after his commander.

Soon came a fun-filled stay in Tahiti, where the French sailors were ecstatic to find an island paradise of sensuous — and decidedly non-sulky — women. After they (most reluctantly) set off, it became apparent that the crew might have partied a little too hard. So Bougainville searched for land that could provide fresh food, clean water and recuperative powers. At one point, he was close — fruit and wood were spotted floating past — but he decided against the riskiness of crossing the coral reef. Instead Bougainville spun north, leaving what was the east coast of France Australe free for a certain James Cook to chart and claim two years later.

For Australian lovers of all things French, the 'what if?' is almost too much to bear. So that's why every time I see bougainvillea, I sigh a little.

I can't help my Francophilia: it's partly genetic. Family lore has it that a leaf on a distant branch of my mum's genealogical tree bears the name Marcel Proust, the legendary author of the epic French novel *In Search of Lost Time*. One of the *beau monde* of the Belle Époque — the so-called 'Beautiful Era' of turn-of-the-twentieth-century Paris — Proust was considered a dandy dilettante who did nothing but eat chilled melon at the Ritz at midnight while hanging onto every fabulous word of his fashionable artist and courtesan friends. But there was much more to Marcel than met the eye. When not indulging in a whirl of wining and dining, he could be found bunkered down in his cork-lined cocoon of a bedroom on Boulevard Haussmann, scribbling his spidery thoughts into notebooks into the wee hours. With a nature that was surely on the obsessive-compulsive side of things, Marcel was driven by an urge to record and reflect on the Parisian world as he experienced and remembered it; to freeze a too-fleeting life through the act of writing. And so, seemingly out of the blue came this brick of a book, spanning seven volumes and 3000 pages.

In these days of sound bites and Snapchat, *In Search* seems rather impenetrable. I'm ashamed to say that I'm still only wading through volume two. But its relevance, for me, lies in the madeleine scene — a madeleine being the classic shell-shaped teacake that's perfect for accompanying a pot of petal-infused tisane. In the first volume, *Swann's Way*, the narrator nibbles on such a cake. The taste and scent trigger a gush of memory, sending him in a sensorial time capsule to his childhood, when he and his aunt would snack together. This leads to more memories still … pages and pages of them.

When you see the term 'Proustian' in a fragrance article, this is what the writer is referring to: how a certain smell can unexpectedly hurtle you back in time to past events and emotions. Science has shown us the mechanics behind this meshing of scent and sentiment: odour molecules waft to the back of the nasal cavity, prompting receptor cells to shoot a nerve impulse to the brain's olfactory bulb, which is situated in the limbic system, and it's here where we also experience emotion and emotional recall.

For example, whenever I smell roasted chestnuts, I'm five again, skipping through the sparkling Christmas markets of Paris.

I've lost count of the number of times I've been to Paris. I used to wonder why I was so magnetically drawn to this city. Was there a deeper reason than the sheer prettiness? What was the plotline beneath the picture-perfect scenery? While strolling along the boulevards or swanning by the Seine, was I starring in my own personal romantic comedy, where I'd bump into the *homme* of my dreams? Or did Paris hold the key to understanding how to grow as a person, as a *femme*? Because this, after all, is a city that has been deeply infused with the spirit of so many of history's most strong, sagacious, seductive women.

'Paris est si *beau*!' my teenage self once proclaimed to a taxi driver, as we turned a corner to see the Eiffel Tower suddenly loom into view.

'Paris est *belle*!' he corrected me. 'Paris est *une femme*.'

I've since found out that Paris is actually historically and grammatically masculine. But, like Monsieur Taxi Driver, I refuse to believe it. All you need to do is look around you in Paris to know that this city can only be a woman. Witness the frilly balconies giving otherwise classic façades a seductive, curvy caress; the street lights as elaborate as vintage drop earrings; the statues of barely dressed nymphs that play peek-a-boo throughout the city's parks. Even the Eiffel Tower, with its cold hard construction of black iron and bolts, appears lithe and lacy from afar, like a fishnet-clad leg kicking up to the sky.

Heck, the men too have feminine flair in Paris, thinking nothing of throwing a mint jumper over a baby-pink shirt, dining under a ceiling frescoed with chubby cupids who dance around roses, or sipping champagne out of delicately etched crystal flutes.

This city, so embracing of the feminine, is naturally welcoming to women — and make that women of all ages. I never feel old in Paris. Perhaps that's one reason Paris never gets old for me.

When the road of life takes me back to Paris, it has often been when I've felt like I'm at some kind of a dead-end, or fork in the journey. I'm attempting to complete a chapter that has gone on too long, hoping to turn a page and begin a new phase, yet I'm unable to find the right words. And then I get lost in Paris's streets once more, recalibrate my inner compass, and eventually find my new life direction.

Paris has guided me through my girlhood and trying teenage times. She has taken me from *mademoiselle* to *madame*, helped me embrace the ageing process, and taught me the true meaning of beauty. I have grown up in this city. From *fille* to *femme.*

CHAPTER 1

FILLETTE

[fijɛt] *nf* (little) girl

In which, at a young age, I learn the values of *liberté, égalité ... fémininité.*

Parisians scurried past us on a rain-glossed Avenue des Champs-Élysées, hunkered down in thick woollen coats and nestled beneath berets, their layers of grey and beige echoing the hues of their mid-winter city. 'Smile,' pleaded Dad, his camera poised as I shivered in pose by a shop window. We seemed to be the only tourists around that day, as the world rushed by, and in a way time did come to a standstill, because the moment Dad was about to capture on film would soon take pride of place in our family's gallery of iconography — those photos and paintings that capture the spirit of a clan, that tell its story to descendants.

I'm the first to admit I have a tendency to read too much into a situation, to search for signs and symbols that probably aren't there, but over the years that photo came to acquire near-mythic status to me. When I look at the five-year-old girl I was that day, I see a head that's shyly tilted down, yet eyes looking up with hope. As I'm standing at the intersection of hesitation and confidence, if I can take an analogy that far, the background seems somehow allegorical: for starters, there's the grand ascending avenue, suggesting life's journey to come, and there seems to be the promise of a happy ending, in the form of that glorious icon of Paris that is the Arc de Triomphe de l'Étoile.

The city's triumphal arches were inspired by Ancient Rome, when such monuments commemorated victory in battle, and as such ignited pride and patriotism. My dad had another theory as to their power: surely such majesty literally lying at the end of the road encourages a city's people to aim high?

Not much that my dad does is spontaneous. He's methodical and considered almost to a fault. So I've sometimes wondered if he art-directed that day's photo well ahead of time, as a kind of visualisation of his hopes and dreams for his only child. He was certainly chuffed enough with his artistic efforts to enlarge, frame and hang that photo in several places, including his office. 'Oh, it's the little Parisienne,' his colleagues would invariably exclaim on meeting me in person. At the time, I didn't really know what it signified to be à la parisienne, but I certainly liked the sound of it.

Most of my first Parisian memories faded, but enough remained suspended in a shimmering blur — like my souvenir snowdome, with its frenzy of glitter swirling around a miniature Notre-Dame and Eiffel Tower. For a girl living in the hazy humdrum of 1970s suburban Melbourne, Paris was a scintillating parallel universe, the place where everything shone, where every tilt of the head revealed a golden dome, glossy cherubs smiling down, or shutter-framed windows offering tantalising flashes into chandelier-lit salons. Paris was my City of Light, before I'd even heard the expression.

My dad might have been a newly converted Francophile, but it was my mother who really made me fall for France. When I first realised, on that trip, that she was speaking a different language, one so lusciously melodious, she may as well have been chanting a magic spell. I looked up in awe at this glamorous woman, swathed in a floral scarf, her lips painted an exotic red, and suddenly saw a new side to my mother — the French one, no doubt. There and then, I signed up for lessons in Gallic chic, ones that would continue long after our holiday. Mum bought me *Madeline* books, took me to Jacques Tati films, and taught me how to eat everything from frogs' legs to crème brûlée. That might all sound a little affected, but it was only natural — my mother being genetically predisposed to a passion for all things French.

Mum's great-grandfather, Georges Armand Proust, was born in France, although the staunch royalist had to leave the republic after it was discovered that he had conspired in a plot supporting the pretender to the throne (*le scandale*!). I've often wondered what was on the minds of the luxury-loving Georges and his wife Berthe as they sailed into Sydney Cove, a cargo of French antique furniture and three young boys in tow, soon to set up a new life amid the dust and flies of this former convict colony. Although they must have managed to live well enough, because their taste for the finer things in life filtered down through the following generations. The Australian Prousts have long been brought up to believe that all good things come from Paris, or else very close by. They sniff at cars not marked Renault or Citroën, eat the stinkiest of cheese, and ensure their champagne is always the real thing. The Prousts, as my dad says only half-jokingly, are snobs.

My parents are like chalk and *fromage*, and they love Paris — and France — for different reasons. My mum was destined to take to it, of course; she studied French and committed herself to blitzing school and forging a formidable career, her reward for which would be the good life, complete with beautiful clothes, exquisite food and nights at the opera — and holidays to the place where such glamour originated. 'One day, I'm going to go to Paris and treat myself to a Chanel jacket,' she'd sometimes say, with a dreamy look in her eyes.

Mum was inspired by the lofty luxury of high-end Paris, but my dad admired Paris as the city for the man of the street, as the capital of liberty and equality for all. Where my mum adored the social life, Dad preferred socialism, and couldn't care a toss for fancy clothing (he would have been horrified to learn that the ties Mum sometimes bought for him were Hermès, and as such eye-wateringly expensive). Dad was a lawyer, in the field of industrial relations, fighting the good fight for workers who had been unfairly treated by the powers-that-be. It only made him more committed to the cause of socialism.

'Did you know the French invented the concept of left wing?' he would often ask. And I'd hear the story once again: during a debate about the king's powers in the early years of the French Revolution, the group in opposition moved to the left side of the assembly chamber, and so the political terms left and right took hold. Originally the distinction was about whether you were against or for royalty, but it evolved to denote whether you supported social reform or a more traditional society.

Still — as my dad would note, approvingly — even the conservative French presidents have shown a certain commitment to the notion of fairness. It was just one of the many Gallic paradoxes, Mum once observed, explaining that only the French can reconcile the seemingly opposing ideals of grandeur and democracy. Only the French — and my parents.

It took us another eight years to find our way back to our beloved France. Dad had been busy building up his practice, while Mum had spent several years studying and strategising her career, before taking a job as adviser to the Premier of Victoria. They were both feeling burnt out, and Paris seemed the perfect reward for years of toil. Of course, I was more than happy to hitch a ride.

A dreamer of a girl, an only child who spent hours imagining my future life, Paris had remained my fantasy world since my first visit. Nevertheless, at thirteen years old, I was at the threshold of an age when you start to sense that life isn't a fairy tale after all — that a happy ending isn't as solid as a triumphal arch at the end of a grand avenue, and life is actually a bumpy road that might take unexpected twists and turns. While my parents' marriage seemed as content as ever, many of my friends' parents had divorced. It was the 1980s, and nobody could deny that the world was changing. Women, too, were evolving, wanting more, with feminism — supposedly — finally setting us free. It was a confusing time for girls who had grown up reading *Cinderella*. On the cusp of womanhood, we looked around and realised 'happily ever after' now meant something else altogether. The future was less certain than ever — both more, and less, in our control; and it was both exciting and daunting.

One of the most powerful displays of Parisian girl power, I discovered, can be found in the Louvre, in the enormous *Liberty Leading the People*, Eugène Delacroix's celebration of the July 1830 Revolution. Its intensity floored me, quite literally — I had to sit down on the museum's parquetry to take in the canvas. I could all too well understand how this painting might have inspired Victor Hugo to write *Les Misérables*, the musical version of which we had just seen in London. I'd found *Les Mis* heart-stirring enough — 'The French had revolutions,' said Dad, 'because they dreamed of a better world' — but Liberty seemed to make the fight for a fairer future personal.

Liberty is an allegorical goddess-like figure, holding aloft the *tricolore* flag as she guides the people of Paris to victory. But this is no delicate maiden playing a pale-skinned muse from afar. Liberty is right in the thick of the violent action, her other muscular arm brandishing a musket as she strides barefoot over the bodies of fallen comrades, her fired-up face urging her army of followers onwards. Oh, and her dress is falling down, revealing a pert pair of breasts.

I was at once seduced and confused. Liberty was strong and sturdy, yes, and I loved that. But she also had to play the sexy card to get attention. The mixed messages somewhat messed with my young feminist-in-training mind.

My mum was a feminist from way back. The eldest of nine children, her mother hadn't been allowed to consider a career, and she wanted her daughters to make up for those lost opportunities. Nana refused any help in the kitchen or laundry (which surely would have been tempting given she had eleven mouths to feed and bodies to clothe); instead, the girls had to study. And then study some more. There were no mirrors in their bedrooms; the emphasis was on a beautiful mind. Mum came to like beauty products as much as the next woman, but her workday look was classic and groomed: a tailored suit with sensible heels, accented with a rose-beige lip. She knew how to get ahead in a man's world, and it didn't involve cosmetics or cleavage; her real weapon was her intelligence.

I was proud of my mother, who was my ultimate role model — and yet I knew from an early age that I was a different girl from the one she'd been. A very girlie one, I was wired to obsess over prettiness — floral wallpaper, pink velvet bedspreads, frilly dresses ... I'd begged for a Barbie collection for years, and Mum, who herself had, quite unregretfully, missed the influence of such a doll at a formative age, finally gave in, albeit with much reluctance. By the age of thirteen, I'd long stopped playing with the dolls, but they still sat pretty on a shelf by my mirror, into which I'd often sigh, wishing my hair could be longer and blonder.

If Barbie was the ideal girl in Australia, in France it was Marianne, whom I'd recently learned about in my French classes. Delacroix's Liberty was an early depiction of Marianne, the ultimate French woman, the symbol of the French Republic whose bust is on display in town halls around the country. Not one particular woman (the name was chosen as it was so common at the time), Marianne is in fact *every* woman. But, of course, Marianne is beautiful. Every now and then, the French state chooses an iconic identity as the personification of the Marianne ideal, to lend her features to a new generation of busts and illustrations that will end up on stamps and postcards. Real-life Mariannes have included Brigitte Bardot, Catherine Deneuve and Laetitia Casta.

Studying Liberty in the Louvre that day, I wondered if French women sensed a pressure to be both sexy and smart. Perhaps they felt just as Liberty might have: frustrated that she'd broken free of her corsets, only to find she couldn't escape from society's expectations that women should be, above all, seductive. Or did they simply accept that women were a package of contradictions, complicatedly wrapped up in layers of lace and feminine frills?

We emerged from our hours in the Louvre, blinking several times to adjust our vision in the searing sunshine. In high summer in Paris, the sun is so golden it's practically molten, and the days seem to go on forever. We headed into the neighbouring Tuileries Garden, once a pleasure ground in which queens, princesses and empresses danced, and passed the manicured lawns and parterre gardens to take shelter within the grid of horse chestnut trees. This, to me, seemed like a wooded fairyland, with its whimsical touches of art, including a white marble statue that made me smile for its pure playfulness. Sitting atop a plinth was the bust of a man, his serious, line-etched face offset by a mass of youthful tumbling curls. Children skipped and twirled around the base, while a cat wearing a natty hat and cape stood to the side, one booted toe elegantly turned out.

Meet Charles Perrault, the seventeenth-century author who recorded a number of popular fictions that had been passed through the generations for centuries, adapting and collecting them in a book he called *Histoires ou Contes du Temps Passé. Avec les Moralitez* (*Stories or Tales from Past Times with Morals*). Soon this genre would be known as fairy tales, and Perrault immortalised some of what are now the most famous and best loved, including *Le Chat Botté* (*Puss in Boots*), *La Belle au Bois Dormant* (*Sleeping Beauty*) and *Cendrillon* (*Cinderella*).

'Can't you just imagine Cinderella running along these paths in her ball gown and glass slippers?' I sighed. I might have been coming to the realisation that real life wasn't a fairy tale, but it didn't mean I couldn't be nostalgic for another time, even one that never existed. 'Don't forget the moral of the story,' Mum reminded me, as she had done so many times before, 'the importance of kindness.'

Disney might have produced a Vaseline-lensed, blissfully-ever-after adaptation of Perrault's *Cinderella*, but the original story doesn't dwell much on the wedding or even the groom; rather, the happy ending is in *Cinderella* forgiving her step-sisters — who are not in fact ugly, just less beautiful in character. Indeed, Perrault finished his tale with this moral musing: 'That which we call good grace, exceeds, by far, a handsome face.'

While my parents are different in many superficial ways, they have always been united by substance, by values — one of which could certainly be termed 'good grace'. They believe in civility and decency, for one, but also the religious definition of grace: the peace of mind and strength of soul that come from love of God. I, on the other hand, was never the most committed of Catholic girls. Perhaps because I went to the local public school, I hadn't been indoctrinated in Catholicism to the same soul-searing extent. Despite sharing a Sunday Mass ritual, I could never seem to achieve my parents' beatific state of mind. I jiggled on the uncomfortable wooden pews. My thoughts wandered … Still, I guess I was Catholic enough to feel guilty about not being Catholic enough.

'Now here's a good role model for you, much worthier than Cinderella,' pronounced Dad, as we headed out of the Tuileries and over Rue de Rivoli. I looked up to see a statue of a woman astride an armoured horse, holding a flag as though poised to charge into battle. It was the original, golden version of the statue I walked by every Saturday, when Mum and I visited the State Library of Victoria: Saint Joan of Arc, the legendary girl warrior of the fifteenth century.

Born into a rural peasant family in 1412, just as the Hundred Years' War with England was about to ramp up again, a teen Joan started hearing voices of saints urging her to fight for the French heir, Charles VII. It was a harsh time when hope was in desperate need, so word soon got around. Upon theological examination, Joan's divine inspiration was officially accepted, and she was allowed to fight for France, her hair cropped and her tiny body dressed in knight's garb. At the helm of what was now effectively a religious war, Joan led the troops to various victories — until she ran out of luck and found herself in the hands of her enemies.

Joan could have stayed at home spinning wool with her mother and sisters, but instead fought against the limitations of her gender, noted Dad, who as the father of a daughter often displayed admirable feminist traits. 'She also shows the importance of following your convictions,' he added. I wasn't quite convinced. Joan, after all, had been burned at the stake for witchcraft, and for generally being a woman who didn't know her place. But at the very least, I figured, the story of Joan reminded me that I was lucky to live in modern times, in an enlightened era that offered women so many choices. I would probably never have to opt for the particular role of girl warrior — but Joan proved we all had one within if we ever needed to fight against injustice. Our own inner Liberty, ready to storm the barricades. Frilly dress or not.

One of Dad's favourite stops on a Paris Left Bank walking tour is a cute cobblestoned lane just off Boulevard Saint-Germain. The Cour du

Commerce Saint-André is the picture of prettiness, festooned with fairy lights and lined with shops bearing quaint signs and colourful slatted shutters. Few would guess this little strip is so heavy with symbolism, having helped to pave the way to modern France. Behind a hefty green door, a certain Dr Joseph-Ignace Guillotin invented the mechanical decapitation machine that would kill off Old France. Just across the way, the champion-for-the-poor Jean-Paul Marat printed his radical paper, *L'Ami du Peuple* (*Friend of the People*), an incendiary read that fired up Parisians and helped send the monarchy up in flames.

If you twist around a corner down to the Rue de l'Ancienne Comédie, then take a right, you find yourself outside a restaurant called Le Procope. This is where the expression *'liberté, égalité, fraternité'* was coined, according to my father. Peering through the windows of Le Procope, I found it a stretch to believe that such a lustrous setting could inspire radical thoughts. One of those famous French paradoxes, perhaps?

When Le Procope opened its gilded doors in 1686, it set the scene for a new type of Parisian institution, the literary café. And a luxury one at that. A world away from the city's traditional tavern — a rough and rowdy, ale-drenched affair of a place — Le Procope was all chandeliers reflected in mirror-coated walls, and marble-topped tables adorned with silver pots of steaming coffee, newly imported from the East, and plates of pretty pastries. The Age of Enlightenment was flickering into life. Patrons could peruse the newfangled newspapers, and openly discuss politics, philosophy and other pressing issues of the moment, all the while ordering endless cups of caffeine to keep the conversation buzzing. Add to this percolating brew a sprinkling of the greatest minds in the city who frequented the café, and you had a potent recipe for a social and political phenomenon.

French socialism has always had a uniquely intellectual bent to it, Dad explained. The movement didn't begin among the working classes so much as the coffee-quaffing intellectuals who idealised the notion of social equality. That's why they wanted to democratise knowledge, he explained, adding that this was the very place where a group of philosophers came up with the idea of the modern encyclopaedia.

My mind reeled at the thought of how thrilling it must have been to fill all those blank pages. I pictured these men as the literary equivalent of the early explorers who charted the globe, sailing back to Paris with gobsmacking stories to report, inspiring a new generation of scientists — for these writers must have felt as though they were also charting new territory. My pangs of envy almost hurt. I had recently decided I wanted to write for a living, but about what I had no idea. In bookstores, I'd wander around the various sections and look at the different genres, wondering where I could slot in — but everything seemed to have been penned on paper. What more could there possibly be to say?

Still, I felt compelled to write in some shape or form. It seemed like the perfect method for making sense of a complicated world. And — I won't lie — it also appeared to be such a romantic way to eke out a living. An insular, independent job, it appealed to an only child — yet it was sufficiently connected to society by virtue of its analytical and observational activities. I pictured myself scribbling away in a pink notebook, for hours on end, in glamorous cafés ... I should have known early on that I would end up writing about the more aesthetic side of life.

Interestingly, most philosophers of the Enlightenment — such as the charming and vivacious Voltaire — while challenging their world and the very basis of human existence, weren't revolutionaries. They argued the case for fairness, certainly, but within the current framework of French life, complete with the monarchy and the growing middle class. I came to believe that they simply liked the modern pleasures of life —

including their silky culottes and the velvety hot chocolate they sipped from porcelain cups while lounging on cushy couches.

Talking about social justice while savouring truffle risotto and sipping vintage champagne in a five-star restaurant only makes true sense in Paris. Because the French believe as much in the concept of equality for all, as they do in luxury for all. Everyone can — and should — aim high.

High in French is *haut*, an adjective that Gallic types love to link to all the important things in life, to raise them to greater heights and infuse them with a haughty demeanour. For example, *haute couture* (high fashion), *haute parfumerie* (fine fragrance), *haute culture* (high culture), *haut bourgeois* (upper middle class) and, of course, *haute cuisine* (fine dining).

It's a delicious irony that French restaurants became posher after the Revolution, the very event that was meant to level things out socially. Once modest establishments that dished up restorative broths (*les restaurants*), a sophisticated new generation opened shop after the 1789 Revolution, as chefs once employed to concoct lavish banquets for aristocrats found themselves out of work and in need of a career rethink. For a price, all Parisians could now wine and dine at marble tables, under chandeliers. The French, you see, do not believe equality means sinking to the lowest common denominator.

Ledoyen is a pretty, buttery-yellow pavilion nestled in greenery at the foot of the Champs-Élysées. It was also the scene of my first deluxe dinner out. Cue all my 1980s finery: a puffy taffeta skirt paired with a velour bolero jacket. My parents and I sat on high-backed, velvety chairs, our table dressed formally in starched white linen, the brightening glow of the candelabras lightening up the delicately etched ceilings as the sky darkened to a perfect shade of French navy just beyond the ruched curtains.

Our meals came out nestled beneath silver cloches, which were then dramatically lifted by a trio of faultlessly in-sync waiters, revealing such delights as a *mille-feuille* of seafood swimming in a silken purée, an artful array of vegetables as colourful as paint on a palette, an intricately designed roulade, swirled and sliced to perfection.

'There's a wonderful French expression, *gauche caviar*,' Mum said, during a conversation about the contradictory country we had all come to love. 'It literally means "caviar left", although we tend to say "champagne socialism" in English, referring to socialists who have certain expensive tastes,' she explained. 'Yet another French paradox.'

'Isn't that a little hypocritical?' I wondered aloud.

'There's nothing wrong with living the good life from time to time,' said Mum.

'If you work hard for it,' noted Dad.

'And you're grateful for it,' Mum added.

I was certainly grateful for the dessert trolley that was wheeled over, laden as it was with fruit tarts glossy and bright, as though studded with huge gemstones; chocolate in every possible guise of cake and tart; and sculptural, sugar-encrusted confections.

We made up for our extravagant dinner by eating baguettes by the river for the remainder of the holiday, but I lived off that grand meal for months. It had nourished more than my appetite, and had been an exquisite taste of the French philosophy of pleasure — something worth fighting for, saving for, in this complex world. Life, I was learning, was as layered as French pâtisserie — but this only gave it more flavour and richness. I would have to contend with all sorts of contradictions and complications in the future, and I might not always have the answers, no matter how many notebooks I filled in Parisian cafés, in search of inner enlightenment. That fabled happy ending was going to be harder work than anticipated. But the point, I was sensing, was not the destination but the journey, and how enjoyable, how picturesque, I could make it.

CHAPTER 2
JEUNE FILLE

[ʒœn] *adj* young [fij] *nf* girl

In which, aged sixteen, I fashion a Parisian alter ego for myself.

Having finally reached the fabled age of sixteen, I was desolate to find I hadn't blossomed overnight into a fragrant bouquet of femininity. I was still the same shy, awkward teenager whose social life extended as far as my weekend job: I worked at the local deli, serving up soggy coleslaw, slices of sweaty salami, and fried-crisp chicken, the carcasses of which I had to string onto the rotisserie. Forget Sweet Sixteen — life seemed positively unsavoury at times.

I had an inkling that the key to the life I wanted to live, the woman I wanted to be, would be found in a certain city on the other side of the world, where girls wore smart pinafores and plaits fashioned from long silky hair, and grew into beautifully styled women who wrapped themselves in scarves and trailed alluring fragrance.

French girls don't tend to celebrate a Sweet Sixteen, I've found. Their coming of age is, rather, a graceful evolution that begins with the tender moment *mamans* start to teach their mini-mes how to groom. My part-French mother was genetically programmed to pass on a few beauty pointers early on, but her escalating workload meant that I was mostly left to my own devices, to experiment with my look as I saw fit. While I appreciated her unerring belief in my ability to self-express, my clumsy attempts to style a more mature, glamorous me usually misfired. (A geometrically tiered bob, anyone?) I began to count down the days to our next trip to Paris, dreaming of the future me I would discover there.

It was late autumn, and the golden leaves of the Parisian plane trees rippled in the light breeze, the shimmering effect making the city seem all the more lustrous. On days like this, Paris seems ephemeral, as though you're in a hazy, glazed dream. You almost pinch yourself to check she's real.

The city proper is divided into a twirl of twenty districts, and we were staying in Passy, in the 16th arrondissement. Once a hilly hamlet of winding pathways and fields lush with grapevines and thermal springs, Passy came into its own in the mid nineteenth century, becoming home to many of the grand buildings that now define Paris — the Haussmannian apartments, named after Baron Georges-Eugène Haussmann, the prefect charged with modernising the city.

'Your beloved Baudelaire would have hated Passy,' Mum commented as we explored the area on our first day, pointing to the apartment blocks, all variations on a classic beige theme.

Forget boy bands; my crush at the time was Charles Baudelaire, the lyrical genius of French Romanticism. Nineteenth-century Romantic poems — gloriously exotic creations that I could only semi-decipher after flicking through my Collins Robert French dictionary multiple times — were what made me really fall in *amour* with the French language. It was by sounding out the heart-pounding verses that I learned how to deliver French, so apt for discussing things of beauty, with a suitably passionate tone. I also eventually worked out how to navigate my tongue around the various Gallic growls and purrs — no mean feat when your mouth is packed with heavy-metal braces.

But how could any sixteen-year-old suburban girl not be seduced by France's answer to Lord Byron? An arrogant aesthete who was living it up on a well-endowed trust fund, the velvet-suited Baudelaire carried off urban cool and bohemian chic thrillingly well, stalking the seedy streets at night for inspiration. He was a party guy and a lady's man, but he was also a boy genius. By the age of twenty-one, he had already penned many of the poems that would one day be collected and called *Les Fleurs du Mal* (*The Flowers of Evil*).

The melancholy poet despised what Haussmann was doing to his beloved Paris — remaking the medieval maze of dark and winding lanes into a big city of broad avenues and bright, cheery façades. 'My dear memories are heavier than stone,' he wrote mournfully. It is to Baudelaire that the expression *épater les bourgeois* (shock the bourgeois) is usually attributed. And Passy, by most accounts, is still considered Bourgeois Central.

The word bourgeois derives from *bourg*, Old French for a fortified town, which Paris once was. As France morphed into a capitalist economy, Paris boomed and bankers, merchants and artisans prospered. The aristocrats, whose power had been guillotined during the 1789 Revolution, scoffed at the *nouveaux riches* (which is why the term bourgeois came to have an accent of insult to it), but as the industrial age cranked into gear, the middle class became richer than ever.

In English, we quip: 'The more things change, the more they stay the same.' The saying was originally French, coined by Jean-Baptiste Alphonse Karr, a critic and journalist, in 1849, at the very height of the French bourgeoisie's influence. Monsieur Karr might well have had in mind the uppity pretentions of the middle classes, who pored over old etiquette manuals that instructed them on how to behave to the château born even if they lived in a city apartment — the bourgeoisie took to aristocratic habits like they were going out of fashion. Speaking of which, dresses were billowing back out to wide-hipped proportions not seen since the heyday of Marie Antoinette. Women wore crinolines — hooped petticoats made from horsehair (*crin*) — under dresses drenched in the vibrant new dyes of the age, creating the appearance of full-bloom flowers. It was a gilded corseted cage, however; women had fewer legal rights than ever before, and their role was little more than ornamental.

As we meandered around Passy, I imagined the ghosts of these women a few floors above, curled up on *chaises longues* in the steamy greenhouse rooms that were all the bourgeois rage at the time, dreaming of a more exotic life under the teasing fronds of palms while wrapped up in their Indian shawls. I wondered if they also read Baudelaire, and yearned for his lands of 'luxury, calm and voluptuousness'. Perhaps that's why I, too, swooned over Baudelaire; he was an escape from bourgeois boredom.

There's a French term I love: *jardin secret.* Secret garden. Marcel Prévost was a society novelist at the turn of the twentieth century who was adequately in tune with his feminine side to specialise in the subject of women's psychology. One of his books, *Le Jardin Secret*, tells the tale of a woman who comes across her old diaries and realises that she left her real self behind upon marrying her cheating husband. After pages of inner struggle, she decides to present a brave face and keep her true self — and feelings — hidden away.

Le Jardin Secret didn't go on to become a cult classic, but at the time it tapped into the zeitgeist enough to give its name to a new expression, one that denoted someone's inner life — their private realm of unexpressed thoughts, greatest fears and wildest dreams. The French believe one's private grounds, so to speak, are what create a sense of allure and mystery. The exterior might appear classic, but lurking just behind that discreet façade are all sorts of verdant nooks and crannies.

If you wander off the beaten tracks of Passy, you come across hidden emerald-green gems, literal secret gardens — leafy enclaves and vine-embossed laneways that seem to wind back into Old Paris. Mum and I were on our way to one such gateway: Maison de Balzac, the literary museum and only remaining abode of one of France's most revered writers.

A man of his age, Honoré de Balzac was particularly suited to reporting on the rise of the bourgeoisie, being obsessed with money and its effect on society and individuals. Balzac himself certainly lived a swish lifestyle. Continually on the run from the creditors knocking at his various Parisian doors, he ended up moving to Passy in 1840, which was at the time just beyond the city of Paris, and thus the reach of its law. The wily writer had not once worked in a legal office for nothing.

Maison de Balzac, a green-shuttered eighteenth-century cottage perched upon a hill, recalls the pastoral Passy of old. The entry is via a stairway that winds down from Rue Raynouard to the terrace garden. Originally there was a building up at street level that camouflaged the front gate; a handy ruse when Balzac needed to slip out of sight from his numerous pursuers. Despite its sweet appearance, Balzac's home was a serious fortress. Renting it under his housekeeper's name, the author placed guards at various doors, who would only grant a visitor access if they uttered the correct passwords (say, 'The plum season has arrived'). If all else failed, Balzac could scoot to the bottom level and flee through the back door and down the cobbled country lane in the manner of a shady character he might well have dreamed up himself.

The prolific Balzac, lauded as the father of Realism, was the man responsible for my mother's love of the French language (*of course* my modern-minded mother was into the Realists, while I was all about the Romantics), and she often urged me to read his work. It wasn't just for the language lesson. I spent countless hours scribbling angsty teenage musings in my diary, or lost in the soul-searching thoughts of the heroines of my preferred books — and Mum probably hoped that Balzac's style of social commentary, his visual attention to detail, would inspire me to better observe the world around me, to look outwards more than inwards, to be more realist than romantic. All I really needed, it turned out, was a session at a Parisian café. There's no better place to learn the art of people-watching.

&

Later that day, we pulled up a rattan chair at a nearby café, next to a group of girls who were alternating sips of black coffee and gasps of slimline cigarettes in a manner that made the dual vices seem the epitome of sophistication. They were about my age but seemed so much more poised, sure of their place in the world. Even the way they spoke to the waiter was with an adult-like confidence, but also with a touch of world-weariness, like they'd done so much and seen so much already. I envied their self-assuredness, if not necessarily their style. They wore blouses, blazers and trousers, accessorised with pearls and structured handbags, and were the very definition of *bon chic, bon genre.*

Literally translated as 'good style, good sort,' *bon chic, bon genre* is France's version of preppy. It was immortalised in 1986 by a top-selling handbook to BCBG style, but the look had in fact been around for several decades. Another term could have been upper-class chic. True BCBGs inherited their fashion flair, along with their country château, from their aristocratic or *haut bourgeois* ancestors. Balzac would totally have aspired to being a BCBG had he been born a century later, especially as Passy was prime BCBG stomping ground. You could easily spot a member of the style tribe: men wore jumpers knotted over pastel shirts, while women threw an heirloom Hermès scarf oh so casually over a stone-hued trench coat. It's perhaps because of this classic style of dressing, instilled from a young age, that many Parisian girls don't seem to go through an awkward period. Transitioning from *mademoiselle* to *madame* is not a matter of before and after, it's a continual evolvement of elegance.

A black-vested, white-aproned waiter loomed over us. '*Mes*dames,' he muttered, peering down his carved aquiline nose, as stone-faced as a statue, eyes squinting as though in pain.

'*Un café au lait, s'il vous plaît*?' It was my best Parisienne impersonation, although my Australianness was unmissable, thanks to the loud addition of a question mark, and a large goofy grin. For my effort, I was rewarded with the *mère* of all eye rolls.

French waiters had quite the reputation for rudeness at the time. Looking back, I later figured that I'd committed a couple of social sins that afternoon. Firstly, milky coffee is usually only consumed at breakfast, often in a big bowl, into which one can dip a croissant or chunk of baguette. My other faux pas might be that I was too, well, Aussie. In Australia, we're brought up to be appreciative of those who serve us. In France, where the ideal of equality sits perhaps a little uneasily with the industry of service, and all the subconscious associations of servitude, that extra dollop of polite can come across as condescending, even disrespectful. Rather, the server/servee relationship should be a matter-of-fact, professional transaction and, as a result, you're meant to simply state your order, clearly and concisely, *sans* any supplementary sycophantic smiles or apologetic tones.

I evidently still had much to learn about the innate complexities and codes of the French language.

I have loved French from my very first class. It had me at *bonjour.* Something about the poetic way the short and snappy *bon* and the long, lingering, sigh-like *jour* met and flirted over that seductive *zhhhhhh* sound.

Like an enduring relationship, I just never got bored. At every turn, there was something new to delight in — an unexpected grammatical twist that would keep me on my toes. French is captivating for its pure whimsicality: quirky flourishes, like silent sneaky letters, that do little more than look pretty, and lovely lilting accents that might seem like a folly in today's world of frantically bashed-out texts and emails, but finish things off like a ruffle on a dress.

Flourishes and follies aside, French is a surprisingly easy language to learn, speak and read once you get on a roll. The French are taught to talk the way they write, rather than write the way they talk. This makes it fairly easy for students of the language to understand the spoken French word. The flipside, however, is that you're often corrected if your French is not textbook-perfect. Make a grammatical faux pas, and many a Parisian will visibly wince, as though in physical distress.

The next day my parents and I ventured into the heart of Paris to visit what could be described as the soul of the French language. The Institut de France is the baroque beauty that sits just over the Seine from the Louvre, with its soaring columns and gilded cupola. Its most famous tenant is the Académie Française, the legendary guardian of the French language. Originally a literary group that would get together over petits fours to talk poetry and puns, this fancy early version of a book club was eventually made official, and charged with the duty 'to give clear rules to our language and to render it pure, eloquent and capable of dealing with the arts and science'.

And so the Academy has filtered the French language of any nasties for over four centuries. The forty *immortels* — as the members are loftily called — meet regularly under the dome, in what was the old college chapel, to debate which new words are fit for consecration into French, as well as to work on the official Académie dictionary — which isn't to record how French is spoken, rather how it *should* be spoken. And this, for example, excludes such Anglicisms as *le jogging* and *le week-end.*

My friends in French class and I used to joke about our 'franglais'. If we didn't know the French version of a certain word, we'd just go with the English, whacking a *le* or *la* beforehand, tweaking it with an accent or two, and hoping for *le best.* But in France, Anglicisms were no laughing matter. In 1964, a French scholar, René Étiemble, dropped a cultural bombshell with *Parlez-Vous Franglais?*, a book that raged against the Anglicisation — and particularly the Americanisation — of the French language.

Americana was influencing more than just French words at that time. Wardrobes, too, were falling under the New World spell. The grandparents of the 1980s BCBGs — like the girls I had admired in that Passy café — belonged to a generation that rejected the super-stiff tailoring of their parents, clothing in preference for the sporty separates worn so strikingly by the American tourists who flocked to Paris after the Second World War. By the 1980s, a simple white shirt and sleek indigo-blue jeans had completed their slow but steady one-way transatlantic journey, crossing over from trusty American workwear into the ultimate uniform of easy, modern French style.

The French government could hardly ban blue jeans, but it could try its darnedest to stop its people from saying *le blue-jean* — a phrase that purists must have found particularly galling, considering that denim originated from the French city of Nîmes (*de* Nîmes). Throughout the 1970s and 1980s, all sorts of acts had been initiated to control the borders of the French language, and make sure it didn't stray into enemy territory.

The French language hasn't always been so rigid. In Roman times, the original Gaulish merged with the new regime's Latin to produce a kind of street-speak known as Gallo-Roman, which was in turn moulded and reshaped as various invaders, including the Franks, came into power and influence after the fall of Rome. France was in a state of chaos for centuries, reflected in the total absence of control over its language. Make that languages: there were as many French dialects as there were regional cheeses, each with its own distinct, often pungent and profuse, flavour.

In English, we sometimes use the word Rabelaisian. It means, according to the Merriam-Webster dictionary, something that is 'marked by gross robust humor, extravagance of caricature, or bold naturalism'. The adjective originates from François Rabelais, a French star author of the early 1500s. Keep in mind, this was an era before Paris was considered the global capital of refinement. She was a dark and dirty town back then (when she was still definitely a 'he'), and Rabelais' work echoed his world. He wrote with little grammatical care whatsoever, taking liberty to make up words and mess around with sentence structure, and he then spiced it all up with a copious dose of bawdiness. It was Rabelais who came up with the term *bête à deux dos* a good half-century before William Shakespeare (who experimented with English in a similar jocular way) would write about 'the beast with two backs' in *Othello*.

All of this Rabelaisian madness must have pained the poet François de Malherbe, who was born a couple of years after the lewd writer's death, in the midst of the raucous century. By the turn of it, Malherbe had scored the gig of official poet, and unofficial literary critic, of the royal court, and set himself the almighty task of ushering in a new epoch of language purity. The eloquent aristocrat was passionately averse to such extraneousnesses as synonyms. He argued for the use of elegant yet also simple, clear and precise language. Both a stickler and a snob, Malherbe's official position and friendship with two kings gave him major social clout. Contemporary authors fell in line by writing according to his dictates, and literary salons hung onto his every declaration — and this is how his philosophy, and style of language, came to lie at the very core of the French Academy.

Malherbe's prim and proper ways notwithstanding, French is the language of romance. Literally. At its roots, it's a Roman language, which is why it's known by linguistic types as a Romance language. But there was a time when the word romance didn't convey thoughts of red roses and long walks on the beach. In Old French, *romanz* was the everyday speech of French people. While Latin remained the lingua of religion, science and philosophy, *romanz* was used to tell the tales of chivalry and heroism so beloved by medieval courtly types. The word morphed into *roman*, which to this day means a novel. And when post-Revolution novelists, disillusioned by the failure of the Age of Enlightenment and all its now-tarnished talk of rationality, began to pen their sweeping, emotional sagas, it made sense to call them *Romantiques*.

The term 'romance novel' today brings to mind bodice-ripping reads of the Mills & Boon variety, but French Romantic types were not necessarily concerned about the heady ups and downs of love affairs. They did, however, tear off a corset of their own — that of strait-laced Classicism, which was too starched for them to fully express their emotions. The Romantics were all about feelings over logic, and they explored new terrains in the form of imagination-charged historical novels or tales of the emotional journeys of everyday heroes. Romantic literature rode a rollercoaster of sentiments, from swooning depths to soaring heights, before plunging once more into the next literary trends: gritty Realism (think Balzac) and dark, disillusioned Decadence (where my poet-crush Baudelaire eventually, despairingly headed).

The Romantics were rebellious at the time, but their names are now some of the most esteemed in French literature. They might have been ridiculed for their excessive emotions, but their passion has always been undeniable, and seductive even to modern readers. They certainly inspired my own *amour fou* with the French language.

&

My parents gave me an hour to myself, and I ambled by the Seine, stopping at every bridge and pouting theatrically, for no particular reason. I was in a moody mindset at this stage in my life, much to the chagrin of my poor, ever-patient father. Hormones were wreaking havoc on my emotions, for one, but it was mostly a textbook case of teenage-girl malaise. Fast growing out of girlish fantasies, I could no longer pretend to be some leading lady in a film (even despite the cinematic setting of Paris). Nobody was going to dress and direct my character, nor map out a neat plotline for my life. Perhaps that's why I gravitated to books about women. I was searching for heroines who could guide me on how to script my life.

Paris's second-hand book dealers, the *bouquinistes*, have been plying their trade from their weather-beaten, wagon-green quayside boxes for over a century. Among the trash-and-treasure trove of trinkets and fluttering displays of posters, you can find most classics of French literature. One in particular called to me that day, with its melodramatically plaintive title, *Hello Sadness.*

Bonjour Tristesse by Françoise Sagan, the publishing sensation of 1954, tells the tale of teenage Cécile and her widowed, libertine father, who have escaped the bourgeois boredom of Paris to live it up in the South of France. The father has his young trophy girlfriend and Cécile embarks on an affair of her own. When a friend of Cécile's late mother comes to stay, assuming the maternal, disciplinarian role, Cécile hatches a plan to restore her old way of life, with fatal consequences.

Over the next few weeks, I ploughed my way through the novel, with my French travel dictionary at my side. I still have the copy; almost half of it is highlighted — yellow for phrases that moved me, pink for words I intended to translate and transfer into the long-term file of my memory. And I returned to the beguiling opening line over and over — with its haunting melancholy and beautifully grave sorrow — as I got to know the precociously worldly Cécile. By book's end, I felt an odd envy for her sadness. I wanted a source of my own dolour, something that would justify a life hedonistically devoted to beachside holidays and chichi cocktail parties.

This sounds perverse and bratty, but it only turned out to be a short, confused phase of my teenage life. At the time, I didn't realise how fortunate I was to have a stable home. I translated the steadiness of my life as boredom, sometimes fantasising about what might happen if my neatly tied-up existence began to fray or unravel, and how this would plunge me into a rollercoaster of emotions, from ennui to exhilaration, in true Romantic heroine style. At first I figured *Bonjour Tristesse* appealed because it held the key to a more interesting life. But true joy, I came to realise, was closer to home than I had imagined. I needed to redefine happiness, and I think that's why a book about sadness beckoned to me that day, from the thousands of other books lining the banks of the Seine.

The French philosopher Montesquieu once remarked that France excels at doing frivolous things seriously, and serious things frivolously. That's perhaps why the *bouquinistes* so seamlessly sell old fashion and celebrity glossies amid the high-brow literature. I certainly had no problem with this. I'd started to buy women's magazines myself, dreaming about the day my life might be as glamorous as the world within their lavish pages.

So I spent some time flicking through the various piles of vintage *Vogue* and *Paris Match*, with their impossibly glamorous cover girls. One in particular took my breath away; she had quite possibly the most beautiful face I had ever set eyes upon. Two capital letters in bold gave the clue to the 1959 cover star: BB.

I was instantly smitten. Brigitte Bardot was everything I suddenly wished I looked like: large eyes elongated with inky-black liner for a feline effect; pouty lips painted rosy-pink; a bouffant of blonde hair that glistened in the sun's rays and cascaded past shoulders bared by a low-cut gingham dress.

When you pronounce the curvaceously feminine letters BB in French, it sounds like *bébé*. Baby. It was the perfect nickname for Brigitte, who was often described as a *femme-enfant*. Woman-child. Indeed, she was a heady mix of girlish sweetness and womanly ease, and seemed to me the very personification of the transition from *fille* to *femme*, the one with which I was having so much trouble.

Most women adopt a style icon or two along the way to honing their own look. I'd occasionally, and lamely, attempted to emulate a fashion or beauty trend I'd spotted in a magazine, but I didn't really have a personal style to speak of. I was still trying to figure out who I was — or who I hoped to be. But suddenly I had a clear idea of how I wanted to try to look; I had the first image for my inspiration wall, which would soon be covered in posters of Brigitte.

Over the coming years, I would commit myself to the cause of *bardolâtrie*: slicking and smudging kohl along my lashes, piling pink lipstick on my mouth (which was forming itself into a suitably pouty protrusion after years of braces), teasing and tonging my hair into Brigitte's famous bedhead style. And I became a self-appointed expert on the subject of the woman herself.

Brigitte was born in 1934, into a typical Parisian bourgeois family. They lived in — where else? — Passy, and holidayed annually in the South of France, following the upper-class tradition of summering out of the city. The heat in Paris in August can be stifling. For this reason, Parisian aristocrats used to up and leave for their country châteaux, not returning until at least October. The bourgeoisie made the ritual their own, taking fancy new trains to seaside destinations, such as Biarritz or Saint-Tropez, where the Bardots occasionally stayed. In a neat plot twist, Brigitte would one day put the quaint fishing village on the glamour map, after a stint there in 1956, when she worked on her breakout film *Et Dieu … Créa La Femme.*

… And God Created Woman was the creation of director Roger Vadim, who also happened to be Brigitte's new husband. He had spotted the young ballerina-turned-model on the cover of French *ELLE*, dressed in the role of perfect Parisian daughter; ironically, this shoot had caught the eye of the very man who would help Brigitte break free from her bourgeois existence. Vadim had picked up early that Brigitte 'was a girl who seemed to be ahead of her time' — as he wrote in his modestly titled *Memoirs of the Devil* — 'in rebellion against her parents' morality and milieu, endowed with an innate instinct for love'. Inspired, he transposed Brigitte's own character onto her on-screen alter ego. Juliette is an eighteen-year-old orphan who slinks around the Saint-Tropezien streets like a kitten on heat, looking for love in all the wrong places. In the final pivotal scene, she performs the mambo barefoot in a basement bar, her skirt unbuttoned and hair free-flowing, whipping the air as her steps become increasingly frenetic. Dancing like nobody's watching (except they are, utterly entranced), her message is: it's my life, and I'll move to my own beat if I damn well want to.

The movie shocked global audiences unaccustomed to women acting in such a pleasure-seeking way. When I discovered Brigitte, of course, times had long changed; women felt empowered to dance and dress as they saw fit. In this respect, Brigitte caused the first ripples of third-wave feminism, a wave that began to undulate all those years ago by the beaches of Saint-Tropez. Even Simone de Beauvoir took BB's cultural impact seriously. The legendary mother of second-wave feminism, which swelled to a crest in the 1970s, thought Brigitte a truly liberated woman of the future, not just for her natural sexuality, but for her utter genuineness.

It was that authenticity that spoke to me. The wild hair and the insouciant sundresses. The living life on her own free-spirited terms. The continual questioning of the status quo: she had first busted out of the bourgeoisie and freed herself of social constraints, and she then threw off the trappings of celebrity life to devote herself to animals. Brigitte was true to herself, regardless of the consequences, and so alluringly self-assured, too. She could well have been a Sagan heroine come to life.

The author and actress were fellow social disrupters from an early age. Like BB, Sagan hailed from the bourgeoisie (and Passy), from which she too dreamed of breaking free. She wrote her first novel at the *enfant terrible* age of eighteen, when she was meant to be studying for her exams. Instead she spent her days at cafés filling her notebooks, then partying the night away at Left Bank jazz bars. Critics were torn between admiration for the nervy Sagan's raw talent, and dread that her book would tarnish the good name of French women. Étiemble, the guy who wrote *Parlez-Vous Franglais?*, put her up there with Coca-Cola as 'an evil of our time'. Sagan's Cécile talks about love in a matter-of-fact, often cynical way that shocked French society as much as Brigitte's breakout film did. Women — especially young, well-bred women — were just not supposed to be so savvy about sexuality, nor defy well-delineated social parameters.

I've sometimes wondered why I came across both Françoise Sagan and Brigitte Bardot that day. What message of theirs did I need to heed? It's not like I necessarily wanted to rebel myself, to fling myself into a world of wild hedonism. But there was something about these women that fascinated me. They had symbolised a new social era at the time, but their ongoing resonance for me was on a more personal level, in the way they had themselves transitioned from good bourgeois girls to self-assured, true-to-self women. In both a physical and emotional sense, they were inspirational muses, at a time when I was searching for the future me.

Since my previous trip to Paris, I had developed a love of old things, riffling through countless vintage bookstores and bric-à-brac stalls, fossicking for anything with an air of faded glamour that suggested it might have hailed from olde-worlde France. My French ancestors' heirlooms had, heart-wrenchingly, long disappeared, and perhaps on some level I was trying to locate a missing piece of the patrimony puzzle. I collected tufted velvet poufs and mirrors with gilded curlicue borders, even though I knew they looked ridiculously out of context in my suburban Australian bedroom.

The flea market is called the same in French: *marché aux puces* — it was so named in the nineteenth century when a new appreciation of the concept of cleanliness (thanks to public hygiene pioneers such as Louis Pasteur) changed the way people looked at clothing. Suddenly fabric had to be fresh; anything that wasn't brand-spanking new or regularly sent to one of Paris's many *blanchisseuses* (laundresses) was tossed out, to become the rich pickings of French fleas and bargain hunters alike.

The next day I hopped on the metro — Dad reluctantly along for the ride, playing security guard more than shopping partner — en route to Paris's largest such infestation, the Marché aux Puces de Saint-

Ouen. Alighting at Porte de Clignancourt, we ventured north of the *Périphérique* — the ring road that encircles Paris — and veered up Rue des Rosiers, with its large airy halls brimful with antique dealerships as organised and ornate as miniature museums, and detours into alleyways tumbled over with ivy and a jumble of antiques. We wandered past curvaceous nymphs that would have once adorned flowering gardens but now served as handbag holders, precarious towers of Louis Vuitton trunks etched with the initials of glamouristas long gone, and veritable zoos of animals that had danced and pranced around carousels in their glory days.

I wasn't sure what I was searching for, but found myself gravitating to the clothes strung up along the walls, rubbing shoulders with candelabras dripping with gems and eighteenth-century paintings of blush-cheeked shepherdesses cavorting with cherubs. I strolled past a timeline of French fashion: flapper dresses heavy with beads that would have jingled gorgeously to the Charleston; skirts in the full bloom of Dior New Look luxuriousness; short and shiny tunics of the swinging sixties, when Parisian designers experimented with space-age style. These second-hand clothes might have seen better years, but there was a glimmer of personality that appealed, a tease of an invitation to step into their previous owners' shoes and live up to a former glory.

And then I saw the dress that had been waiting for me to come along and breathe it back to life. Swaying from an old coat stand, it seemed to sashay its hips of its own accord. Held up by ribbons at the shoulders and along its fluttery sleeves, the dress then swooped downwards, cupping the chest and cinching in the waist, before flowing down to the knees. The flowering-vine print tried to give the impression of innocence, but I wasn't fooled. She was a total minx, the Brigitte Bardot of frocks.

I can trace my dress obsession back to this very moment. Dresses have a reputation for being fussy or prissy. But they're actually the most practical clothing option around; one second and you're dressed — literally. But you're so easily undressed, too. And therein lies their subtle sexy charm.

French women do dresses particularly well. It arguably began with Cinderella, who showed the transformative powers of a glamorous gown. Think also of Coco Chanel and her little black ones. Parisiennes of the 1940s who so stylishly survived wartime rations, pairing flippy little floral frocks with cork-soled wedges and painted-on 'stockings'. And, of course, there was Brigitte in her flirty sundresses.

One of Brigitte's favourite labels was Chloé, the pioneer of *prêt-à-porter de luxe* (luxury ready-to-wear). Founder Gaby Aghion, a wealthy Egyptian who had emigrated to Paris high society, launched the label after tiring of being a lady who lunched. She herself dressed in haute couture (along with some couture copies whipped up by her local *couturière*, or dressmaker) but sensed that fashion change was in the air.

After an initial offering of six pretty cotton-poplin dresses in 1952, Chloé came to define the modern Parisienne with a wardrobe that worked from day to night, from smart office-friendly shirtdresses to light and frothy frocks perfect for dancing the night away. To this day, Chloé still creates the city's most stunning dresses — and is for many women the ultimate in Parisian femininity.

The story of prêt-à-porter is interwoven with that of the Parisian bourgeoisie, both having come into their own after the Revolution. Ready-to-wear could develop once the authorities dismantled the rigid regulations covering the city's various guilds. Dressmakers and tailors, whether small-time or high-society, were the original designers, but as the industrial age took off, sewing techniques were enhanced. Production lines of seamstresses, cutters and fitters assembled themselves into workshops, and produced large numbers of cookie-cutter clothes, often copied from the big names of haute couture.

Then came the department stores, which opened along the grand new boulevards and catered for the consumer age's fashion-savvy clientele, the bourgeois Parisiennes who couldn't afford haute couture, yet wanted to look the part and live the dream. Increasingly, anything could be imitated and mass-produced, from patterned shawls to porcelain cups to gilt-framed mirrors. The French might have invented luxury in the first place, but they have long excelled at faking it, too.

We met up with Mum for afternoon tea at Musée Jacquemart-André — the place gilded in the type of luxury that could never be described as *faux*. The museum showcases the ultra-chic life of a Belle Époque star couple, banking heir Édouard André and society painter Nélie Jacquemart. The haut-bourgeois power duo obsessively collected art, especially of the Italian variety, and showcased it all in their Boulevard Haussmann abode — actually more a mini château, with staircases carved out of rippled marble, ceilings painted with scenes of celestial beauty, and flashes of gold at every turn.

After ordering coffee and cake in the delightful tearoom — the mansion's former dining room — I excitedly pulled out my new purchase. 'It smells like moth balls,' said Mum, crinkling her nose. She instinctively picked up her cup of floral tisane, as though to clear her nasal passages of such olfactory nastiness.

My mother's fashion taste has long been what you'd call modern. Not in the sense that she slavishly follows the latest trends, rather that she has always chosen clothes that will let her live the fast-paced life of a woman with places to go, things to do. She has little time for skirts that are too tight or sleeves weighed down with details. Ever the onwards-and-upwards kind of woman, she has never worn clothes that look backwards, clothes burdened with the trimmings of the past.

True, Mum was having slight trouble shaking off her shoulder pads from early on in the decade, but only because they seemed so well suited to the act of barging into the future. She would eventually streamline her fashion look, and actually dress in a more typically French fashion than I'd ever adopt. That's because modern French style is surprisingly simple.

There's a telling self-portrait of Nélie André. She's wearing a dress in a shade of cocoa-brown, in what seems to be velvet, its only adornment a flutter of white lace at the sleeves and neck and a softly folded bustle at the back of the skirt. Her casually upswept hair is offset by a delicate yellow rosebud. Despite living in such exquisite surroundings (her preference for eighteenth-century rococo paintings would have made a royal mistress feel at home) Nélie chose to style herself in a most understated way.

The paring down of personal style was a trend taking hold among the Parisian *haut monde* towards the end of the nineteenth century. Thanks to ready-to-wear, the bourgeois masses could now easily copy high-fashion looks, crinolines and all. As they kitted themselves out more and more elaborately in an attempt to look all the richer for it, those whom they were imitating reacted by eschewing obvious displays of wealth. While the middle classes splashed on a rainbow of colours, widely available due to breakthroughs in synthetic dyes, the upper classes — who had long been able to afford gowns tinted in rare natural pigments — began to literally tone things down.

The bourgeoisie eventually caught back up with their high-society counterparts, dressing down so as to balance fashion out across the board. This emergence of a subtly stylish national uniform was a fitting social leveller for a country equally obsessed with the tenets of equality and elegance. Some say that the signature Parisian style of discretion threads back to the French Revolution, when even a hint of aristocratic luxury could cost you much more than money. But in fact, modern Gallic chic came a century or so later, when Madame André and her friends showed that the truly stylish did not need to prove their point. It was an early example of the famous Chanel motto 'Elegance is refusal'.

These days, most Parisiennes conform to dressing in simple shapes and shades: dark, sleek blue jeans; a crisp white shirt; the horizontally striped top known as the *marinière*; cashmere in soft, muted tones; a well-tailored black tuxedo jacket; a trench coat in the same classic colour as a Haussmannian façade.

One of the most celebrated French style muses is Jane Birkin, the English it-girl who hooked up with Serge Gainsbourg, the singer, songwriter, pianist, poet, painter, actor, director and all-round national treasure of France (with his dapper suits, gravelly growl of a voice and mesmerising way with words, he was also nothing less than a modern-day Baudelaire). Wearing little more than lithe-legged jeans, sheer T-shirts and long, swinging hair, Jane the honorary Parisienne sold sleek French style to the world, especially when the house of Hermès designed a bag for her. The Birkin is to this day a top bucket-list item for many women. Despite having a cult luxury bag named after her, Jane continued to flit around Saint-Germain with a simple straw basket her only accessory — one of those women so ridiculously stylish they don't need to over-emphasise it.

I've sometimes wished I'd discovered Jane before Brigitte (perhaps Serge did, too; he had tumbled in lust with BB after they collaborated on '*Je T'aime … Moi Non Plus*' — a song so steamy that Brigitte begged him not to release it for fear that her third husband, German playboy Gunter Sachs, would discover the affair; a heartbroken Serge went on to record the tune with Jane). It would have saved me a lot of money, at the very least. As a fashion icon, Jane inspires a considered, if simplified, approach to style. Brigitte, on the other hand, is all impulse and frills. Ever since I fell for that flea-market dress, my wardrobe has bulged with all sorts of gowns, kaftans and frocks. I shop with my heart, not my head, which has led me to an oversupply of flounces and florals, and a serious shortfall of classic separates. One of my most glaring Francophilic failings is surely my inability to wear jeans and a pristine shirt. Still, I don't regret it too much. I might never have carried off a frock — or filled it out — quite like Brigitte, but she taught me, at an emotionally formative age, the importance of feeling physically free, comfortable in your own skin.

On our last day in Paris, I once again had some time to myself, before meeting my parents for dinner. Beneath my winter coat, my new dress swished around me as I strolled along the Seine. This time, by that river, I felt lighter, more liberated. As the famous Parisian magic hour imbued the sky with an amber glow and transformed the Seine into a length of rippling golden silk, the future indeed seemed brighter, and sixteen sweeter. I might not have taken many steps closer to understanding the woman I wanted to be, but I at least knew how I wanted her to dress.

CHAPTER 3

INGÉNUE

[ɛ̃ʒeny] *nf* innocent, unsophisticated young woman

In which, aged almost eighteen, I enter
a Belle Époque of my own.

I felt like I was floating on that first day back in Paris, on such a high that my toes seemed to hover above the cobbled streets. Although today it was my hands, not feet, that needed grounding. I was en route to a manicure appointment I'd made months before, when the stress of Year 12 started to take its physical toll. I'd filled so many notebooks throughout the year that the skin on my hands eventually cracked and bled. I had to cover them in plasters for my exams lest any red smears detract from my words. Serious pampering à la parisienne was in order.

The beauty salon was located just behind the Champs-Élysées, up near the Arc de Triomphe, and I paused at the foot of the avenue to admire the vista that ended in the triumphal arch, the iconic monument that had, for me, become so symbolic of goals and dreams. For the moment, however, I had no immediate objective other than tending to a different kind of extremity.

This was no ordinary nail bar. After stepping through the gilt-trimmed doors, into the rose-scented atmosphere, I was ushered over to a brocade-covered armchair.

'*Une coupe de champagne, mademoiselle?*'

That would be a *oui*. Conveniently, the legal drinking age in France was sixteen.

The manicurist soon returned, perched herself on a velvet stool, and placed a silver tray, topped with myriad bottles of red and pink nail polish and a flute of champagne, on the gilded table between us.

As I took my first sip, I felt like I could dissolve with pleasure. I'd dreamed of this very moment for months. It had been the single incentive propelling me through the torture of my final school year. Still, it all seemed surreal. I couldn't quite believe that my parents had allowed me to go to Paris on my own. When I'd originally formulated this grand schoolies plan, they'd simply nodded noncommittally, no doubt hoping that 'Organise Paris Trip' would drop off my to-do list at some point during the frantic year. It didn't. As I saved up every cent possible, I wallpapered the study in posters of Paris, believing in the powers of visualisation, and somehow the trip morphed from wishful thinking into accepted fact. In the end, I think Mum and Dad simply decided they had enough faith in me, as they did in the world (or, at least, Paris) to set me free for a short while, although Mum did experience a moment of qualm at the airport. It was only after I solemnly promised to collect-call her twice a day, as well as check in daily with a former colleague who'd recently relocated to Paris, that her grip loosened, and I fluttered into customs with the nervous excitement a bird must feel when taking its first tentative flaps before swooping into the wide open sky.

'*Rouge ou rose*?' asked Madame Manucuriste.

Would it be possible instead to have *une manucure française*?

'*Mais non*!' she exclaimed, sensibilities clearly offended. '*Ce n'est pas du tout chic*.'

I'd later discover that the so-called French manicure — where glossy pink nails are tipped with a thick white line — is as American as apple pie. Some clever Yank came up with the look and a do-it-yourself kit, and gave it the misleading moniker in the knowledge that most women easily fall for anything à la française.

An hour later I was strolling back down the Champs-Élysées, my nails painted a Parisian-esque pink, no particular destination in mind. And it suddenly hit me: I was not only in Paris on my own for the first time, but in life, too, and I could do whatever on earth I wanted. School was the trodden path behind me, and the coming years stretched before me like a grand avenue. My own Belle Époque had begun.

It might be difficult to sense the former glamour of the Champs-Élysées, now largely a strip of flashing cinemas and fast-food joints, but the avenue was an epicentre of action during the original Belle Époque, which dawned just after 1871 and drew to a dark close on the eve of the First World War. The era was so named after the fact, by a post-war generation looking back through a filter of colour-saturated nostalgia. But idealised reminiscences aside, the period was uncommonly glamorous, and surprisingly so given that it came so soon after the devastations of the civil war known as the Siege of Paris.

Perhaps it was a case of post-traumatic frenzy. Paris has never been as hedonistically happy as she was during these 'beautiful' years, a time when she became the undisputed global capital of pleasure. Life was as bubbly as a magnum of Moët, and Parisians partied in the gardens at the foot of the avenue, in the pretty pastel pavilions there, and at the legendary *café-concerts*, open-aired wonderlands where singers serenaded patrons by the electrified twinkle of fairy lights. Along the avenue, dotted with elegant lampposts and stately elm trees, carriages swept courtesans to and fro, their seductive silhouettes echoing the feminine curvature of the buildings.

I crossed over to Guerlain, the famed beauty brand whose vanilla-sweetened fragrances perfumed the Belle Époque as much as my teenage years. For the past few Christmases, my grandmother had gifted me Guerlain Météorites, a jewel-like box of violet-scented, iridescent powder pearls designed to ignite the face with an ethereal luminosity. To this day, the aroma of violet fills me with the sense of pride I felt on receiving such a grown-up gift, as well as an aching longing to live up to its glamour — and for me Guerlain will forever be the essence of Parisian womanliness.

I made to push open the glass doors, into the glossy marble foyer illuminated by chandeliers cut from the same Baccarat crystal as Guerlain's perfume bottles, but suddenly stopped, transfixed by the scene before me. It was like looking into a hothouse of rare and exotic birds. The boutique was filled with beautiful Japanese women, wrapped in exquisite kimonos and obis — glossy fabrics saturated in fuchsia, mint and raspberry, and bright prints of cherry blossom, butterflies and dancing cranes. They struck me as *maikos*, or geishas in training, although they weren't wearing the usual tell-tale thick white rice-powder face paint. Their skin in fact looked fresh and scrubbed clean, and I saw that most of them were close to my age. Still, I was too awestruck to shatter the mesmeric image and venture inside. So, sadly, I'll never know the true story of their visit. Although I'm sure it has something to do with the universal desire to learn the beauty secrets of the women of the world's most seductive city.

The word geisha literally means 'art person', and a successful geisha is a true entertainer. She dances beautifully, her delicate fingers flit lyrically over traditional instruments, and she excels in the arts of flower arranging and calligraphy. She pours tea for the table, but she can also lean in, being confident enough to chat about a wide range of subjects. People often consider geishas a type of courtesan, but sex is not part of the deal. French courtesans, on the other hand, despite priding themselves on their conversational skills, were ultimately all about sex. They weren't called *grandes horizontales* for nothing.

French courtesans were also known as *demi-mondaines*, creatures of the *demi-monde*, a term coined by writer Alexandre Dumas, fils. It was the half-world of women who flirted at the shadowy fringes of society. Ignored and unacknowledged by high society, they nevertheless made their extravagant presence felt. If you knew where to look, it was easy to spot them — parading along the Champs-Élysées or attending opening nights at the opera in full finery, a neon-bright billboard for their own business.

The courtesans were creatures of their century. They were women who fought to redefine what a woman could be, after the Parisian patriarchy had tried to put her in her powerless place. As seductive as hell and tough as nails, it's little wonder they left a lasting impression, influencing what it means to be a French woman. The most successful courtesans were beautiful, yes, but they had to have so much more. They invested wisely, patronised the arts and forged lasting friendships. They were the complete package. To this day, the ideal French woman is a direct descendant. She's a bundle of serious substance — confidence, intelligence, eloquence — wrapped up in a seductively soft bow.

At the time, I was still to appreciate the multifaceted French definition of feminine allure, and the hidden codes of Parisiennes' stylistic and social demeanour, which is for the most part modest and unassuming. French girls are traditionally schooled in all facets of etiquette by their mothers, and from a young age they learn what's appropriate and what's not. While my mother was a stickler for manners, she preferred to let me experiment and find my own way when it came to my personal style. At the time, Brigitte Bardot was still my icon. I asked myself only one question when I shopped: would BB wear this? I'd yet to realise that the 1960s sex kitten had been expressing *herself*, and a moment in history, and perhaps that wasn't quite the right statement for me to make in modern times.

But also, I wasn't self-aware enough to truly express myself. I was certainly far from understanding what the full package of femininity entailed. Naïvety played a role, for sure, but it was more that I was taking a while to grow up socially. I'd had a few boyfriends, but none that serious. Romance for me existed mostly between the yellowed pages of vintage books. I might have dressed in a somewhat flirty manner, but it was without artifice or intent. Unlike my icon, I wouldn't have been able to follow up easily on the seductive messages I seemed to send out. Then again, I wasn't so interested in the physicality of romance. I would have been too much of a prude for the free-love era of Brigitte Bardot and I certainly wouldn't have made an overly enthusiastic courtesan. The idea of dating was downright daunting. In an ideal world, I would meet my soul mate by chance, early on, just as my parents had.

One of my favourite movies as a teenager was *Gigi*, the musical about courtesans set in turn-of-the-century Paris. I'd watch it every year with my grandmother, and it was only on the third or so viewing that I realised, with a blush, it was a movie about the selling of sex. I'd thought it simply a pretty tale about one girl's journey to become a true Parisienne. I melted for the gilded snippets of Belle Époque Paris and the frill-laden gowns while singing along to Maurice Chevalier's 'Thank Heavens for Little Girls' (without sensing how faintly creepy the signature tune is). Over time, however, I came to an appreciation of its subtle subversiveness: when Gigi ends up marrying the reformed playboy Gaston, rather than take the role of his concubine, she becomes his equal, and a woman of the twentieth century.

As the veiled curtain came down on the Belle Époque, a new era began in which women would take greater control of their destinies. This was the world in which Colette, the author of *Gigi* (and many other lauded titles of French literature) came of age. Born in the countryside of Burgundy, Colette moved to Paris at twenty, upon marrying a family friend known to all as Willy. He was fourteen years her senior, very much the man-about-town, and determined to show his innocent young bride, with her knee-skimming braids and wide-eyed wonder, the ways of a racier world.

As the legend goes, Willy, a journalist and editor, discovered his wife's talent for writing and encouraged her to record her schoolgirl memories —

albeit with a heavy-handed dose of spice sprinkled throughout. He then took credit for what became the spectacularly successful *Claudine* novels. I'd read Colette's *Claudine at School* but I was far from this mesmerising French schoolgirl who confided her story in this diary of a book, so breathless with excitement and exclamation marks. I didn't have, shall we say, such a liberally minded view when it came to matters of love.

As Willy's fame grew, so did the number of women who threw themselves at him, often dressed and tressed up as saucy schoolgirls. Colette was miserable, as you can imagine, but the marriage wasn't all doom and gloom. It was through Willy that she met the city's avant-garde and eventually learned to find and assert her own voice. With her kittenishly heart-shaped face and a newly chopped mane of permed curls, Colette had a feline-like intensity to her. Once divorced from Willy, she threw herself into the philosophy of free love with a ferocious passion, and became a trailblazer for women who wanted to live and love with the freedom that men had always had (just as would Brigitte Bardot, whom Colette saw as a modern Gigi). Scandalous lifestyle aside, Colette was just as famous for her brilliant, poignant prose. She wrote about love and its intricate ins-and-outs with the same pure, raw emotion, not to mention lush and heartfelt detail, as she described the beloved Burgundian landscapes of her childhood. You can hear her heart beat as much as smell the sun-sweetened strawberries and touch the velvety green woods, and it was these evocative descriptions that so entranced me and kept me dreaming of life as a writer.

&

I had booked myself a room in a small hotel not far from Colette's final Parisian residence, the Palais-Royal. And so the next day I made a pilgrimage there, crunching over the gravel towards the tall, elegant windows of her former apartment. It was by this glass, overlooking the rows of clipped lime trees and the immaculately manicured, rosebush-trimmed lawn, that Colette penned *Gigi*. Luxuriating in her sofa-bed that doubled as a desk, in the aromas of the floral bouquets that garlanded her room, and in the outside sounds of rustling leaves and fountain spray, she must have felt as happily at home as she once did in her childhood village.

Don't be fooled by the bucolic prettiness of the Palais-Royal. This primly elegant park, so tastefully edged in colonnaded arcades, hides some shady memories. The gardens date back almost 400 years, when Cardinal Richelieu built his sumptuous residence on the site. The palace eventually passed to the royal family, ending up in the hands of the cadet branch and eventually the Duke d'Orléans, who was immensely more popular among Parisians than his ill-fated cousin, King Louis XVI. In the early 1780s, the cash-strapped duke decided to convert his backyard into a kind of forum of fun. He rented out the ground floor spaces of the arcades to shopkeepers and restaurateurs, and the floors above to all manner of shifty operators. Everyone was allowed in, from courtesans to countesses, pimps to puppeteers — everyone, that is, except the police. Not surprisingly, the Palais-Royal became a kind of revolutionary hotbed, with students and *sans-culottes* flocking there to read illicit pamphlets and brew radical ideas over coffee. But politics paled in significance next to its role as Paris's ultimate pleasure palace, a den of debauchery.

Spanning the grounds of the Palais-Royal — just next to the infamous Daniel Buren art installation: pillars painted in black and white stripes for a liquorice effect — is a twin row of columns. It's all that's left of the Galerie d'Orléans, one of the earliest ever shopping malls. There ladies could come to buy frilled parasols or rosewater perfumes, and if they knew where to look, they could also surreptitiously slip an erotic novel or packet of condoms into their shopping bag. No wonder Parisiennes became such passionate shoppers.

I click-clacked my way around the shopping arcades that remain. These days, the Palais-Royal is a hallowed high-fashion address, but back in the early 1990s there was still a musty air of yesteryear, its dusty boutiques crammed to the rafters with random and eclectic bibelots, like toy soldiers, antique medals, or made-to-measure, elbow-length gloves. I stopped in front of a store called Didier Ludot, and marvelled at the vintage haute couture on display. I was myself in a 1960s fashion phase, courtesy of Brigitte Bardot. I recall wearing a black-and-white hound's-tooth coat wrapped over a turtle neck sweater, vinyl tunic, and thick tights with shiny high-heeled boots, all in some shade of black. In the sixties, Bardot had slipped out of her girlie floral dresses and into French space-age style: mini dresses in shiny high-tech fabrics by the likes of André Courrèges and Paco Rabanne, one of whose sequin-laden party dresses sparkled in the window before me. I heaved a sigh and headed for the exit. Today was my day for Christmas shopping, and I doubted I'd have any francs left over for such fripperies of my own.

Just north of the Palais-Royal is Galerie Vivienne, an exquisite covered passage way. In the early nineteenth century, many Right Bank streets were connected by a series of such graceful glass-topped and marble-floored boutique-lined galleries, inspired by the Palais-Royal. A shopper's heaven at a time when the city was lacking in footpaths, these gas-lit arcades allowed women who preferred not to plunge ankle-deep in Parisian mud to glide through, leisurely admiring window displays brimming with hats, twinkling with jewels or perfumed with bonbons. Galerie Vivienne, with its swirling mosaic floor, is the most elegant, and it was especially so on this day, festooned in flickering Christmas lights.

I spent the rest of the morning weaving in and out of this arcade, and the few that remain nearby. The Passage Jouffroy is perhaps most like falling down a rabbit hole into old Paris. There's a whimsical toy store, where you can buy doll palaces (no mere doll houses there), a dainty *salon de thé* serving up frothy, creamy delights, and the quirky Hôtel Chopin, still trussed up in all its lacy Romantic-era glory. It's a veritable time capsule of curios, a flashback to a quieter and quainter Paris, just before it bloomed into Belle Époque grandeur.

Few phenomena have transformed the cityscape and psyche of Paris like the boulevards. I took a right from Passage Jouffroy onto Boulevard Montmartre, which leads into Boulevard Haussmann, named after the man who made Paris the city famous for its grand tree-lined streets complete with wide, stroll-worthy footpaths where Parisians could see and be seen. Cafés spilled over onto what is now a Parisian institution — *la terrasse* — and patrons would sit and spend hours watching the world — clattering carriages and misty-eyed window-shoppers — go by.

Some say the repetitive nature of Haussmann's streetscapes make for mind-numbing monotony, but I've always found they induce a state of harmony, as you can walk endlessly, almost in a trance. Unless, of course, you're wearing boots that aren't made for walking. So this is why Parisiennes wear comfortable little ballerina flats, I realised that afternoon, adding a pale-pink pair to my mental shopping list. Luckily, I was about to reach shopping nirvana.

It might by now come as no surprise to learn that Paris invented the department store. Multi-levelled retail meccas, divided according to product categories, sprang up along the grand boulevards. They were temples of commerce for a new consumer culture, houses of worship topped with a dome through which light could shine. I walked into Galeries Lafayette and stood in the perfume-hazed atrium, in awe beneath the stained-glass cupola, a prismatic jewel atop the golden, crown-like interior. You feel as though you're in a treasure chest. Your head spins and your senses are dazzled. No wonder I never come out of there *sans* shopping bag.

On this particular trip, I bought my parents a scarf each from the accessories department (it's impossible not to come home from this city without such a souvenir, the ultimate symbol of Parisian panache), then glided up an escalator to find myself in the lingerie department. The word *lingerie* in France once meant 'things made of linen'. No longer. These days Parisian lingerie is more likely to be slinky, silky slips of sweet nothings in a spectrum of shades; there is always the classic black, often in lace, but also a selection of delicious *macaron* hues. I couldn't help but be tempted, walking over and picking up a balconette bra made from whisper-light tulle, tinted a shade of apricot sorbet.

'That would suit you, Mademoiselle,' said a tall saleswoman, made even taller by a beehive of a hairdo.

'Oh, I'm not sure, I've never worn anything like it,' I replied.

'Have you ever been fitted?' she asked, looming over me. And before I knew it, Madame Lingerie had whipped out a tape measure and bustled me into a change room. It had been a good five years since I'd been measured for my first bra, and I self-consciously peeled off my top.

'*Oh là là*, that is not right for you,' she tut-tutted, looking at my black elastic-edged triangle bra with equal parts sympathy and disdain. 'You need some oomph, Mademoiselle.'

It was true. I could have done with some help in that department. I just always ended up spending all of my money on *outer*wear.

'*Voilà*. See how this style of bra gives you shape, but still appears natural?'

I looked in the mirror and couldn't believe it: I actually had cleavage. It was subtle, granted, but it was most definitely there. The French, I'd later find out, abhor overly engineered push-up bras. They like tricks, sure (what is couture if not clothing that makes the body look better?) but those whose effects fall within the realm of nature's possibilities.

'It's very pretty but I don't really need it,' I protested, but only half-heartedly, my powers of rationality fast dissolving in the face of such feminine allure.

Madame sensed me weakening. 'One doesn't have a need for beautiful lingerie, one has a desire for it!' she declared, triumphantly.

'But I don't even have a boyfriend ...'

'You don't buy lingerie for a man,' she replied scoldingly. 'You buy it for yourself, because it feels good. When you wear even the simplest outfit, if you have beautiful lingerie underneath, you feel better in your skin, you walk more seductively. You will see.'

So that's the secret to the swaying, sashaying stroll of Parisiennes.

'And you must buy the matching culottes,' Madame added. 'You should never wear mismatched lingerie.'

I blushed at the thought of the beige cotton briefs beneath my tunic.

My funds being so unexpectedly and dramatically depleted, I decided to cut my losses and head for the exit. The ballerina flats would have to wait. Anyway, I apparently now had the real Parisian secret to a seductive swagger.

&

Later that week, I went to Angelina for breakfast. The iconic tearoom, having opened in 1903 in the fading years of the Belle Époque, retains the diffused golden glow so symbolic of those times. And you can still order the *chocolat à l'ancienne dit 'l'Africain'*, the famous pot of decadently thick hot chocolate. Which I promptly did. It was all I could do not to dollop the whipped cream on top.

I had pretty much starved myself all year, recording every ingested kilojoule in a slim notebook I carried around with me. I'd only recently realised how crazy this was, as I emerged from the pressure-cooker that was my final school year. I guessed it had been my way of trying to control the situation. Plus, I swore that an empty stomach seemed to sharpen my mind. Fortunately, it wasn't a true eating disorder, as it disappeared overnight. Literally. I woke up one day and knew that I no longer needed that notebook, which I proceeded to toss in the bin — before smearing butter (butter!) and jam (sugar!) all over my two (yes, two!) thick slices of toast (carbs!). Still, I was wary not to go too far to the other extreme. I knew my limits — and whipped cream atop molten chocolate was definitely one.

The waitress placed a tiered tray of petite pastries on the table. Now these, these I could do. I mean, how could anything so little and so pretty possibly do any harm? As I nibbled the mini croissant, at once buttery and flaky, I could have melted with happiness. Really, I thought, where better to get reacquainted with the utter joys of eating than Paris?

After breakfast, I walked around the Tuileries Garden just across Rue de Rivoli. As in many French parks, statues of nude nymphs seemed as common as trees. I wondered how this shaped the impressionable minds of young girls, still coming to terms with their changing bodies. Surely it would give a certain perspective to the issue; the commonness of all this nudity would, you'd think, make for a shrugged-shouldered sense of the *c'est normale*. At home, one barely dressed stone maiden would probably have everyone up in arms, railing at this immodest attack on

Australian girls' virtuous minds. And yet, Australian women generally flash much more flesh than Parisiennes, who can often seem prudish in their simple, classic wardrobe choices. And yet! Parisiennes are the ones who come across as most comfortable in their own skin, so at ease with their body that they don't feel they have to show it off for reassurance from the crowd. Incidentally, wolf whistles seem non-existent in Paris; in their place, a subtle smile of appreciation.

I was wearing another mini dress that day: a thigh-skimming red shift, worn with black tights and my trusty boots. A leopard print faux-fur coat topped it all off. It was not what you'd call a subtle look. Nor very Parisian. I felt very much out of place that day. Fashion is all about finding yourself, but it can just as effectively be about working out who you're not, and I was starting to not feel like myself. What's more, my clothes felt out of sync with my body, which I was still trying to understand, if not control. I wasn't sure I liked my legs, my thighs and calves having bulked up from a year's worth of daily step aerobics. Or my chest, which I was increasingly wishing was a little larger, to rebalance a figure with bottom-heavy tendencies. Or maybe I just hadn't grown into my own skin.

I wandered over to the Louvre, where I planned to spend the rest of the morning. I began with the Venus de Milo, the Ancient Greek sculpture depicting Aphrodite, the goddess of love. The marble-carved, semi-draped Venus is a figure of breathtaking beauty, even without her arms. And even when judged in today's world of body perfection. Venus is what women's magazines would somewhat derisively term a Pear. And yet, for centuries this very figure has been the ideal, because this Venus — who was sculpted in the second century — boasts the magical waist-to-hip ratio of 0.7, which to this day tops the lists when it comes to men's preferences.

Evolutionary biologists would say it's something to do with childbearing hips signalling fertility. And they must be onto something, because the art world, like the Louvre, is filled with examples of naked women whose waists measure approximately 70 per cent of their hip circumference. Think of the sinuously satin-skinned *Une Odalisque* by Ingres, or his curvy women of *The Turkish Bath*, or the various mythical Three Graces, sculpted or painted in all their fleshy glory.

I watched a group of school children, aged around thirteen, as they sat before Pradier's sculpture of the trio of Graces, listening attentively as a teacher explained the history of the work. Not one schoolgirl squirmed with discomfort, not one schoolboy sniggered from embarrassment. To them, nudity — both artful and natural — was as much a matter of respect as a mere matter-of-fact affair. I couldn't imagine the same scene taking place at home, which made me feel envious. I wished I'd grown up in a country where there were enough displays of natural bodily beauty for a girl to know that it's perfectly normal to have hips. Maybe then we'd have a healthier respect for our bodies, and not torture them with daily aerobics and occasional starvation. Instead, we'd nourish our bodies with the right amount of good food, keep trim by simply walking — and enhance the rest with great tailoring.

My last stop at the Louvre was the Winged Victory — or Nike, Goddess of Victory. If I get to the Louvre right on opening, I run straight to her, so as to have her all to myself even if only for a few seconds. But I also always visit her at the end, as she's such a high note on which to complete a tour. Like the Venus de Milo, Victory dates to second-century BC Greece, and she is also incomplete, missing her head. But this only lends so much momentum to the rest of her. She stands at the top of a dramatic sweep of stairs, and you sense the power of her body before you start to climb; the beautiful drapery can barely contain her force, while her majestic wings are set to take flight.

Nike, the winged goddess, happened to be the emblem of the university in which I was enrolled for the following year. It was a cleverly chosen symbol, because Victory represents a journey into the unknown, a bracing of self against the winds of resistance. Still, I wondered if I was on the right path. I'd worked so hard all year to get accepted into the same law school my parents had gone to, yet when I received the letter of acceptance, it felt anti-climactic. I mean, I liked the law well enough, and I was very much the law-abiding citizen, never even daring to cross against a red pedestrian light. But it's not like I wanted to make it my life. The first thing I did in Paris was not visit the tomb of Napoléon to doff my beret to the man who created the Civil Code; *non*, I went and got myself a deluxe manicure. Paris and my hands knew my future. I should have accepted my fate and switched from law to beauty school then and there. Perhaps Winged Victory up there was trying to tell me to lead my life with my heart, not my head.

That afternoon, I explored the Les Halles district. Once the area around the city's old markets, the patchwork of higgledy-piggledy streets was now studded with eclectic boutiques. One caught my eye, its windows crammed with vintage mini dresses made from all sorts of light-flashing fabrics, from vinyl to spangles to lurex. In this city of subtle tailoring, I exhaled with relief to finally see myself reflected somewhere. Experiencing an overwhelming need to feel like I belonged, I walked inside, happily inhaling the patchouli incense that filled the air and smothered my senses, already under assault from the sounds of the Rolling Stones and the sight of a riot of colours.

'Bonjour, petite BB.'

I swung around so swiftly that I almost lost my footing, and certainly my composure, because peering at me was a pair of dark-brown eyes, narrowed with curiosity. They belonged to the most handsome face (dark eyes, chiselled cheekbones, pouty lips: check! check! check!) I'd seen in, well, I could barely remember how long.

Hang on, did he just call me a *bébé?* I wondered. Baby. I mean, he did seem old — perhaps even thirty (*mon dieu*!). But then I remembered that Brigitte Bardot's initials, in French, are pronounced *bébé*. He'd called me a little BB.

'I wish!' I laughed, a little self-consciously, if embarrassingly gratified by the compliment.

We introduced ourselves. His name was Marc and it turned out this was his shop, which he filled with vintage clothes from the 1960s.

'Brigitte Bardot must be more popular in Australia,' he said. 'Parisiennes don't dress like her that much. It's difficult to sell the 1960s look here.'

'Then why do you do it?' I asked.

'I don't find the other eras appealing,' he replied, with a shrug. 'Paris was at its peak in the 1960s. It was all about the future. Since then, everyone has been looking backwards.'

'But you're looking back, too,' I pointed out.

'Well, true, but I try to really live the period. The optimism. *Le free love*.'

I could feel my cheeks turn as red as my dress.

He laughed again. 'I'm just teasing. Hey, I'm just about to close up. Let's go grab something to eat. You can practise your French.'

I nodded, cheeks still flushed, heart fluttering; I didn't know the right words to say in English, let alone French.

Café Costes was an impossibly hip restaurant with an ice-cool interior courtesy of the *enfant terrible* of design Philippe Starck. We sat outside, *en terrasse*, and Marc ordered two kirs royales — champagne tinged with crème de cassis, just as a tint of pink infused the grey of the cool winter light. The sky was steadily darkening to jet-black, and soon the lamps flickered into action. The heady romance of the moment would have whirled my senses into overdrive had the champagne not already done so.

'That is the Fontaine des Innocents,' Marc said, pointing to the square before us, in the middle of which was a sort of triumphal arch, set upon a tiered, illuminated pedestal down which water cascaded. And then he chuckled: 'Innocent, like you.'

'I'm not that much of a child!' I exclaimed. 'Okay … maybe a little,' I conceded, in answer to his raised eyebrow.

'Don't worry, I'm a true gentleman,' he said, at which he lightly took my hand, and bobbed his head over it so that his lips hovered just above, close enough that I could feel his breath on my skin.

Marc might have gone on about the 1960s, but like many French men, his in-built codes of behaviour can be traced to long before then; he is a product of centuries of traditions and customs. As I'd find out that evening, he was proud of his city's heritage, weaving historical tidbits into his wide-ranging conversation.

'It's the oldest monumental fountain in Paris,' he continued, one of the many facts I'd learn on our evening's tour. 'It actually used to be called the Fontaine des Nymphes — see the sculptures?'

'Of course it was,' I said rolling my eyes. 'You French and your naked women.'

'We just like to celebrate the beauty of the female form,' he murmured, leaning back in his three-legged bucket chair, as though to take in more of me.

'Some gentleman!' I joked, trying to make light of the situation, but he continued to stare. Instinctively hugging my coat around me, I shivered, perhaps a little too dramatically. 'It's cold,' I declared, partly in attempt to change the course of conversation.

'Really? It's hot where I'm sitting. Or maybe it's just this heat lamp.' He was clearly enjoying the situation. Parisian men probably didn't get to toy with naïve Australian girls all that often.

'Don't be embarrassed,' he said, laughing. 'Everyone flirts in France. It's a national game.'

Marc had used the term *flirter*. The French borrowed the term from the English, although they're flirts from way back, because the English word was pinched from French in the first place. In Old French, *fleureter* meant to talk sweet nothings. You can still say *conter fleurette* — to talk of little flowers. It's one of my favourite French expressions, bringing to mind a hand-in-hand walk through a field of daisies. Speaking of which, when the French pluck daisies, they don't simply alternate between 'he loves me' and 'he loves me not'. Plucked petals correspond to one of the following: *Je t'aime un peu* (I love you a little), *Je t'aime beaucoup* (a lot), *Je t'aime tendrement* (tenderly), *Je t'aime passionnément* (passionately), *Je t'aime à la folie* (madly) or *Je t'aime pas du tout* (not at all). Matters of the heart are not *noir* and *blanc* in French. Love is a much more nuanced game.

The curious thing about French flirting is that there might not even be a particular aim in mind. The French, I've learned, naturally like to charm, and in their language, *la séduction* is not the same cold, hard calculated play that it is in English; it's about pleasing for the sheer joy of both parties. Men make an effort to talk to women, and not because it's a means to a certain end. Often dialogue is the end in itself.

Like the water trickling down that nymph-adorned fountain, our stream of conversation flowed naturally. Marc spoke slowly so that I could understand him, and jotted down words I didn't know on a serviette.

'So what do you want to do with your life?' he asked.

'I have no idea. I'm still recovering from the exhaustion of school.'

'I know what you mean. School in France is fierce, too. How you perform affects the rest of your life, the jobs you get. Luckily I knew what I wanted to do, so I didn't let the pressure get to me.'

'I was solely responsible for my pressure,' I said. 'But I think I burnt myself out. I'm not quite sure I'll ever be able to work that hard again.'

'Well, I can tell you studied your French — you speak like a textbook! Very formal and 1800s, it's rather sweet.'

It was around this time that I realised I'd been addressing Marc as *vous* — the formal form of 'you' — while he had been using the familiar *tu* all along. That might not seem such a big deal in English, where everyone is the same kind of you, but in French, *tu* versus *vous* is a serious power semantic. (So much for all that *égalité*.) Adults *tutoyer* kids, who in turn *vouvoyer* their elders. At the office, your boss would probably be a *vous*, and you a *tu*. But it gets tricky when you're closer in status and age. If you start off with *vous*, changing to *tu* is a huge jump; you're moving into a new level of intimacy. But what did it suggest, I wondered, that Marc saw me as *tu* from the start — and was happy to be a *vous*. He considered me to be young, that was obvious. I couldn't work out if it was also a respect issue. Should I be offended? Or should I just be a grown-up and simply *tutoyer* him back. But I just couldn't bring myself to say *tu*. Perhaps he awed me with his apparent worldliness. Or maybe I was still overly governed by the rigid rules of high-school French. Interestingly, Marc never suggested I *tutoyer* him. He probably liked that subtle imbalance of power.

&

After dinner, we wandered around Les Halles. As I tried to keep up with the ever-veering subjects of Marc's conversation, I soon lost my bearings around the swerving streets. I wondered how geography shapes a person's outlook on life. My home city was a neat and tidy grid, with one best way to get anywhere, and I was used to linear lines of discourse. In Paris, you could choose any number of interesting routes to reach the one destination. Could that be the reason the locals flit so easily from one seemingly random subject to another?

As we stepped into a particularly lively street, I leaned closer towards Marc, trying to make out his barely audible words. And then a little closer still. And before I knew it, he had turned me around and pinned me against a wall, right between two cafés filled with outdoor diners.

'*Embrasse-moi*!' It was my first French kiss and it was *magnifique*.

'Let's keep walking,' Marc said, after a few minutes, ever so nonchalantly. I felt like a hot breathless mess. I looked around self-consciously, but nobody was staring. Nobody else's world had spun off its axis. We hadn't put anyone off their meal. Scenes like this — which I'd usually only seen in movies — obviously happened all the time in Paris.

Marc continued chatting, as before, but he'd taken my arm in his. I noticed that he made sure to always walk on the street side of the footpath, which required fairly regular arm-holding rearrangements. It was a little clumsy, but also endearing — his commitment to an apparent vestigial custom from the days when the muddy Parisian streets would play havoc with women's dresses.

French chivalry dates back to the Middle Ages, when the knights — *les chevaliers* — ritualised a new romantic love for a new kind of woman, one who craved worship. With their lords away fighting the holy wars, ladies took charge of their castles, which lent them an erotic new prominence for the younger, more handsome nobles left behind. Adultery was officially a no-go zone, but that didn't mean that star-crossed lovers couldn't indulge in long lingering looks, and playful, if complex, rituals of courtship. Men had to prove their worth and devotion in new and entertaining ways, from music to jousting. Courts became the centre of attention, their ladies sitting upon throned pedestals, adored by their fans and serenaded by troubadours, whose love stories were recited and sung all over France. This new style of romance became known as courtly love; its rules developed at court, but it was also very much like a game that two might play on another kind of court, batting *bons mots* and eyes at one another. Its modern-day descendant is *courtoisie* — courtesy: men opening doors for women, and the like.

'Come, I want to show you something,' said Marc, taking my hand and leading me down a cobbled street. We stopped before a huge wooden *porte-cochère*, which creaked open after Marc punched in a door code.

'You live here?' I asked, somewhat hesitant.

'No, I just know the code. There is the most beautiful hidden garden.'

'But that's illegal.' I knew I sounded lame, but a mild sense of panic had flicked on my flight-or-fight sense, and I was starting to think I might need a getaway strategy. And a hefty coach door would not have been helpful to the situation.

'Ah, the law is not so serious here. We are the land of *liberté*, remember?' Spoken like a true citizen of a city where pedestrians race across the road at any given time, regardless of the risk that a car might be zooming the wrong way down that one-way street.

We had walked through a vaulted entryway, into a cobbled courtyard, a wonderland of fairy lights, topiary trees and statues of nymphs (but of course). A row of lean and elegant, leafless trees stretched to the sky, their stark branches making patterns with the exposed beams of one of the buildings, while a stone building opposite was covered in a luscious coat of glossy green ivy. The semi-shuttered windows looked down upon us with window boxes of chrysanthemum, valiantly a-bloom despite the winter chill, in vibrant oranges and yellows. It would have been delightful had I not been so suddenly overcome with nerves.

'I want to show you what's down the end here,' said Marc.

And that's when I knew I had to get out. I can't remember what I said, but I stammered every excuse under the stars why I shouldn't be there — in frightful franglais, as my French vocabulary is only accessible when the rest of my mind is totally calm and clear.

Eventually Marc gave up trying to lead me down the garden path (literally), and emitted a huge Gallic sigh. 'Okay, let's get you back to your hotel. I told you I am a gentleman.'

Oddly, we reverted to our previous banter, as though nothing untoward had just occurred. Perhaps this was simply part of the French game of love. I had a sneaking suspicion that an Australian guy, in the same situation, would have stormed out.

We finally found ourselves in front of my hotel.

'So, can I come up?' asked Marc, pouting his lips, cocking his head and generally trying to be as irresistible as possible.

But I had a visceral need to feel in control of my life once more. 'I have to get to sleep,' I replied artlessly, feeling every bit the unsophisticated Australian.

'*Tant pis pour toi*,' he muttered, turning on his shiny heels and walking off into the night. Too bad for you.

So much for chivalry.

&

I woke the next morning with that same hazy sense of disorientation you have after a dream that has spun out of control — you know, those ones that begin well enough, yet suddenly go off in strange and random directions, and you find yourself saying or doing the exact opposite of what your higher self is screaming. And then it dawned on me that what I was unravelling and replaying in my mind had actually occurred. A one-two of mortification hit me in the pit of my stomach, and I instinctively curled into the foetal position, pulling the bedspread over my head in a kind of denial reflex.

Not that I thought I should have invited Marc up to my hotel room, or stayed in that secret garden of his. I didn't regret saying *non*. But I couldn't shake the feeling that I had taken a misjudged turn at some point, said the wrong thing, failed some kind of test. I felt gauche, like a silly kid playing dress-ups, acting at being worldly and seductive. And perhaps I'd falsely advertised myself, with my thigh-skimming dress and knee-high boots. I wondered how a Parisienne would have acted. She probably wouldn't have worn vinyl, for one. And then never got herself into a situation she didn't want to be in. She would have been one step ahead — which is always easier when wearing little ballerina flats, of course.

From my observations of Parisiennes in their natural habitat — what they wore, how they chatted with men in cafés — I was starting to enviously sense that these women might have the right balance of seductiveness and self-preservation. Just like those medieval ladies, they were active and equal players in the court of love, but always in control — knowing when to lean in and when to pull back. How much to reveal, how much to hide.

As decidedly non-Parisian as I felt that morning, I didn't think it was something I couldn't learn, that these subtle seduction instincts were exclusively innate to Parisiennes. I had a hunch that courtship remained very much a coded affair; when there are rules, anyone eager enough can learn how to play, with time and practice. I also needed to learn the secrets to Parisienne style, I sighed, as I slipped into a hot-pink pinafore, belted up a faux-leather coat and zipped on my high boots.

After stomping and scowling my way around the local streets, I took a turn onto Avenue de l'Opéra, looked up to see the old opera house and couldn't help but smile. Every lovesick girl knows the feel-good powers of cake, and the Palais Garnier is like the most glorious gâteau you could dream up, a tiered and domed, marble-rippled confection, drizzled with mint icing and garlanded in gold. As a building, it's voluptuous almost to the point of vulgarity. Its creator Charles Garnier, in the mid nineteenth century, mixed all sorts of design references to come up with an entirely new kind of architectural splendour, one to symbolise a new age where princesses and prostitutes continually one-upped each other in the glamour stakes, one where the nouveau riche gorged themselves on opulence. Garnier, a son of a blacksmith and a lace maker, was the perfect man to refashion the definition of luxury, setting the scene for the grandiose Belle Époque, where life was more a stage than the stage itself.

I decided to venture inside — it seemed like a suitably melodramatic thing to do, given the tortured, operatic drama playing inside my head. I knew that I was going to be wowed, but I was not prepared for how knee-weakeningly lavish the interior would be. You can barely breathe for the opulence: curvaceous bronze statues brandishing a galaxy of lamps, exotic mosaics underfoot and florid paintings above, a kaleidoscope of coloured marbles, gold paint and crystal-heavy chandeliers dazzling your eyes at every turn — and mirrors to multiply the sumptuousness all the more.

'Zee Pariziens came 'ere not for zee show, but to zee an' be zeen,' the tour guide was saying. We stood at the base of the grand staircase, an exuberant sweep of marble and onyx that splits in two, ascending to a ring of gilded balconies. 'Men came 'ere wiz zeir wives on a Monday, and zeir mistresses on a Friday. Or zey came looking for a mistress. 'Ere was zee best place in town to pick up. You can imagine how seductive zee ladies looked, walking up zeze ztairz wiz zeir *robes à faux cul* [bustle dresses — literally: fake-butt frocks], wiz zeir diamonds glitterrring on zeir décolleté, sparrrkling under zee chandeliers, *non*?'

The Palais Garnier had been the home of both singing and dancing until recently, when the Opéra de Paris had decamped to the Place de la Bastille. Twenty years later, I still haven't been, partly because the hulking Modernist building leaves me cold — as does what goes on inside. Despite my mother's impassioned efforts, I've never fallen for the opera. I mean, I get it if you feel like singing about love — but when your aria concerns what you're going to eat for dinner, I can't take that seriously. I've always been more of a ballet kind of girl. I'm a sucker for a tutu, for one. But I also love the mystique of ballet, the power of what is not said, the focus on the universal language of the body. Ballet for me has a subliminal poetry, elegant demureness and subtle force; it's just more, well, French.

Sure, there's French opera, but that's really just a tweaking of what was originally an Italian import. The Italian language, so rhythmic in even everyday banter, naturally lends itself to the lofty highs and dramatic lows of opera.

But ballet is French at every pirouette, right down to its slipper straps. It was the French who originally thought to have women dance during the *entractes* of Italian opera, and this eventually spun off into its own art form of classical ballet. When we think of ballet, most of us imagine flutters of frothy white tulle, for which we must also say *merci* to the French; during the height of the Romantic era, ballerina Marie Taglioni so entranced with her turn in the ultimate *ballet blanc, Les Sylphides*, that we gush over this ethereal style of ballet to this day.

We were ushered into the red-velvet auditorium, lush and lustrous under the magnificent gilt-bronze and crystal chandelier ('az tall az two 'ouses!') and the capricious colours of Chagall's painted ceiling. 'Monsieur Garnier loved rrrred,' our guide purred. 'Eet waz a sexy new colour for a passionate new age. Not everyone waz 'appy at zee time, as eet iz zo sexy. Eet 'az a little of the bordello about it, *non*?'

Turns out, the Palais Garnier was very much the pick-up joint. For the price of a subscription for three seats a week, any rich top-hatted Parisian could buy his way in, and stalk backstage as though it were his very own hunting ground. Most of the ballerinas found themselves working double-shift at night for a patron. 'Zay must 'av been exhausted,' exclaimed our guide. 'But art loverrrz were usually more lucrative zan zee art itself.'

The tour over, I wandered down Boulevard des Capucines, its simple stone façades soothing after the sensory overload of the Palais Garnier. The old opera house captured an outrageously over-the-top moment in time in the city's history, but Parisian architecture soon reverted to its prevailing theme of classic chic. Parisiennes, too, began to eschew outward displays of showiness, a simple black dress masking a set of lacy lingerie in the same way that their deceptively plain windows belie a brilliant extravagance within. Parisiennes love their gold and glitz, but mostly in intimate settings.

On reaching Place de la Madeleine, I sat myself down on the steps of the church it's named after. You could be mistaken for thinking the colossal colonnaded Église de la Madeleine has time-travelled in from Ancient Greece. Originally designed as a temple to the greatness of Napoléon's army when the antiquity trend was in full swing, it was later consecrated as a church dedicated to Mary Magdalene, the patron saint of repentant prostitutes, which is fitting, as one of history's most celebrated courtesans prayed in this very church. Marie Duplessis was the real-life Lady of the Camellias, the prostitute with a heart of gold made famous by Alexandre Dumas, fils, who mythologised his former lover in his best-selling *La Dame aux Camélias*, a book that in turn inspired *La Traviata*, one of the most iconic operas, and has triggered the tears of countless French-learning school girls. The flower in the book's title was Marie's symbol. She would carry a bouquet of white camellias, except for those days of the month she was 'indisposed', in which case the camellias were red. Only a Parisienne could come up with such a pretty yet witty way of warning guys to keep the hell away.

Marie Duplessis wasn't your usual frills-and-feathers kind of courtesan. She dressed modestly, cladding her slender frame in understated gowns of black or white, and saved the bells and whistles for her glamorous apartment. Marie was both stylistically and intellectually ahead of her time. She could mix it with the smartest of men, having taught herself to read (and read all the classics at that) and she could hang at cafés with leading editors, writers and musicians, and keep the cultured conversation flowing. It's not difficult to understand the enchantment. Like a ballerina, her dainty demeanour veiled sheer grit. No wonder the book Marie inspired was reimagined as a ballet. She was the ultimate Romantic heroine, her deathly pallor enhancing her otherworldly beauty, her premature passing a tear-jerking tragedy.

Marie was the precursor to the fabled French woman, the subject worshipped in so many future books and articles. The literary genre that could be termed Gallic Chic didn't exist back when I was still learning the true story of the real Lady of the Camellias. I and the rest of the world were still clueless about how these French women, so alluringly sexy yet also stylishly demure, managed to carry off such *je ne sais quoi*. But I was starting to appreciate that Parisiennes rarely show their true colours; they don't wear their hearts splashed on their monochrome sleeves. In Paris, love, like fashion, is a subtle game of strategy, with a dash of intrigue thrown in for good measure.

&

I was, of course, a mere rookie when it came to games of *l'amour*. What's more, I was competing in another language; even if there had been instructions, I probably wouldn't have been able to interpret the subtleties and unspoken codes. But what was the point in strategising when I only had limited time to play? If I wanted to make another move, it had to be now or never. I returned to Marc's boutique later that afternoon.

After having psyched myself up with a glass of champagne in a nearby café, I walked through Marc's door with a force that was pure bubbly bravado; inside I was still quaking in my boots. Marc, nestled in a corner, swung around at the sound of said boots marching in, and a look of pleasure — or was it amusement? — flickered across his face. 'Ah, BB,' he said, with a smile. 'You returned.' He didn't sound at all surprised. Nor seem sheepish that I'd found him *tête-à-tête* with another girl.

'I, uh, wanted to, uh, say hi,' I stammered, failing miserably in my plan to act cool and collected.

'Hi, I'm Lulu,' said Marc's friend, walking towards me with a friendly smile, and earning my eternal gratitude. She must have been ten years older than me, and undoubtedly felt sorry for the gauche Australian girl sweating it out before her.

Lulu was a gorgeous slip of a thing, lithe as a ballerina in black leggings matched with a caramel cashmere sweater, and Parisian style personified. Her long curtain-fringed chestnut hair swung like silk around the chiselled frame of her face, her eyes were defined in inky liner, and her lips pale and pouty. She had the whole breezy Jane Birkin thing going on and I, dolled up like a poor-man's Brigitte Bardot, suddenly felt horribly overdone, like I'd arrived at a fancy-dress party having misinterpreted the theme.

'Marc told me about you,' she said. 'We love Australians!'

Marc was strolling over, all snake-hipped in a pair of slim, striped trousers, worn with a matching waistcoat. Oh *zut*, I thought, my heart thumping and skin burning, he's going to do that French-cheek-kiss thing. Sure enough, he took my shoulders and moved his lips towards my right cheek. I should have done the same. Flustered from failing to quickly recall the intricate Gallic greeting rules, I instead made for his left cheek, the result being that our foreheads clunked together.

'Oh sorry!' I exclaimed, my cheeks by now well and truly on fire.

Marc laughed. 'You have lots to learn. In Paris, we *faisons la bise* by starting on the right cheek, and we kiss twice. And you never actually make contact with your skin,'

So now I knew.

'We're about to close up and go for a drink,' said Lulu, with a sympathetic smile. 'Come with us? We're meeting a friend there.'

Awkward doesn't quite do justice to how I felt, although fleeing the scene seemed like the more mortifying option. So I agreed to go for a (much-needed) drink. At least there would be four of us — I wouldn't be the third wheel, or candleholder, as the French say.

As Marc locked up, Lulu led me around the corner, chatting away about everything she knew of Australia (Kylie Minogue and koalas was pretty much it), her manner so airy and nonchalant that I wondered whether my boots hadn't stomped on her relationship turf after all ... That, or I was not a threat in the first place.

We walked into a bar hazy with cigarette smoke. '*Salut, Louis*,' purred Lulu to a boy who looked like the fifth Beatle. He wore pageboy hair, a stovepipe trouser suit and the dreamy look of all those who wish they'd been born in another era. He greeted me with the requisite double-kiss.

'Isn't she a mini BB?' said Marc, as he arrived and pulled up a chair.

'All French men love Brigitte Bardot,' Louis said to me. 'Sadly, not enough women dress like her.'

'Bardot's look is not very Parisian,' declared Lulu. 'It's more Southern French. There's a big difference,' she told me, helpfully. Did I mention the bit about feeling like I got the dress code wrong?

Still, it was a pleasant enough evening. Lulu spoke English so she could help me navigate my way through the fast-paced conversation, which ranged from the sublime to the ridiculous in true Gallic style, debating everything from bidets to bouillabaisse.

'We French are a complicated bunch, aren't we?' Marc said, with a laugh. That was one word for it. I still couldn't work out if he and Lulu were a couple. However, I soon had the answer.

'*Alors*, I must be going,' said Marc, feigning a yawn.

On cue, Lulu stood up, too.

'It was lovely to meet you,' she said to me. 'Keep up the French.'

'*Au revoir, BB*,' Marc said, placing a kiss on each cheek with each B. 'Come visit me again.' Even though he knew I was leaving in a couple of days.

I watched him walk down the cobbled lane, his arm casually slung over Lulu's petite shoulders. Their slinky black silhouettes melted into the shadows, and my heart sank a little more with the beat of each step.

A dog was sitting by the table next to us, also peering out the window, and I suddenly felt like a pathetic puppy myself, wagging her tail for attention, desperate for the grown-ups to take her out. Snap out of it,

I silently barked at myself. It's not every night you get to hang in a Parisian bar practising French with a guy who looks like a cute young Paul McCartney.

Louis and I chitchatted a little more, but I just couldn't hold it in. 'Are they boyfriend and girlfriend?' I blurted out.

He looked at me curiously, but worked me out within seconds, his face softening with sympathy. 'Sometimes, yes.'

'He shouldn't be such a flirt,' I scowled, sulking into my glass of wine.

'That's just Marc,' Louis said, with a shrug. (French people love to shrug, the body's way of saying '*C'est la vie.*') 'He's living the dream. *Le free love.*'

'I don't think I could ever be so free with love.'

'I prefer monogamy, too. I just haven't found The One.'

'What's your type?'

'I'm not really sure. She doesn't need to look a certain way. Marc's superficial like that, girls need to dress the part. But I'm open. She could be anyone. Australian even … Relax! I'm just joking. You're too young anyway. Perhaps next time you visit?'

I was truly rattled by now. It was time to walk back to my hotel — alone — so I made to say *bonne nuit.*

'Sorry, I embarrassed you. But I had fun tonight. I've never met an Australian. Shall we keep in touch?' And so we swapped addresses and promised to be penpals. 'You can practise your French with me and I'll tell you all about what's happening in Paris. And I promise I won't mention Marc's name.'

Sigh. Why do we never like the nice friend?

&

It was my final *soirée* in Paris. I decided to go out in style, albeit solo, and spend the evening — and my remaining traveller's cheques — at the bar of the Hôtel de Crillon. Overlooking the Place de la Concorde — once the blood-soaked scene of the city's most overworked guillotine — the hotel was home to nobility before the Revolution. Like the bars and dancehalls that proliferated just up the road, it eventually opened its doors to a new Paris, one where anyone could buy into a glamorous life, even if just for a night.

I perched at the mirrored bench and ordered a glass of Perrier-Jouët, which I proceeded to sip languorously while flipping through the French magazines I'd just bought down the road at WH Smith, once again attempting to decipher the secrets of French style and seductiveness in the models splashed over the glossy pages. The combination of the golden bubbles popping in my head and the exquisite world showcased in the glossy pages before me equalled pure intoxication.

Just as I had drained my glass, the bartender placed another flute of champagne in front of me. 'From Monsieur over there,' he said, and nodded to my right.

Sitting a few seats down from me was a dapper gentleman of sixty, give or take. He made a gentlemanly gesture, as though doffing an invisible hat.

'*Merci*,' I said with a smile. '*C'est très sympa*.' That's very kind.

He reminded me of the suave-as-velvet Maurice Chevalier. And there I was, a Gigi, waiting for my own Belle Époque to begin.

'What are you celebrating, Mademoiselle?'

'Life, I guess. I'm about to go home and begin it.'

'Tell me, what kind of life do you want?'

'I'm not exactly sure. I first need to work out if I'm on the right path.'

'Ah,' he smiled sympathetically. 'I'm of the age where I can dispense wise words, so let me just say this: *la vie est courte*.' Life is short.

And with that, my very own Monsieur Chevalier buttoned up his long woollen coat, swirled a long cable-knit scarf around his neck and walked towards me. Oddly — as I was barely practised in the art of French embraces — I instinctively held out my right hand. He reached for it while lightly bending forwards, and air-kissed it in the most dignified way imaginable. It could have been a signature Maurice move straight out of *Gigi*.

'*Au revoir, Mademoiselle.* Never forget to listen to your heart.'

The French don't blindly 'follow' their heart, as we do. They 'listen' to it, and try to understand its language. I was still deciphering mine, although I could make out a few words. And they most certainly sounded French.

CHAPTER 4

MADEMOISELLE

[madmwazɛl] *nf* miss

In which, aged twenty-one, I discover you can be both feminist and feminine.

I dragged my suitcase up and around a spiral of stairs, the *thwack!* at each hollowed wooden step echoing off the cold musty walls. The building, with its façade of sooty stones and crumbling shutters, had evidently seen better days — some time back in the eighteenth century. I finally reached the top floor, dust particles dancing in the air of the past, and, guided by the dim wintry rays filtering through the skylight, I found the way to my door.

My apartment was once a *chambre de bonne*, a room for one of the maids employed to tidy and polish the fancier floors below. It was not hard to imagine the lives of my ghostly roommates. The studio furniture consisted of a single bed draped with a nubbly floral quilt, a wardrobe with a look of wilting grandeur, and a battered old desk propped by a dormer window under the sloping ceiling. The kitchen contained a bar fridge, microwave and a few rickety shelves. To the left, a door opened to a sliver of a bathroom (on seeing the tiny tub shower, I mentally calculated how little I could get away with washing my hair for the following few months); and to the right, a gas heater clung tenuously to the wall, as if unsure of its ability to warm up the chilly January air permeating the room.

The maids eventually moved out — as fewer families could afford live-in help — and the tiny apartments were rented out to hopeful artists and students who came to Paris to live the dream, just like me. My building was nestled in the fringes of the Latin Quarter, an international mecca for graduates since the days when scholars still spoke that ancient language. The fabled Sorbonne University was founded back in the twelfth century, and a plethora of bookstores, printers and publishers followed suit. The quarter had another resurgence after the French Revolution, when education became the great social leveller — for men, at least. It was a rite of passage, even for sons of wealthy families, to slum it there while studying, warmed by their dreams and their latest dancehall *grisette*, a working girl of the fashion industry who dated in order to supplement her meagre income. Some students aspired to creative greatness, hoping for acclaim as a poet or painter. This was the birth of the myth of the struggling, suffering artist in the garret.

It's no surprise that the opera *La Bohème* is mostly set in the Latin Quarter: the characters' real-life counterparts who inspired the book (the 1851 Henri Murger novel *Scènes de la Vie de Bohème*) that in turn sparked the opera, did too. Murger labelled the unconventional lifestyle of his protagonists as bohemian, a word that at the time evoked the Roma gypsies who originated from the central European region of Bohemia. He did such a great job of romanticising the image that the term bohemian was soon sugar-coated in sentimentality. Generations to come would fantasise about living à la bohémienne — at least for a few months.

So there I was, wrapped in a fringed shawl, my freezing hands desperately trying to fire up the heater, doing a great impersonation of Murger's Mimi. I was cold, I was hungry and I was the happiest I had been in a long time.

I'd taken some time off university. My attempt to study law had been a dismal failure. All that got me through the first couple of years were my French classes and part-time job in a fashion boutique; in contrast, I just couldn't get excited about constitutional complexities. When a favourite professor told me that I didn't have a lawyer's brain (in the nicest possible way) I didn't need a second opinion. I quit the faculty the next day, and opted for all sorts of practical arts subjects like Gothic Literature. But after a couple of years of analysing the symbolism in *Jane Eyre* and debating the Postmodern-feminist agenda of fairy tales, I started to wonder the big Why? Not to mention What (was I doing) and Where (was I going)? I was about to turn twenty-one, and had to at least start pretending that there was some grand plan on my horizon.

The only solution: I took a term off and took myself off to Paris for a few months, under the official guise of intensive language studies. My real aim, however, was to spend as much time as possible pondering and musing anything and everything over endless cups of coffees in Parisian cafés. If you're going to work through an existential crisis, it might as well be in the city that created the concept in the first place.

After a tepid — at best — shower, I quickly dried off and layered myself in an outfit that seemed appropriate for the romantically woeful weather: tights and a thermal spencer, a long dress followed by a just-as-long cardigan, all of which was topped by a thick wrap. Let me point out that this was the era of grunge, a kind of bohemianism of the early 1990s. I laced on my Doc Marten boots and headed out.

I was walking in the steps of so many other cold feet, heading for the warmth of one of Saint-Germain-des-Prés' famous cafés. The quarter is the spiritual French home of coffee, which was first consumed in public at the old Saint-Germain fair back in the 1670s. Once upon a time, the area was covered in fields (*prés*) where students would come to duel, but it eventually developed into a village-like neighbourhood of elegant apartments and colourful cafés, where students now had a new weapon — their mind — to sharpen with heated and caffeinated debates.

I stopped outside Les Deux Magots, the legendary café in the midst of it all. In its 1920s heyday, American author Ernest Hemingway spent mornings writing away over café crème, and held meetings over dry sherry in the afternoon. Just opposite the quaintly cobbled square is the oldest church in Paris. In such sacred grounds, the huge Emporio Armani across the boulevard looked as jarring as a priest swapping his black robes for bedazzled ones. Throughout my stay, I'd hear grumblings that Saint-Germain was no longer the hive of serious intellectual activity it once was, that the publishing houses were abandoning the area and leaving, of all things, high-fashion boutiques to take their place — Prada was nearby, and Dior and Louis Vuitton would soon materialise. Perhaps the real writers and thinkers had moved off to new pastures, finding fertile ground in less salubrious surroundings. But Saint-Germain still exerted a magnetic power over wannabe intellectuals, who dreamed of buying a book at the iconic La Hune and flicking through it at the next-door Café de Flore.

The Flore was my destination that morning, a shrine at which to worship the legacy of my French feminist icon Simone de Beauvoir, one of the café's most fabled former customers. My mum had passed on her adoration of SDB, who famously proclaimed, 'One is not born, but rather becomes, a woman.' Mum had once told me that the quote helped her 'question how far to buy into femininity'. As an up-and-coming businesswoman she had more to prove than the male majority of her colleagues. To play men at their own game, she couldn't afford to commit too much time to feminine frivolities; she preferred to spend her mornings reading the newspaper rather than battling with hot rollers.

Madame de Beauvoir might have had pride of place on the shelves and in the hearts of my household, but she was considered old hat at university, where I studied feminist philosophy for a while — until I decided that my mother was my best teacher.

'You can't take French feminists like de Beauvoir seriously,' one fellow student declared during class. 'They live in the shadow of their men.'

'Not to mention the shadow of the Eiffel Tower, that ultimate phallic symbol,' added another.

'But how could a tower not be phallic?' I countered. 'I mean, it has to be tall and skinny for practical design purposes.' I was ignored. We were all girls on the verge of womanhood, vacillating between confidence and confusion, but most of my classmates seemed to prefer to dwell at the angrier end of that spectrum.

'And they wear so much makeup,' said another, with a roll of an unadorned eye. 'De Beauvoir must have spent hours on those updos of hers.'

I didn't respond, as I was also letting the sisterhood down on the hair and makeup front. I'd rarely leave the house without a few layers of lipstick and shiny, iron-straightened hair. I was a feminist firmly entrenched in the camp of Naomi Wolf, the author of *The Beauty Myth*, who had insisted women can wear makeup without a finishing dusting of shame. Wolf would defend her book from being charged as anti-beauty with these stirring words: 'For I conclude that the enemy is not lipstick, but guilt itself; that we deserve lipstick, if we want it, AND free speech … we are entitled to wear cowboy boots to our own revolution …' Or Doc Marten boots, I assumed.

I hovered outside the Flore. The waiters must have seen my type countless times before: starry-eyed students dreaming of other worlds, either utopian ones of the future, or those long gone, when SDB and her philosopher guru of an unconventional life partner Jean-Paul Sartre would hold court at this very café, their personal office during the Second World War, when they spent days and nights working by the heat of the pot-bellied stove.

I reverentially took a seat by a heater in the enclosed *terrasse*. The air seemed electric, and I was awestruck by the realisation that I was not only in such close proximity to the ghost of SDB, but also sitting in the very café that had incubated Existentialism, the philosophy that had recently jolted me out of a rather big university funk.

I'd never really got into most of my philosophically minded subjects. I didn't want to spend hours wondering whether I really existed. It was enough that, to me, I did exist. So the real question became: what on earth was I going to do about that? I needed my life and myself to have meaning. Having become disenchanted with religion, I'd stopped attending church, even though I was envious of my parents' ongoing faith, their peace of mind in the acceptance of a higher power, in the knowledge that God was guiding them where they were meant to go. But I craved something more empowering. And then I started studying Existentialism. It was like a light bulb went *ping!* in my mind. Life suddenly looked different; it felt more real.

Basically, Existentialism states that we are all free to choose our own path in life. In the seminal essay *Being and Nothingness*, written at this very café in 1943, Sartre came up with the catchcry that would define his new philosophy: 'existence precedes essence'. We are not pre-programmed in any way, it's in our power to become whoever we want. And the journey is ongoing. We're all works in progress, open to continual reinvention. Of course, we're all in certain situations, and some are more spoilt for choice than others, who might be constrained by societal expectations, morality, religious beliefs, finances ... Nevertheless, we can all determine how to act within our personal parameters. Don't be a victim, in other words. Be who you want to be in this short and precious life, and make it count.

Existentialism initially went hand-in-hand with a decadent lifestyle — beautiful young black-turtleneck-wearing things dancing to jazz in the smoky basement bars of Saint-Germain, drinking their grim wartime memories to obliteration — and that's what gave the movement its depraved reputation. It also had a certain darkness to it if you looked for the shadows. You could take from it the idea that we're all alone in this world, which is inherently devoid of meaning. That could be an anguishing thought, as the implication is that every choice we make weighs on our conscience alone. Therein lies the much-discussed angst of Existentialism: the price of freedom is incessant anxiety. Personally, it didn't bother me too much. I've long felt that this life we are so lucky to have should be taken seriously, that a little bit of fear propels us to be our best. And I found it inspiring that Existentialism believes we humans can make the right decisions. When you scratch the seemingly dark surface, there's a bright optimism at the core, because Sartre himself was unwavering on the ethical front: a devout atheist, morality was his religion; a committed humanist, authenticity was his goal.

JPS was not technically handsome. He was excessively short, and his crumpled face featured bulging lips and protruding eyes that seemed to waver in all directions. Yet once his ideas got under your skin, he was utterly alluring, then as much as now. '*Alors*, who will you be?' I'd imagine him whispering to my higher self, in a gravelly growl. The realisation that I had complete control over my answer was terrifying, exhilarating and liberating all at once.

I watched the Flore waiters glide around, taking their jobs suitably seriously, and recalled what Sartre once wrote about waiters. He said that those who come across as too typically waiter-ish are merely play-acting, submitting to a predefined role and therefore rejecting their innate freedom. In adopting such false values, these waiters demonstrate what Sartre called bad faith. For Sartre, we live in bad faith whenever we are not living up to our unique potential. Don't be a fake, in other words. Was I pretending to be someone I was not, or being true to myself, at that moment in time? Was I a one-dimensional cookie-cutter or a fully-fledged three-dimensional being? Was I dumbing myself down? It would become something I asked myself again and again over life, throughout my future career in women's magazines.

Existentialism was out of date at the time. At university, everyone flocked to Postmodernism, seduced by its sardonic, ironic take on life, and blinded by its glitzy catchwords. I didn't understand most of it; my main take-home was that we are pastiche-like products of our environment, pure social constructions. But I didn't buy its pretentious world-weariness. Because, really, where would that get us? After the heavy, shoulder-padded conformity of the 1980s, the 1990s needed a rebellion and refreshment of thought as much as dress. Grunge was a kind of counter-cultural bohemianism that attempted to live a more authentic life, but in urging you to opt out of consumer society, it was hardly a realistic philosophy. What if you wanted to stay in the real world? How would you navigate it, especially given the escalating level of pressure, expectation and choice in that world? Perhaps it was time to bring back Existentialism and take life excitedly back in our own hands; to re-evaluate our realness and rediscover the joy of living; to experience the exhilaration of freedom and self-empowerment of options. As an only child whose parents had mostly let her determine each step of the life path she was forging — despite occasional potholes — Existentialism made perfect sense.

I was deep in thought — and, yes, I'm well aware that I might have merely been playing the role of a postulant intellectual in Paris, and thus displaying an egregious amount of bad faith. But it wasn't as pretentious as it might sound. Affectations such as long, thoughtful stares into one's black coffee, or furious scrawling in one's Moleskine notebook, feel completely normal in Paris, because the French love to think they think. This is the birthplace of 'I think, therefore I am', don't forget. French intellectualism traces its illuminated roots to the days of the Enlightenment, when philosophers questioned the status quo, but it was after the Revolution that intellectualism became the new religion. Ever since, all high school students have had to undertake compulsory philosophy studies. Writers and even artists are expected to double as intellectuals; politicians pen deep and meaningful books in their spare time. On French television, there's a mind-numbing amount of time filled with panels of clever people talking over each other. And all this highfalutin' intellectualism filters down to the street, to the footpath terraces of cafés, where even the average French Joe has high-minded ideas on each and every subject.

'*Merci*, Mademoiselle,' said my waiter, after noting down my order. I would one day yearn for the days of being a 'Mademoiselle', but back then it irked me that I was defined by my marital status. You see, there is no Ms in French. You're Mademoiselle until you're either married or a certain age, at which time you graduate to Madame.

And don't get me started on the subject of gender in French. My female classmates and I had twisted ourselves in knots trying to work out why a knife was masculine (*le couteau*) and a fork feminine (*la fourchette*). After much deliberation over many glasses of red wine, our befuddled brains concluded that there's no real rhyme nor reason nor conspiracy theory to it. Still, we abhorred the inherent sexism in a language that defaults to the male setting; if you want to say that both he and she are beautiful, you use the masculine *beaux*, not the feminine *belles*. We'd shake our heads in disbelief that France was the country that gave the world the wonderful Ms de Beauvoir.

As I drizzled honey (masculinely gendered, despite the sweetness that many would assume to be better matched to femininity) on my baguette (curiously feminine, given its phallic appearance), I thought about SDB, and how she had turned the notion of gender on its head. In her trailblazing tome of 1949, *The Second Sex*, she argued that woman is not a natural concept, that we women have been moulded in opposition to men for centuries, that we are a product of myths and tradition and, above all, a patriarchal society. She urged us to rethink our destinies and claim control of our lives, to work in order to support ourselves and our freedom, and she set the scene for the worldwide women's liberation movement of the 1970s. SDB had articulated the anger and resentment of so many women who felt constrained in their roles as frail, frilly females. The book was nothing short of revolutionary, and certainly the most successful practical application of Existentialism.

With such a formidable founding mother, it's surprising that French feminism gets a bad name. 'It's like the Revolution never happened in France,' claimed one fellow feminist student. 'Women seem so retro there, demure and deprecating.' To be fair, French women haven't had the easiest run; they've had to fight particularly virile patriarchal forces. Despite the pivotal part they played in the French Revolution, they were sidelined by the word brotherhood in the motto '*liberté, égalité, fraternité*' — and relegated to the legal status of children by Napoléon's Civil Code of 1804, which fortified the foundations of the patriarchy. The term 'feminism', coined in 1837, might have originally been French, but that century saw French women suppressed to such a degree that breaking the shackles proved arduous; they weren't granted the vote until 1944 — 1944! — and men remained the official heads of Gallic households until 1970. Who could blame *une femme* for being exhausted after such a slog?

Or perhaps French women simply like to cling to some of the traditional womanly wiles, in true *vive la différence* style. 'It's more like feminine-ism,' another classmate scoffed. Indeed, many French women consider themselves as feminist as they are feminine. They would never burn their beautiful lacy bras, for instance. SDB had written that elegance is bondage, that the definition of female beauty had been created by men for their own viewing pleasure. But the fine-featured aristocrat — who was rarely seen without her uniform of tailored chic complemented by lipstick and nail polish — admitted that the allure of glamour was difficult to resist. To me, the contradictions within her only made her more real. And also, she was a Parisienne, born in the global capital of fashion and beauty. Surely living up to the exquisite image of that city is a kind of civic duty?

As a young feminist who liked the feminine things in life, SDB also spoke to me with her more embracive style of feminism. She did not hate younger, prettier women. She had praised the liberated spirit and true-to-self honesty of Brigitte Bardot, which scored her major brownie points in my book. BB was not living in bad faith, because she was living for herself. She didn't see herself as an object; she was in total charge of her image and life. Hardcore feminists often attacked the femininity of my two French icons, but it didn't bother me that they obviously spent some time in the morning applying makeup and choosing an outfit that made them feel good. For me, it was what they did with the rest of their day that counted. As Existentialism asks, *What are you going to do?* With a postscript: *Make it good.*

That afternoon I stopped for food supplies on Rue de Seine, at the little market there just on the doorstep of Hôtel La Louisiane, an establishment so peopled with A-list ghosts you could faint from star strike. Just some of its past guests are the jazz gurus Miles Davis and Chet Baker, while Simone de Beauvoir lived there for a while. I wondered if she'd also shopped at these very stalls, indulging her appetite for life after the hungry wartime years.

I quickly walked past the rotisserie of chickens, as my stomach churned in empathy. Ever since I had to work a similar device in a deli years before, I'd been vegetarian, getting my protein fix from bowls of chickpeas and tofu steaks. My previous trips to Paris had proved how difficult it was to eat well there meat-free. I once thrilled to discover a restaurant advertising lentil salad, only to have it served up on a layer of salami, so I'd come to accept that these few months might not be my healthiest. As a token attempt to nourish my body, I bought a bag of glossy clementines, hoping the vitamin C might stave off the chills. For no reason other than pure greed, I next chose half a dozen wedges of cheese from the *fromagerie*, which displayed its stinky wares on tables covered in red-and-white chequered cloths. And, of course, I added the requisite baguette. Oh, and a half-bottle of red wine. And that was pretty much the extent of my French diet for the coming while. Sustenance, I figured, also came in the satisfying form of *joie de vivre.*

For the past few years, I'd regularly corresponded with Louis, originally as a ruse to glean something of the life of his heartbreaker friend Marc, but eventually for the pure vicarious thrill of it. Remember, these were the days when other countries were shrouded in mystique. There was no Facebook connecting you with people on the other side of the globe, no digital pathways that allowed you to drop in on another city at a moment's notice. Louis kept Paris tangible for me at a time when my classes theorised it, boxing it into a cultural study.

We met up for lunch the next day, Louis — who still looked like the fifth, French Beatle — doing a double take as he walked through the café door. '*Mon dieu*,' he said after he had kissed each of my cheeks, shrugged off his duffle coat and sat down. 'I almost didn't recognise you. What are you wearing? What happened to our baby Brigitte?'

In one of his letters, Louis had asked, 'Do you still have Bardot hair? You must be a *bombe sexuelle* by now.' I didn't mind having a Parisian guy see me as some kind of antipodean bombshell, so I neglected to respond that I'd stripped off the baby doll dresses and combed out the bouffant hair, deciding that I was not a convincing sex kitten, after all, and that I was trying on some new styles for size. Grunge, for instance. That day, I was wearing my chunky cardigan-coat belted over a footpath-trailing floral dress, cherry Doc Martens and a knitted beanie pulled down tight. My hair was long and lank, framing a pale face punctuated by dark-brown lips. I loved grunge for its dark romanticism: it was feminine but with a feisty spirit that spoke to the university student in me; it was poetic in its nostalgia for past fashions, like 1930s tea-dresses, and angry in its defiance of the modern world. I hadn't anticipated that the look would not translate to Paris, or at least the Latin Quarter. After all, grunge was basically the new bohemianism, a rebellion against bourgeois good taste.

Louis laughed, and said, '*Le grunge* hasn't taken off in Paris. Even bohemianism isn't what it used to be. You really should have lived in Paris decades ago.'

I agreed that, yes, I would have loved to have belonged to a past Paris, but isn't Paris the city of always looking back? History hits you at every step of the foot and tilt of the head; you can't avoid it. Anyway, he still looked to be very much into the 1960s, I pointed out.

'*Touché*!'

'So … how's Marc?' I asked, in my most valiant attempt at a nonchalant voice.

'Ah, I wondered if you were going to ask me about him! He's fine. Same old Marc. Juggling a couple of girlfriends at the moment.'

I couldn't help but pout into my wine. And then he said the words that every guy knows to bring out, to console a girl whose heart has been a little bit bruised by his cad of a friend: 'You're too good for him anyway.'

We rugged up against the cold in our respective retro-inspired coats, and wandered our way around the Latin Quarter, my chunky boots clomping and his pointy lacquered shoes clacking along the cold cobbles.

'Let me show you something that gives me goosebumps,' said Louis. Or chicken skin, as the French say. We turned down the skinny, crooked Rue Gît-le-Coeur, with its lackadaisically sloping façades, a street that was first mapped out in the twelfth century, and stopped outside the seventeenth-century stone building that was number 9. Now fancied up as a four-star hotel, it was once the most squalid boarding house in town, and from 1958 to 1963 home to a cluster of American beat writers on the cusp of international stardom. It was there that these on-the-road cool cats with their scraggly beards and black berets cooked up some of their most acclaimed poems and books in an acrid haze of mind-bending fumes. 'What I would give to have been one of them, indulging in the psychedelic craziness of life,' sighed Louis. I crinkled my nose. My idea of bohemianism was one that involved clean sheets and perfumed air.

'So you are more bourgeoise-bohème than bohémienne, I see,' chuckled Louis. It was true: I was Bobo, not Bébé. I laughed along but couldn't shake the feeling that he was disappointed in the reality of his little *australienne*. We were worlds apart — eras, too.

Darkness was falling, the pale pearl-greys of a Parisian winter's day morphing into shades of slate and charcoal. Pleading lingering jetlag, I said goodbye. I didn't want to use the term *au revoir*, which means see you again. Instead, I used *adieu*. Literally, 'to God'. I'd leave it to fate as to whether we'd catch up once more.

&

My language school was situated down a charming little lane. So I was somewhat taken aback by the utilitarian classrooms and mechanical approach to teaching. I'd imagined us lolling around on lounges, sharing nuggets of wisdom while nibbling on caramel éclairs. Instead, we spent our days under fluorescent lights, taking dictation while watching documentary shows or wearing bulky headphones as we listened to disembodied voices drone on about the weather. I wondered if it would have been more effective to enhance my French by attempting to dissect the meaning of life with the city's waiters.

My fellow students were mostly older, retirees clutching their bucket-lists to their cashmere-clad bosoms, ecstatic to finally make it to Paris and polish up their rusty high-school French. But a cluster of us in our early twenties were drawn to one another. Our shared desire to live the Parisian dream seemed to make the possibility more real. There was Lucia, an Italian knockout à la Sophia Loren, with glistening dark-cocoa hair, scarlet lips and a figure that defined the word voluptuous. She tried to dress in a subdued way — cable-knit jumpers and denim jeans — but she couldn't camouflage her inner siren; everywhere we went heads would turn and tyres would occasionally screech. Martin was from New York, but looked as Gallic as they come: a swish of hair, pastel shirts and corduroy pants, always a scarf wound around his neck. And then there was Hugh from Canada, the scruffy, anguished artist who dreamed of being a writer, and had come to the place where aspiring authors have long pilgrimaged.

By Friday, we were the firmest of friends and made plans to meet up that evening in Montparnasse. Situated south of the Latin Quarter, Montparnasse started its ascent to legendary heights in the late nineteenth century, when creatives such as Picasso moved from the overly fashionable, and expensive, Montmartre, converting the stables and sheds of the pastoral Montparnasse into light-filled artist studios. Soon the place was teeming with talent from all corners of the globe. After the war, which shattered the old ways of thinking and doing, the avant-garde of Montparnasse boomed. Writers flocked there, too, and cafés competed to attract the coolest crowd. Arguably the birthplace of Modernism — ironic for an area so recently rural in character — Montparnasse was populated by those who spent their days exploring novel ways to express and enjoy themselves.

We met at the Carrefour Vavin, the intersection of boulevards Raspail and du Montparnasse, which was the very heart of the social universe back in the 1920s, and gravitated towards the ruby warmth of the fabled Café La Rotonde, where we squeezed into a booth and ordered a bottle of wine in a shade matching our surroundings.

'I'm so awestruck right now,' sighed Hugh. 'This is the very place Ernest Hemingway wrote about in *The Sun Also Rises*. Henry Miller used to hang here, too.' Hugh certainly had the Henry Millers about him. That night he was wearing a crumpled mackintosh coat and a black brimmed hat.

'I read that the owner used to let artists and writers stay here for hours for just the cost of a *café crème*' said Martin. 'He loved all of the creatives who moved here to make the most of the cheap franc, although the locals called them Parisites.'

'Which is I guess what we are,' I noted. At the time the franc was as cheap as *pommes frites* against many other currencies.

'Montparnasse is still a bit too dirty for me,' said Lucia with sniff. She was staying just over the river, in an apartment that I enviably pictured to come with a luxuriously usable shower, going by the unfailingly shiny bounce of her hair. 'And how hideous is that tower?'

She was referring to the Tour Montparnasse, a 58-floor monolithic shaft of black starkness. Opened in 1973, it was so instantly and passionately reviled that it triggered an urban planning ban on city-centre constructions exceeding seven levels.

'I think it's totally fitting to have such a monument in the spiritual home of Modernism,' remarked Hugh.

'I wouldn't call it Modernist, but a failed attempt to capture the future,' argued Lucia. 'Everyone hated it from the start, and they still do, which proves that they got it wrong.'

'Unless the architects are so ahead of the curve that we all start to love it in another twenty years,' said Martin. 'Good art is about shocking people.'

'I disagree,' I said. 'I think it's about seducing them. Giving them what they don't know they desperately want.'

'But art also has to serve a need sometimes,' argued Martin, a New Yorker at heart beneath his Parisian-inspired clothes. 'A true international city needs skyscrapers or it becomes a fossilised museum that can't work in modern times. It's crazy that Paris sends its workforce so far out of the city every day.'

'But that's exactly why I love Paris,' said Lucia. 'Here it's about living aesthetically above all.'

'The way Paris needs to go forward is to find a way to merge the practical and the beautiful,' countered Martin.

'That's so un-French of you,' responded Lucia, laughing.

France is a country of extremes, and Paris a city of polarities. Binary opposition was how a linguistics teacher once explained it to me. The French, it's said, love to think in black and white, to divide everything in two; everything has a perfectly contrasted partner. Paris is, after all, the hometown of the Left Bank and Right Bank, not to mention the city that created the concept of left wing and right wing. The desire for duality explains the strict Gallic delineation between public and private lives — and why French women only venture outside once immaculately groomed and dressed. But the ultimate coupling is the mind and the body; equally important, each requires TLC and attention, which is why Parisians hang around cafés for hours, chatting and eating — they're dining on food for the soul as much as the stomach.

It was René Descartes, the *père* of modern Western philosophy — the guy who originally proclaimed, 'I think, therefore I am' — who crafted the concept of mind–body dualism, back in the seventeenth century. The maths buff's brand of thinking was sceptical rationalism, and he argued along the neat lines of deductive reasoning. Cartesian thinking is all about elegance, clarity and confidence. It has a mathematical organisation to it, and it has long shaped the Gallic view of the world. I've never quite got my irrational, romantic, non-lawyerly, maths-failing mind around the notion, especially as my introductory French philosophy classes seemed to sell Existentialism so much more effectively to me. And the core of Existentialism is basically the binary opposite of Cartesianism; instead of 'I think, therefore I am' it's 'I am not, until I think'.

Certainly, any attempt at Cartesian conversation was a dismal failure that evening. It was fortunate that Lucia spoke English well, because even though we all started the night trying our best to converse in French, our efforts, and grammar, deteriorated in direct correlation to the amount of wine consumed. Clear-headed Cartesian types would have reasoned that it wasn't wise to keep drinking — and probably wouldn't have ordered more than a couple of bottles in the first place. But we were still learning how to think French as well as speak it, and it seemed like a good idea to kick on for cocktails.

We wandered down Boulevard du Montparnasse to La Closerie des Lilas, named in homage to a nearby nineteenth-century dancehall that was set within a candelabra-lit, lilac-scented garden. A frenzy of cancan dancing and champagne bubbles, this is where the students of the Latin Quarter came to take their pick of the *grisettes* who so fragrantly decorated the leafy arbours.

Just as we were about to step inside, Lucia and Martin bashfully made an apologetic retreat. Hugh and I watched them walk off arm-in-arm into the wintry night. 'I didn't see that coming,' he said. I hadn't either, possibly because we'd been engrossed in one another. I didn't find Hugh attractive so much as fascinating. He was a walking encyclopaedia on Paris, and his passion for the city was infectious.

He also dreamed of a past Parisian world, when a so-called Lost Generation found itself in the interwar period, a time of frenetic creativity and debauched denial. While I tended to fantasise about the languorous fashions and the subdued self-contemplation of the 1930s, Hugh was obsessed with the preceding decade known as the *années folles* (crazy years). 'I like to party,' he explained with a shrug.

We made our way into La Closerie, through a blur of Gauloises smoke, and sat down at a glossy mahogany table in the red-amber lushness of the piano bar, its burnished glow enhanced by glass bottles twinkling away against the mirrored wall. I ordered a French martini, Hugh a dry one, 'just like Papa'.

Papa was the nickname of Ernest Hemingway, who would often write in this very bar, seeing as he lived around the corner. There, he met with a new friend by the name of F. Scott Fitzgerald, who read him some of his latest book, *The Great Gatsby*. 'I mean, this is what I love about Paris,' said Hugh. 'It's soaked with history. You can almost smell it, it's palpable.'

I lost track of the time we spent singing the city's praises, and suddenly I realised we were the last couple in the room. Should we have one last drink, I asked? Hugh scrounged around in his pockets, then shrugged. 'I have no money, no resources, no hopes. I am the happiest man alive.'

Uh, this was getting a little deep.

'Don't tell me you haven't read *Tropic of Cancer*?' he asked incredulously.

'Ah, got it. Well, I do love Anaïs Nin and tried to read it when I got into her. And there are some beautiful sentences in there, but I just couldn't get past the filth. I know I sound like a prude, but it just makes me feel ill.'

The feminist in me — even if she was a feminine one — hated the misogyny of the book, even more so because I suspected it was one big put-on. It smacked of a desperate attempt by Miller to appear manly and virile so as to cover up some Freudian neurosis.

'So,' Hugh whispered, leaning close, his gin-and-vermouth-scented smile lopsided and louche, 'you're not going to be my Anaïs?'

Nin had edited *Tropic of Cancer* for Miller. During countless bouts of passionate lovemaking.

I hadn't planned on looking for *l'amour*; I was in a determinedly single — and self-reflective — phase. Hugh wasn't my type; he was too cocksure, a little too brutally direct at times. And I had a hunch it would be a most unbalanced pairing. *En amour, il y a toujours celui qui donne les baisers et celui qui tend la joue*, goes one French proverb. It means that in love there is always the giver (of kisses) and the taker (who turns the cheek). But then again, perhaps it just meant we were binary opposites.

I woke up surprised to feel my skin against lemony-fresh, starched sheets. Turned out, Hugh was staying in a four-star hotel. So he wasn't as much the struggling bohemian that I at first thought. I smiled. I guessed I was playing the part, too. Bad faith be damned.

Hugh was still asleep, the matted hair over his face barely stifling his drunken snores, so I got up and padded about for a while, enjoying the central-heated air and the plush carpet beneath my feet. I picked up Hugh's coat, which he'd strewn on the floor, and noticed a book poking out of the pocket: *The Outsider*, by Albert Camus. He was a bit of a poseur, I thought, but rather adorable in his earnest pursuit of Frenchness.

I didn't know much about Camus at the time, otherwise I might have wondered if this was a warning sign of sorts. In the cult book, the protagonist kills an unnamed man, and goes to trial, with a blood-chilling lack of emotion. The Algeria-born Camus was an Existentialist, but, unlike Jean-Paul Sartre and Simone de Beauvoir, he never felt as though he fitted into the world, certainly not Paris. He disagreed with them, too, that life had real meaning — for him, human existence was no more than an absurdity. Not the happiest of chaps, in other words. But his scarringly tortured childhood goes a long way to explaining the grim outlook.

At the time, I thought, how apt. We were two outsiders, desperately wanting to belong. We were perhaps both a bit lost. I wasn't sure I wanted to try to merge our particular Parisian dreams — my romantic, feminine one with his modernist, masculine one — so I made to leave. 'I need some air. Our usual at twelve?' I wrote on a piece of paper. While unsure that I wanted to meet up again so soon, I didn't want to be rude to someone who could at least be an amusing friend. So I left *la balle* in his court.

Later that morning, I cleared my head in the Luxembourg Garden, the icy air having a purifying effect. A light snow had just fallen over the gravel paths and the bare branches criss-crossed against the pale-grey sky, and I felt as though I was walking into an old black-and-white photograph. The original 1923 chairs were still scattered around the park in those days, and there was even the occasional design from earlier days, its delicately poised curves standing out from the more masculine sturdiness of the others, like a *grisette* amidst an admiring cluster of students.

I noticed a vintage set of scales but couldn't get them to work. I'd later find out these machines used to be dotted throughout the gardens, installed in the late nineteenth century when the French were becoming weight-conscious; a few are now left purely for show. I officially weighed nothing, I decided with a smile, but realised that I did in fact feel rather flimsy. I'd barely eaten a proper meal in two weeks, let alone remembered to take my iron supplements — and I had a gaunt look, complete with moody under-eye shadows, to prove it. Back in Romantic times, pale and weak heroines were all the rage, and on a subconscious level my inner *bohémienne* was probably relishing the drama of it all, but I suddenly didn't care about starving for art or anything else. I was too ravenously hungry.

A poor Ernest Hemingway used to come to these gardens when he was famished, sometimes to try to catch dinner in the form of an unfortunate pigeon, at other times to escape the tempting aromas of Parisian streets. He'd also take shelter in the museum there, which then showcased the Impressionists. Standing before the Cézannes when he was particularly 'belly-empty, hollow-hungry', the writer's appreciation of the proto-Cubist and Fauvist painter intensified, and the heavy and structured yet bright brush strokes would influence his own art: prose filled with strong words and colourful action, yet sparse in adjectives.

Hunger had also worked for me — for a while. When I was at school, controlling my appetite somehow focused my mind on the main task. In my final year, I lived like an ascetic monk, eating little more than a daily bowl of porridge, studying in every spare second, and often falling asleep on a mattress by my desk. But I got over it, thankfully; Paris had helped me fall in love with food, as it did Hemingway, who blossomed into a great gourmand, if not a glutton of frivolous adjectives.

&

The café was just around the corner from our language school. It was one of those old neighbourhood bars known as *un zinc*, with a long metal counter displaying a stack of hard-boiled eggs, which could be bought for a few coins. In the morning, beret-topped locals would crack an egg on the bar and shake on some salt, then quickly gobble it up before downing a chaser of espresso. The authenticity stretched to old French men — crustier than fresh baguettes — arguing about politics. It was the perfect place to polish up our colloquial skills, and try to delve further into the Parisian psyche.

I had almost finished my cheese-smothered onion soup when Hugh walked in. I must have looked surprised. 'Did you think I was going to *poser un lapin*?' he asked with a laugh as he sat down next to me on the banquette.

'Pose a *rabbit*?'

'It means to stand someone up. Isn't that great? I read it has something to with the days when men ran off on women without paying them their dues.'

I laughed uneasily, the prostitute reference not quite infusing the scene with romance. 'So you're not going to hop away on me?'

I winced at the needy undertone to my question, which I'd meant to come across as light-heartedly rhetorical. And then I mentally kicked myself for being such a girl.

'I'm here, aren't I?' There was a slight edge to his voice, I thought. He might have been trying to sound similarly carefree, but I sensed his wariness at where the situation was heading. But hang on, I ordered myself, did I really want to let myself fall for someone I didn't think could return the favour? I knew from all of his bravado-packed talk that he was not the kind of guy you'd want handling a delicate heart. He was a writer who seemed to like total control of his own life's plotline, who brought characters into existence only when he was ready for them.

This was all getting a bit too complicated to unpack. I decided it was probably best to leave our emotions locked up so early in this particular journey. After all, the only baggage I wanted to take home from Paris was of the sartorial, not emotional, kind.

'Look, let's just keep having fun, okay?' I said after a few moments' silence. 'Whether we see each other much or not. We're both on holiday — it's not like we're going to get married.'

Hugh smiled, a little too much with relief for my liking. 'You know, I wouldn't be the best boyfriend anyway. I'm always running off to write, or lurking around looking for new inspiration. I can't stay put because what kind of boring story would that be?'

I didn't answer 'a love story'. It clearly wasn't his genre.

At least the tension in the air had evaporated. Hugh ordered us two glasses of wine, flung an arm around me, and proceeded to bury his nose in a book: *Sentimental Education* by Gustave Flaubert, a nineteenth-century novel about a selfish womanising socialite. It was all I could do to keep from rolling my eyes. Hugh really should have lived in his beloved 1920s, or earlier, I thought, when men could more easily get away with being so cavalier.

&

No Parisian education — sentimental or otherwise — is complete without a few trips to the movies. The French love their films, which is not surprising given that cinematography was invented in France (by the suitably named Lumière — light — brothers), and the heavily subsidised industry more than holds its own against the might of Hollywood. Of all global cities, Paris boasts the most big screens, and its art house cinemas double as temples to Gallic culture, worshipping classic French films on eternal rotation. There's also little better to do on a blustery Parisian day than bunker down in the velvety-red cushioned chairs of a cosy cinema, head preferably resting on a manly shoulder.

The Latin Quarter, as you'd expect, is spoilt for art house cinema choice. Over the next couple of weeks, Hugh and I worked our way through most of the theatres, often skipping classes in the justification that we were still focusing on our aural comprehension. On a Saturday night, we found ourselves at Le Champo, where we bought tickets for *A Bout de Souffle* — or *Breathless*. Released in 1960, this was the star of the so-called New Wave, a generation of films that rejected the traditional rules of movie-making as much as the old, pre-war world altogether. For *Breathless*, director Jean-Luc Godard worked with hand-held cameras, edited with jump cuts for a jagged, sometimes dizzying effect, and wrote the script only on the very morning of a day's shoot; the result was a documentary-like realness. He also created totally new, amoral characters: youthful but disaffected, both narcissistic and nihilistic. This was the dark side of Existentialism, where it's all too damn gloomy to see the point of living.

Michel is a cop-killing car thief, whose only emotions seem to be the ones he fakes in the mirror. Patricia is an American who's supposed to be studying at the Sorbonne, but is instead selling copies of the *International Herald Tribune* on the Champs-Élysées, while dreaming of spending her money on a Dior dress. He's attracted to her gamine style, she digs his whole gangster bad-boy vibe, and the two hook up despite little shared interest beyond a fondness for chain-smoking and an inclination towards sociopathy. Spoiler alert: it all ends pretty badly.

'He has to be cinema's first antihero,' said Hugh later, as we ordered a bottle of wine at a nearby bar. 'I mean, they've been in books for centuries, but I can't think of a cinematic one before 1960.'

'She wasn't much better,' I pointed out. 'I mean, she only turned Michel in to test whether she loved him or not, not out of moral duty.'

'But imagine how liberating this film must have been back then,' said Hugh. 'To see all of the supposed rules of life being questioned and rejected.'

'I would have been depressed by it.'

'I would have loved it.'

'Of course,' I said, with a laugh. 'You would have run out and bought yourself a jaunty hat at once!'

'You know me too well,' he replied. 'But I don't just mean stylistically. Imagine how amazing it would have been to live at a time when everything was being rethought. I just feel like everything in the 1990s is recycled and retro, like everything has been done before.'

I could have talked to Hugh all evening. He was a hoarder, filling his mind with all sorts of trivia as much as he stuffed his pockets with ticket stubs, logo-laden coasters and matchboxes nabbed from bars, and articles ripped out of *Le Monde*. He was endlessly interesting but I sensed he was about to bring today's particular chapter to an end, and rush off to document his latest thoughts, or venture out in search of more interesting fodder.

'Let me walk you home,' he said, standing up. And sure enough: 'I can't stay though.'

&

I didn't see Hugh again until Monday morning, back at school. I went to walk over to him, but froze when I saw him deep in conversation with a new student. A particularly pretty female one.

'Everyone, say *bonjour* to Kinari, from India,' chimed our teacher as class began. 'Kinari, *comme un canari*!' Like a canary.

More like a bird of paradise. Kinari was exquisiteness personified. Her golden skin was lustrous, stretched over finely carved cheekbones, and her feline eyes were accentuated with sooty kohl. Framing her face was shining jet-black hair, cut into a long bob with heavy bangs, and she wore a black turtleneck sweater and black slim-leg pants. She was an exotic incarnation of Juliette Gréco, the chanteuse, actress and poster girl for Existentialism back in the days of smoky Saint-Germain jazz bars. Hugh, who had manoeuvred himself to sit next to Kinari, was obviously smitten. He had just found his next heroine.

After classes, Lucia and I dined at a cheap nearby pizzeria, the kind that caters more to clueless students than savvy bon-vivant locals. The Latin-looking waiters practically dropped their plates when Lucia walked in, and spent the night gaping at her much more than decency would usually allow. The chefs even took turns poking their *toque*-less heads out of the kitchen to see what all the fuss was about. They obviously agreed with the general consensus: when our pizzas came out, they were in the shape of a heart.

Appropriately enough, we had been talking about *l'amour*. Lucia listened patiently to my rant about Hugh, how he had treated me as a minor love interest, to help build momentum before the real heroine of the story came along. The one before The One, in other words.

'Don't be so dramatic,' she smiled. 'He's a wannabe writer. He'll be off looking for his next leading lady as soon as he needs more material. You never really liked him anyway, remember that. Don't confuse a bruised ego with heartache.'

I wished I could be more like Lucia. She was only a couple of years older, but so much worldlier. And she had Martin wrapped around her elegant little finger. He had already taken her shopping and out to a couple of two-starred restaurants.

'I like him,' she shrugged when I asked how it was going. 'But I wish he was more, well, American. He tries so hard to be French and French men are just too feminised for me. I mean, he wears more pink than I do!'

'It's better than someone in a musty old coat whose pockets are stuffed with dirty napkins and moody books,' I pouted. I figured I could give myself a while longer to get over my heartache, or wounded pride at the very least.

A few hours later, I woke up in agony. Diagnosis: food poisoning. Culprit: one heart-shaped pizza. Now I could really say that love hurt. I stayed writhing around in bed the next day, wallowing in my freezing misery. Hugh was such a louse, I railed to myself, a try-hard Henry Miller out to prove his virility. Were all guys thus? Had literature — and now cinema — celebrated the badly behaving boy character to such an extent that the script was now programmed into male DNA? No wonder my mother's generation of second-wave feminists had had to play men at their own game, with ballsy talk and brutish suits that mimicked guys' broader, more powerful silhouettes.

I recalled Lucia's observation about French men being too feminised. Perhaps that was why French women hadn't felt the need to masculinise themselves; their better halves had already met them halfway, happily buttoning on pastel shirts and sipping champagne and discussing the latest haute couture catwalk shows over dainty hors d'oeuvres. Maybe I needed to find a French guy. Although I had a hunch that they, like their cinematic alter egos, might be just as adept at playing the scoundrel. They would just know how to do it more stylishly. With, say, a jaunty hat.

Gaunter and paler than ever, I was back at school on Wednesday, where I tried to ignore Hugh as he snuggled up to his chirpy, golden canary. Needless to say, the situation did not aid my recovery. So on the Friday, I took a mental, as much as physical, health day. After a hearty breakfast (one omelette, two croissants, a hot chocolate and a look of disapproval from my waiter), I decided to do what Parisians do best: wander and ponder. It was one of those brilliantly blue winter mornings where you almost tingle as the sun energises your very cells with vitamin D. Recharged, I took a different turn from usual, heading uphill towards the Montagne Sainte-Geneviève. I walked past the Sorbonne University, stopping momentarily to envy the students scurrying around dressed in black, their faces furrowed as though deep in philosophical thought. How inspiring it would be to study in a city that has for centuries shaped so much of the world's learning. Australia could feel so far away from the heart of the action that knowledge sometimes seemed one-dimensional, something trapped in a book rather than connected to a wider world. But in Paris, I figured, theory would be as real as the ancient buildings around you, the stones of which seem to be living and breathing with the souls and spirits of generations of thinkers and dreamers. In this context, you'd have perspective on your place in the world; you would be part of an ever-evolving history, continually pushing the boundaries of thought and knowledge forward, for the benefit of the next generation as much as for the glory of your country. Because Paris, this city of grandiose domes and grand monuments, sure loves her glory.

I eventually found myself in front of the Panthéon, the huge Greek temple-like edifice originally conceived as a church dedicated to Sainte Geneviève, the patron saint of Paris whose girl-power cred is up there with

Joan of Arc (Geneviève saved the city from Attila the Hun, which is surely the very definition of kick-ass). It's laugh-or-you'll-cry ironic, therefore, that the building ended up a shrine to French masculinity. Seriously: the inscription above the portico entrance reads 'To Great Men, The Grateful Nation'. (Okay, granted, four women, including Marie Curie, are now commemorated in this house of heroes, but that's out of a grand total of seventy-five, people!) I refused to go in, on principle.

Instead, I made my way back to the Luxembourg Garden, just down the road. Entering this time through the Boulevard Saint-Michel gates, I turned left and soon stopped before a vision in ivory: a statue of nineteenth-century novelist George Sand. The queen of French Romanticism, Sand wrote books to shine a light on women's rich interior lives, exploring an uncharted terrain of lush emotions, exotic dreams and shadowy fears. And in true Romantic heroine style, this sculptured Sand wears a flowing gown, a fluttering shawl and a pensive look on her pretty curl-framed face. But I was confused, because the little I knew of the author was that she was a trouser-wearing, cigar-smoking cougar. Intrigued, I scribbled her name on my mental to-research list, and over the next few weeks would discover just how enigmatic, controversial and iconic this powerhouse of a woman was. She more than deserved such a beautiful statue; her name should be up in lights in the Panthéon.

Sand's novels are mostly forgotten these days, but they can be seen as the first feminist call to arms. She wrote about women's hidden misery in a patriarchal society, their enslavement in unhappy marriages from which there was no legal escape, and her market was the growing number of female readers who could all too well relate. Sand might have dressed up her tales with the usual swoon-inducing trappings of Romantic fiction, but her message was loud and modern — just like Sand. Having been miserably married herself, to a boor of a provincial baron, she had moved to Paris to forge an independent existence as a writer and, extraordinarily, managed to get a court to grant her official freedom, along with custody of her beloved children and ownership of her country château. Her habit of wearing trousers to get around town — at a time when respectable women required a male escort — was not intended to be provocative. It was simply a practical measure, allowing her ease of movement. A woman with a lot on her plate, Sand had to make the most of her precious time.

The trousers might have seemed subversive to some, but it was Sand's multifaceted personality that was truly rebellious. She didn't just demand the right to live like a man, but like a woman, too. Just as she could flit between her actual name — the fabulous Amantine Aurore Lucile Dupin — and her pseudonym, she could quickly fling off the suit and turn on the frilly feminine wiles. Many portraits show her in those early Parisian days, with pale porcelain skin, large soulful eyes, dark hair parted in the centre and spiralling down around her long face. In one celebrated painting, she demurely tends to her needlework while listening to her great love Frédéric Chopin tinkering away on the ivories.

But in the next breath, she would become a gender-bending man-eater, carousing around town with her artistic friends, and catching pretty boyfriends in the same way she might collect colourful butterflies. Attracted to young, elegant men — rather than the gruff old types women tended to be matched to — Sand both loved and mothered her partners. By celebrating and encouraging a more feminised version of men, she flipped gender relations on their head. But Sand was even more complex than that. She proved that a woman could be much more than a lover; she could also be a doting mother and grandmother, a homemaker, a committed professional and a dynamic intellectual. She was a fully realised human being, in an era when women were confined to small, narrow boxes.

But I didn't know that at the time. All I saw that day in the park was a pretty woman. I sat down on one of the slatted chairs placed on the path in front of the statue. An elderly lady was perched on the other one.

'*Bonjour*,' I said, with a smile.

'She was one of our first feminists,' noted my neighbour, nodding her silvery-grey head towards Sand. She had evidently detected my accent and figured I'd need a back-story. Sand might be a heroine in France, but she's little known beyond its borders.

'She looks like a very French kind of feminist,' I replied with a smile.

'Yes, she was very alluring when she wanted to be. She had men worshipping her for her entire life. Even though she could do everything, love was always the most important thing to her. You know, in France, we feminists don't hate men.'

On the advice of Madame Sandiste (as George Sand fan-girls are known in France), that afternoon I caught the train up to Pigalle, then zigzagged a little south to the Musée de la Vie Romantique: the Museum of Romantic Life. How could a girl in a sentimental frame of mind resist that call? At the end of a narrow, paved laneway I came across a pretty pavilion set in a garden that enchanted even in mid-winter, when the tearoom is closed and the twirly iron chairs are scattered forlornly among tangled thickets, the hydrangeas and hollyhocks are in hibernation and the only burst of colour is the pistachio green of the painted shutters. It was inside the jewellery box of a house that I found the exuberance, a treasure-trove of mementos that recall artistic life in the early nineteenth century.

The museum doubles as a tribute to George Sand. Portraits of Sand and her loved ones hang on the patterned wallpapered walls, and her cherished jewellery — a mix of heirlooms and trinkets — is displayed in glass cabinets, along with a mesmerisingly eerie casting of her right arm, pale and elegant as any self-respecting Romantic limb needed to be. A floral-carpeted parlour room re-creates the private world of Sand and you almost feel like you're trespassing, your bulky boots committing sacrilege on a floor that has welcomed so many dainty slippers. It's a most intimate museum, offering a peek into the interior life of the poster woman for feminine emotion.

Paris might be a city of well-known, much-loved monuments, I thought, but it was in the warm, cosy spaces that you felt most at home. Sand might have soared to the ultimate career heights and basked in public acclaim, but it was back in her private realm that her soul was nourished. She most treasured objects that were charged with emotional meaning, and she felt nothing without her family and friends; her collection of miniature paintings of her ancestors in particular caused my heart to contract with a mixture of envy and longing and homesickness. It all moved me in a way that I was not articulate enough to explain, but as I walked back down the moss-flecked path, I sensed that my vision of my ideal future was shifting. I suddenly craved grounding in life. I wanted sturdy emotional roots along with the literal kind, a rambling garden that would perfume a home filled with love and laughter. And floral carpet if I could find a guy to agree to it.

I spent the next few weeks revelling in my personal space, lolling about in bed while eating chocolate and drinking wine, and disappearing into the worlds of George Sand and those of the various other novels I'd bought from the *bouquinistes* or at Shakespeare and Company, the legendary Latin Quarter bookstore. Occasionally, I'd return to reality and wonder about my own life narrative. I mean, yes, I knew I wanted the lovely house and all that, but as for the road I needed to take to get there, the job that would give me the money to make it materialise, that wasn't so clear.

I guessed political journalism was still my best career bet. I'd struck upon the idea after dropping out of law. I knew that I wanted to write, after all, and felt that I got politics well enough, after years of absorbing my parents' sometimes heated dinner conversations. So, hoping for divine inspiration, I'd buy myself the day's *Le Figaro* and *Le Monde* on the way to school, and try to make sense of their lofty words over a croissant and coffee. When I'd drunk too much red wine the night before, I'd opt for the *International Herald Tribune*, as the clear English words wouldn't hurt my brain as much.

But after a while, I found myself loitering by the women's section of the newsstand, and soon my café literature consisted of *Elle*, *Glamour* and *Vogue*. I realised that I was no longer just trying to understand what the women around me were saying, I was also observing how they expressed themselves through their clothes. I was slowly but very surely developing a new obsession: fashion. Occasionally, Lucia would drag me out to a nightclub and I'd near swoon at the glamour of the Parisiennes in their tiny skirts and wispy dresses. On the street, I noticed that they opted for pants. This wasn't surprising, given it was February, and the threat of rain hung heavily in the chilled air. I had managed to avoid pants myself, wearing layer upon layer until I was winter-proofed. Still dress-obsessed, I didn't even own a pair of jeans, and wondered if it might soon be time to fill this gaping hole in my wardrobe. Pants, I realised, were a key ingredient of Parisian fashion. Pants allowed a Parisienne, like George Sand before her, to stride briskly around town. Granted, it took a while for the look Sand started to catch on — mostly because trousers were actually outlawed for women in 1800. Were men hoping to preserve women's delicate image at the dawn of the Romantic age? Perhaps. More likely the patriarchy feared that women would get too swept up in all this post-Revolutionary equality talk — and it's easier to march for women's rights in pants than petticoats. Which goes to show just how radical the wonderful Madame Sand was.

It took another century or so and a few fashion icons to convince the powers-that-be that pants could be feminine and so very French. Think Juliette Gréco slinking around Saint-Germain in sleek black, Jane Birkin breezing through the 1960s in lithe jeans and a clingy T-shirt accessorised with a simple straw basket, and Jean Seberg's Patricia in a pair of capris on the big screen in *Breathless*.

So I should probably have bought myself some pants, but like Patricia I was mostly dreaming of designer dresses. I couldn't afford her Dior, of course, although I sometimes wandered along Rue Saint-Honoré, the celebrated high-fashion street of the Right Bank, and looked longingly into the glossy windows. It was the era of the long slip dress, cut on the bias for a serpentine effect that gave the illusion of curves. I tracked down a high-street version in black satin, which made it look much more expensive than it was; simple yet sophisticated, it was one of the most grown-up items I had ever bought. It was the perfect thing to wear to my birthday dinner.

'It's not every day your only child turns twenty-one,' responded my mother, when I questioned the extravagance of their trek to Europe for the occasion. Not that I was complaining. When I'd bid *au revoir* at Melbourne Airport six weeks earlier, I fancied my maturing self as a free spirit flitting off to her spiritual home, but in the time since I'd come to crave the comforts of home, both physical and emotional, much more than I expected. I'd never been away from my family for more than a fortnight, and the initial exhilaration of freedom soon became a sensation of free fall. So much for existential independence. I realised that I relied on my parents for advice much more than I'd thought. So on meeting up with them again, my world suddenly tilted back onto its rightful axis. I felt realigned and rebalanced, as though our small triangle-shaped unit had been neatly put back together, with three perfectly equilateral sides.

I'd temporarily shacked up in my parents' room at a nearby hotel — so much plusher than my sad, cold little *chambre de bonne* — and Mum and I devoted a good chunk of the afternoon to preening for dinner, shopping for the just-so shade of red lipstick, lavishing on face masks and blow-drying our hair. My dad patiently sat in the foyer bar sipping sherry, having long ago given up complaining about the time-consuming tribulations of women's beauty rituals. And anyway, this was no ordinary night out.

We were on our way to La Tour d'Argent, at the time the Parisian pinnacle of fine dining, which is saying a lot given that this is the city that invented haute cuisine. La Tour d'Argent means The Silver Tower, named after the mica-flecked stone fortifications that once stood at the same location — on the river's edge upstream from the islands — glittering in the sun. The restaurant also shone with a three-star Michelin rating. Ever since the *Michelin Guide* launched in 1900 — the tyre company's genius way of enticing the French to take road-trips — chefs have sweated it out for this ultimate accolade. The pressure to serve up culinary perfection, not to mention a night to remember, is intense.

As we approached the curlicued, wrought-iron door, it swung open grandly and a man in black-tie greeted us with a slight bow. A woman wearing a gleaming gown, who could easily have passed for a model, stepped forward to take our coats. Someone else ushered us into the lift — operated by yet another suavely suited type — and we whizzed in reverent silence to the top floor, on which the restaurant is perched. As we stepped into the warm glow of the dining room, we were welcomed yet again, and led to our window table, where a trio of waiters held out velvet-seated chairs for us. It was quite the entrance.

'Mademoiselle, you must be *la végétarienne*,' said the maître d', as we sipped champagne and nibbled on a selection of *amuse-bouches*, literally mouth-amusers — scrumptious morsels presented before the entrée to tickle the tastebuds and delight the senses.

'*Oui* …' I replied. '*Je suis désolée* …' I'm sorry. After all, I'd come to a restaurant so famous for its pressed duck that on ordering the signature dish you receive a postcard marked with the bird's serial number; over a million of these cards have been given out.

'It's no trouble at all, Mademoiselle.'

Surprise at my dietary requirement had been expressed when Mum rang to book, but if the chefs weren't thrilled at having to limit themselves to plant food, it didn't show. My main course — revealed with a flourish as the waiter lifted the silver cloche — was a veritable city of vegetables. Seriously, little houses had been constructed out of teeny sticks of carrot, mini buildings made from brick-cubes of fried potato, and it was encircled with towers of asparagus, while rivers of sauces meandered here and there, herbs and micro-blooms sprouting along their pea-sprinkled banks. To this day, I've never seen a more exquisite plate of veggies.

Beyond the glass, we looked down to Notre-Dame. The cathedral was lit up from below with a golden light, and the spiky framework of flying buttresses wrapped around its back shone like a medieval crown, a diadem of Gothic glamour. As the barges streamed up and down the Seine, they would momentarily illuminate the night sky, and we watched the newly falling snowflakes swirl against a violet-blue velvety backdrop.

It was such a chimerically wonderful moment that I wished I could bottle it up in my very own snowdome. I silently thanked the Parisian heavens for the evening.

'Will you come to Notre-Dame with us tomorrow?' asked my father. 'We should give blessings that you've made it to twenty-one. Or that we got through it!'

I was well into my state of lapsed Catholicism, but I agreed. The startling splendour of the cathedral always made me gasp in awe and breathe in that familiar, comforting aroma of musky incense. It was all too easy to sense the divine inspiration this church must have struck into medieval Parisians, beneath the series of arches ascending to heavenly heights, where light glowed through the kaleidoscopic windows. Sadly, our parish church, with its 1970s suburban aura and hues of orange and brown, had the effect of dulling, not heightening, my senses. I was pretty sure that if Notre-Dame was my local, I'd be much more pious in my commitment to Catholicism. Perhaps that seems superficial … although why would the French Church have built such glorious edifices in the first place if they didn't appreciate the power of beauty?

The next morning, after my parents had the chance to literally thank God they'd seen me through to adulthood, we crossed the Pont au Double bridge between Notre-Dame and the Left Bank, and ambled around the sinuous streets of the Latin Quarter.

'These were once completely paved with cobblestones,' remarked Mum. 'Sadly, most of Paris's cobbles have been tarred over.'

In May 1968, towards the end of the decade that was supposed to belong to the youth, the students of the Sorbonne began to protest. At first, they were lamenting their cramped, decrepit campus conditions, but the rebellion quickly swelled into demonstrations against an increasingly capitalist society, and into a crippling country-wide strike of millions of workers. In the Latin Quarter, the riot police clashed violently with students, who dug up the quarter's old cobbles for barricades and weapons.

'I remember sympathising with the students,' said Dad. 'It was ten years after Charles de Gaulle had become president, and they were disillusioned. He was seen as old and old-school, and he had too much power.'

'Would you have joined in if you were here?' I asked, recalling old black-and-white photos of a rebellious-looking Dad rocking a black leather jacket and slicked-back hair.

'I became too much of a law-abiding citizen early on,' he replied, with a slightly rueful sigh. 'That's what happens when you study law! Still, I've always warmed to the French for their willingness to take to the streets, and support the workers.'

'I love that there's this beating rebellious heart beneath the calm French surface,' I mused. 'Like the old cobbles that are still lying beneath the asphalt, just waiting to resurface.'

One of the most poetic chants of the 1968 protests was '*Sous les pavés, la plage*' — 'Under the cobblestones, the beach.' The cobbles were indeed embedded in sand, but the students were alluding to the paradisiacal freedom they hoped was around the corner.

We meandered our way to Café de Flore for lunch, and the conversation headed in a direction I'd been anticipating.

'So, what are you thinking about life after university?' asked Mum, as casually as possible, as though enquiring into my intended meal order (goat's cheese on toast, for the record). I was well aware that my mother, who had perfectly planned and executed every step on her career ladder to date, was sometimes a little bemused by the wafty, winding life path that her daughter seemed to be taking. 'As you know, an arts degree is vague and doesn't lead to a specific job, but I thought we could have a look at public service opportunities when you're back.'

I screwed up my nose. 'You know, the French believe it's an honour to work as a civil servant,' Mum replied huffily. 'I wish more people thought like that back home.' At the time, Mum was running Melbourne City Council, relishing the opportunity to serve the town she so loved.

'I still want to write for a paper,' I shrugged. 'Probably politics. It's a public service too, you know.'

'True ... But you seem to be reading a lot of fashion magazines for someone supposedly into political journalism.'

Yes, I had started to fantasise about seeing my by-line on glossy magazine pages, so I knew I'd have to choose sooner or later, before another existential crisis risked setting in. Still, I didn't think the two interests could be mutually exclusive. I believed I could be passionate about matters of state as much as matters of style, just as Saint-Germain was fast becoming a luxury, as well as a literary, haven. In France, the land of beloved binary opposites, contradictions can coexist and it's totally fine to flip between them, as though between two sides of a *centime*.

One of my best loved movies is Audrey Hepburn's *Funny Face*, and it shows how a girl can easily fall into fashion in a place like Paris. Audrey plays Jo, a shy, bookish type discovered by a fashion magazine editor who is looking for a model who'll give a fresh-faced jolt to a photo shoot of the latest French collections. Audrey agrees to a trip to Paris purely as a ticket to pay homage to her philosophy icon — she eventually meets the Jean-Paul Sartre-like character while clad in the intellectual uniform of the day: beatnik-black turtleneck and slimline pants. But it's high fashion that wins out in the end. Divinely dressed by Givenchy, and shot against a backdrop of Parisian landmarks, Jo learns how to really express herself. And find Monsieur Right, of course.

It's obvious and sappy and clichéd and all that, but isn't it every girl's dream to go to Paris and fall in love — at least with a designer frock. I hadn't found my own Monsieur Right, but I had faith that my opposite was out there somewhere, and would appear soon enough.

At least I'd fallen for a few new dresses, and a particularly shapely pair of boots — long and lace-up, and so much sexier than my manly Doc Martens. Mixing up my feminine and masculine suddenly didn't feel right. I was happy to de-grunge myself and delight in feminine frills, without worrying too much about the wrath of the sisterhood. I could wear the pinkest of lipsticks without fearing that my feminist talk was mere lip service. I had rather taken to the French definition of feminism, where you can be both equal and different. This, of course, being the land of opposites, where feminine and masculine (albeit a pink-shirted masculinity) are as hand-in-hand as SDB and JPS, left and right, *la* baguette and *le* fromage.

Towards the end of my stay, I was having lunch in a café, ploughing through my usual pile of magazines with my trusty dictionary by my side, when I gasped at the realisation that I could understand what everyone around me was saying. It was like the fuzzy radio music I'd been listening to throughout a long road-trip suddenly tuned into crystal-clarity as I approached home. Or like that moment in the *Wizard of Oz* when the screen switches from black and white to technicolor. Everything suddenly seemed vividly real. I was truly part of Paris, and that thrilling awareness dragged me right out of my insularity. It was time to stop living in my head, and get on with life — or *la vie*, as the case might be.

'*Voilà*, Mademoiselle,' said the waiter, placing my flute of champagne before me. '*Merci*,' I responded with a smile, as much for my champagne as for calling me Mademoiselle. At that very moment, I felt like a French girl — and it was something to celebrate.

CHAPTER 5

MADAME

[madam] ***nf*** **madam**

In which, aged twenty-five, I find that champagne and cake can get a girl through anything.

To the surprise of nobody really, my plans to become a political reporter didn't quite pan out. My inner hard-nosed journalist ventured off into a parallel universe, and one day I looked in the mirror to see, staring back in surprise, a beauty editor for a women's magazine. I could not have found a more polar-opposite job in the publishing business.

I'd been seduced by magazines' glossy, fashion-filled pages (so much nicer to the touch of a manicured hand than a newspaper's ink-streaked stock) and had moved to Sydney in the hope of getting my pointy-toed, kitten-heeled foot into the door of this glamorous industry. For my first job, I managed the front desk and icy stares of the long-limbed, little-black-dressed editors at a high-fashion title. I tried my best to emulate their style, but eventually had to admit to myself that their world wasn't for me. Fashion trends, by their very nature, constantly change, so to be in fashion you must be brave or self-assured enough to continually reinvent yourself, to carry off all kinds of shades and shapes and hem lengths. And fashion, I found, was not always pretty or flattering; sometimes it was downright ugly (camouflage cargo pants worn with heels, anyone?). So is it any wonder I gravitated to the world of beauty.

As the beauty and lifestyle editor of a mainstream magazine for twenty-something women, I was under no illusions — my primary task was not to dissect the active ingredients of lip balm, but to be amenable to advertisers. My secondary role: to give readers all the tools they'd need in their quest for locking down Mr Right. I dispensed every trick in the book: how to make your eyes more mesmerising (Smoky! Sooty! Sexy!), how to drop a dress size by Friday night (Broth is your friend!), how to small-talk in a beguiling matter (Ask him questions about himself! Act interested!) …

You can only work for so long in such a place before you become part of the system. I spent my spare time on the treadmill or in the nail bar, trying to become the girl I thought I had to be. I got better at the business of looking the part, and soon hardly recognised myself. 'Your hair is amazing,' my managing editor exclaimed one day as I rushed into her office to file copy, her eyes widening in surprise before narrowing once more. 'I hate you.'

I'd spent four hours at a salon the previous evening, having my hair highlighted to shimmering perfection, and blow-dried long and lean so that the smooth cuticles reflected light for an even more lustrous effect. So yes, I knew that my hair did look amazing. As for whether said editor in fact despised me, I had little time to ponder; my taxi was waiting to take me to the airport, where a plane would then jet me off to Paris, where I'd meet up with my boyfriend.

'Ooh, I wonder if he'll propose,' cooed the receptionist as I ran out the door. 'It is the city of love, after all.'

Paris is indeed the undisputed capital of *amour*, the dream destination for hopeful lovers, heavy-breathing honeymooners and die-hard romantics, regularly topping the polls for the world's most passionate city. Her heart-palpitating prettiness — the subject of so many misty-eyed posters on walls the world over — is part of it, sure. But I think the reputation for romance is also inspired by Parisians themselves. This is a city where women parade down the streets in a sleekly seductive manner, while men cast approving and appreciative glances. It is a city where the locals — warmed by a good *verre* of *vin rouge*, or the Roman blood that still races through their veins — feel no inhibitions about public, often lavish, displays of affection. When in Rome ...

So that's why you might feel quite at home in Paris when strolling leisurely arm in arm while whispering sweet nothings into your lover's ear; locking sugar-dusted lips on a bridge as the Seine, and the rest of humanity, gush by; feeding one another spoonfuls of melt-in-your-mouth salted-chocolate mousse; getting all weak-kneed and fluttery-tummied as you sip sparkling champagne together under twinkling lights.

I'm not totally naïve about this romance business. France has worked hard to style Paris as the home of love, peddling the notion that its women were the most beautiful and flirtatious long before the rest of the West caught up to the concept of equality of seductive expression. This amorous branding has been helpful to the French economy for centuries. And the beauty and fashion brands are in cahoots, of course; being linked to the world's most alluring women is no bad thing for business, after all.

As a beauty editor, I knew the power of Paris over women. Every day, my desk filled with goodie-laden bags containing the kind of sigh-inducing gorgeousness that can hail from only one place on earth: the City of Light and lipstick. It had been four years since I'd last journeyed to the beauty capital of the world, and it would be my first time there with a boyfriend. You can imagine my excitement. There was simply no skin potion that could conjure up the glow of being in love, in Paris.

I'd been seeing Zack for a couple of years. We were practically living together, just not officially so. We had fun, sometimes a bit too much, and I could never shake the feeling that we were only mucking around, like kids playing at grown-ups, hosting tea parties in a cubby house, while wearing Mummy and Daddy's shoes and clothes.

At work, we were all about the modern phenomenon known as Impostor Syndrome; we seemed to run some version of the story every second issue. The upshot was basically this: despite how successful a modern woman is, she will never, deep down, feel worthy of acclaim. Was it a self-fulfilling prophecy? I at least tended to believe our own hype.

And turning twenty-five didn't help my confidence levels. We'd recently reported on another condition of modern life (women's magazines love syndromes, as they make for great cover lines): the quarter-life crisis. As such, I'd started to fret about whether my personal life was in appropriate sync with my professional life.

I won't lie. I was getting anxious to take things to the next level. When Zack told me he had to go to an old friend's wedding in London, to which I was not invited (in retrospect, the universe hanging up a huge warning sign, flashing in neon lights), I shrugged it off as casually as I could. Well, I had a bit of, ahem, market research to do in Paris anyway … oh, which happens to be close to London … hmmm, perhaps he could just pop over afterwards? Genius.

First on the itinerary that I'd laboured over for weeks was a couple of days' driving around *la Champagne*, a region just to the east of Paris, to drink lots of *le champagne*. I'd planned the jaunt as an apéritif of sorts to the Parisian feast ahead, something to whet the appetite, so to speak.

After finally reaching Charles de Gaulle, I practically skipped out of customs into the arrival hall, scanning the crowd for Zack's eyes. When I caught them, my heart flipped but quickly fell with a stomach-hollowing thud. I sensed it straight away: a certain *froideur* in his eyes, in fact in Zack's entire body language. His smile seemed forced, chiselled out of cold stone. His arms were folded across his chest, as though in defensive mode, and it was with something akin to reluctance that he opened them to give me a quick hug, before grabbing my bags and leading me away.

As I struggled to keep up on the march towards the hire-car office, I fought an urge to turn and run. For the first time, after a couple of years of lovely, light-hearted camaraderie, I had the distinct impression that our time together might be near its use-by date. That might seem like an extreme reaction, but the sensation was violently visceral at the time. Some people opt for fight, I usually choose flight.

Friends would tell me that my tendency to paranoia when situations start to reveal themselves as less than perfect comes dangerously close to self-sabotage. I, however, like to see my heightened reading of a scenario as a sort of perceptiveness, allowing me to move into a pre-emptive mode of attack that protects me in the long run. I might hit the parachute button too early, but at least I don't crash.

I tried to decode the startling development. Did Zack meet someone else at the wedding? My old-fashioned women's intuition told me no; there was an icy coolness to him that didn't seem compatible with any inner flames of passion. Did the wedding simply freak him out? After seeing his friend get hitched, did he feel like he was next in line? I remembered a recent throwaway comment of his, slurred after a bottle of wine. 'You're just waiting in this little apartment of yours for me to come and rescue you, aren't you?' He was drunk, yes, but the words had rolled off his tongue a little too easily, as though he had voiced the thought several times before.

'It's 120 kilometres to the hotel,' Zack told me as we settled into our car, in a formal tone that would nicely befit a chauffeur.

'Oh … okay.'

'It will take maybe an hour and a half to get there.'

'Uh-huh …'

Silence ensued for a few minutes, although it felt like hours.

Then: 'It's going to be 26 degrees today.'

Oh god, we were already talking about the weather. I needed a drink.

&

I had become quite accustomed to quaffing champagne. My job saw me attending at least one product launch per day, which almost always entailed a line-up of tuxedo-clad waiters bearing silver trays decorated with champagne-filled glasses.

I love champagne for so many reasons, but mostly for its pure sensuousness — it appeals so deliciously to every single sense. First, there's the eye-catching sparkle, and the subtly unique tint: a shade of gold or pale apricot or pearly-grey. Next, bring the glass closer, and you start to hear the effervescent hiss, the sound equivalent of tingles down the spine. Closer still, and a frenzy of bubbles bursts on the tip of your nose, an array of aromas exploding, bringing to mind colour-saturated images of orange blossom, juicy strawberry or green grass. As the liquid gushes over your tongue, still more flavours and fragrances permeate your mouth, perfuming you from within.

Real champagne can only come from Champagne, a region encompassing less than 85,000 acres of vineyards. As Zack and I drove out of Île-de-France — the area that was basically the sum total of France way back in the time of the Franks — and into Champagne, we found ourselves whizzing past sloping hills covered in a rippled carpet of vines, lush and green with hope after a long icy winter.

In springtime, the wines of Champagne can be found underground, furiously bubbling away in their bottles, as though ready to explode. All wines naturally ferment, when the yeast on grape skin meets the sugar in the juice and converts it into alcohol and carbonic gas. In Champagne, the process is halted into hibernation during the winter freeze, before picking up again when spring peps things up and sets bubbles back into action.

Champagne had nothing on my stomach at that moment, which was churning with nervous energy. I tried to fill the gaps in the jagged atmosphere with some conversation. 'Sorry,' Zack said, looking straight ahead, jaw firmly set. 'I need to concentrate on driving on the other side of the road.'

Did I mention that I needed a drink?

Champagne wasn't always bubbly. Winemakers toiled for centuries to keep fizz and foam out of their wine, which was a rather glum pinkish-brown hue. As Paris sparkled into life at the City of Light in the 1700s, winemakers in Champagne worked out how to control the phenomenon of second fermentation, and the drink became as lustrous as the age.

But champagne had its place in the worst of times, too. 'In victory you deserve it,' declared Napoléon, 'in defeat you need it.' The contradictory drink suitably hails from a region that, while breathtakingly lovely, knows much about misery. Napoléon also noted that the gently sloping countryside of Champagne was perfectly suited to battle. From the Romans to Attila the Hun, the Russians to the Prussians, French revolutionaries to German regiments, Champagne has been plundered and pummelled to a shocking extent; it's arguably the most blood- and sorrow-soaked region on earth.

Not that you'd know it, as you wind your way around the verdant fields, as pretty as a postcard with pink and red roses tumbling out from each row of vines. But even this rosy picture is not what it seems. To grape growers, the presence of roses keeps the potential of impending doom top of mind; these ornamentals succumb to disease before most plants, so they signal when grapes might be headed for blight. So much for romance.

We arrived at our hotel, a turreted château rich in fairy-tale fantasy, and disconcertingly at odds with where our relationship seemed to be heading. More awkward still, we were upgraded to a suite, a toile de jouy-lined folly of a room complete with a velvet-curtained four-poster bed. Cringe.

After I had gingerly unpacked, I noticed Zack standing at the window, staring out at the nearby ruins of a medieval fortress (perhaps another symbolic sign, courtesy of my friend the universe?). It was such a forlorn image that I found myself walking over and wrapping my arms around Zack's torso, an instinctive consolatory gesture. 'Okay, let's get going,' he said, a little too quickly, unfurling my arms and leading me towards the door.

We drove to Reims, the capital of the region, for a visit to the house of Veuve Clicquot, that champagne that's like liquid gold, sparkly sunshine in a bottle. So voluptuously full-bodied, it's a blend that could have only been made by a formidably strong woman.

Barbe-Nicole Clicquot is nothing short of a legend in these parts. In the early nineteenth century, the wily widow (*veuve*) — the first woman to run a champagne house, and an internationally successful company, at that — invented *remuage*, a process for easily removing the pesky sediment that used to plague bottles of champagne. It was a game-changer, making champagne more commercial than ever.

Our tour took us down into the depths of the *crayères*, vaults that date back to Roman times. The Romans had their slaves quarry the chalky soils of Champagne for stone with which roads and towns could be built; it turned out, centuries later, that the leftover cavities made for ideal spaces in which to store and age champagne. We were told how these tunnels all link up to form an underground city of winding roads that would stretch for almost 500 kilometres. During wartime, life was thrown upside down. Literally. People sheltered in the cellars for months on end, sleeping side by side, mirroring the bottles lined up in racks.

While bombs tore into the city above, its subterranean residents dined by candelabra in the cold, clammy depths, sipping on the finest champagne as they defiantly continued to live life as best they could. Births and deaths occurred; most probably bust-ups, too.

For the finale of our tour, I finally got my hands on that much-needed drink. Today, however, the champagne tasted bitter, as though my body chemistry had soured. It even seemed to lack its usual sparkle, I thought, holding up my glass with a left hand that was decidedly lacking in any kind of sparkle itself.

Suffice it to say, dinner back at the château that night was not the romantic, oyster-fuelled affair I'd had in mind when booking weeks before. Citing a stomach ache, Zack retired early. I took myself to the lounge and ordered a flute of rosé champagne.

Rosé champagne is typically the syrupy drink of romance, not relationship breakdowns, but I found its creamy sweetness soothing rather than cloying, as though it was restoring my body's emotional balance. These days, the most popular bubbles tend to be dry (or *brut*) but every girl knows the importance of a well-timed sugar fix. Right then, its candied femininity felt fortifying, swirling a surge of feel-good endorphins through my body. I was surprisingly clear-headed for all the bubbles, which was helpful, as I was already mentally rewriting my itinerary, for a Parisian holiday for one.

The next morning, there was a knock at the door. They were most terribly sorry, but there had been a mistake … We'd been given the wrong room and could we possibly move to that smaller one down the corridor. Shocked from the shame of it all, we nodded and — lamer still — proceeded to move our own bags. Down the hall in our dinky new room, Zack went back to bed, dramatically clutching his supposedly sore stomach.

I wandered down to the breakfast room, and was stopped in my tracks by the glamour of a couple checking in. They were evidently the successful claimants to the room from which Zack and I had been so unceremoniously ejected. And rightly so: they looked like movie stars, with their bouncy hair and tailored linen, and were entwined in such a passionate embrace that I blushed. Get-a-room just didn't cut it for them; they were get-a-suite status. Zack and I, as a couple, obviously hadn't fooled the French, those masters of matters of the heart.

I spent the morning lying by the pool, Zack mostly in bed. In the afternoon, I ensconced myself in a velvety couch in the bar, and sunk into a hazy champagne-induced blur. I once caught sight of Zack out the window, wandering around the ruins. I wondered if he got the symbolism.

Later that day, we finally found ourselves back in our room together, unable to ignore *l'éléphant* any longer.

'It's over, isn't it?' I asked.

'I think so.' After pretty much avoiding all eye contact for a day, he finally looked straight at me. 'I'm sorry.'

I didn't need a why, I just desperately wanted to flick past the final pages of this chapter, and propel myself into the next. Zack wanted to move on quickly, too; he'd already booked a flight back to London.

&

An eternity of polite smiles and stilted words later, it was time to check out. I brooded in silence all the way back to Paris (mortifyingly, every radio station seemed to be playing Celine Dion's 'My Heart Will Go On'). Looking determinedly out the side window, I watched the fields flash by and attempted to put my present drama into perspective by reflecting on the horrors that this land has seen: the blood spilled, the countless bodies buried, the deadly gases released and cannons fired …

No wonder the vines there weep. The French call it *les pleurs de la vigne*; in spring, the sap — warmed by the sun — starts to flow, dripping from the wounds inflicted by relentless pruning. And yet, it's the explosion of corks, not guns, that has won out. Champagne has become a symbol of the French will not only to survive, but to survive in style.

My first day alone in Paris, I did what all heart-hurt women the world over do: wallowed in chocolate. I was sitting cross-legged on the cobbled western quay of Île Saint-Louis, shaded by a parasol of leaves held aloft by a gnarled old plane tree. All around me were couples, gazing into one another's eyes and stroking one another's skin under the golden glaze of the sun's rays, but I didn't mind so much, because I had my own guy: Bert.

That would be Berthillon, the city's most famous purveyor of *glaces* and *sorbets*, proudly hailing from this delightful little island. I'd ordered a *double* of *chocolat noir* and *citron* — the rich and sweet dark cocoa creaminess set off by a sour and icy citrus edge. It complemented my mood, which was oscillating between nostalgia and bitterness.

I'd checked into my room, originally — and excitedly — booked for two, in a quaint hotel on the main strip of the island. Straight out of central casting, it could have been a location for a light-hearted rom-com about a couple romping around Paris. Its ceilings were striped with wooden beams from which hung a large chandelier, and its walls papered in florals and dotted with oil paintings of blush-cheeked duchesses — the very picture of romantic luxury. Then again, perhaps the full-blown femininity of it all was a regular Australian guy's nightmare. It was going to push my credit card to the limit, but as a kind of post-break-up therapy, this girlie haven could be worth every *centime*.

Once my senses were filled with feel-good cocoa vibes, I wandered across the bridge that links Île Saint-Louis to the larger island, Île de la Cité, past a busker wringing yearning wails out of his violin. A kind of magic starts to happen as you cross there, as the chiselled arches and elaborate spires of Notre-Dame soar into view — a gravitational pull, as though Paris is drawing you towards its very heart.

This is where Paris began, when Julius Caesar and his troops marched into town in 52 BC, conquering the Celtic fishing tribe known as the Parisii. Lutetia Parisiorum was a boomtown waiting to happen; as an island, it was naturally protected from enemies, as well as boasting a prime position as a trading port. Lush fertile land stretched for miles, and plentiful stone reserves allowed the Romans to build their majestic arenas and famously efficient highways, spreading the city southwards.

After the collapse of the Roman Empire and the so-called Dark Ages, Paris began to come back to life, as stone masons, sculptors and stained-glass artists conspired to beautify the island city. It's almost impossible to imagine what the Île de la Cité looked like in the Middle Ages, as much of it is now lumped with staid government buildings. But look around and you can catch an occasional peek into the past. As I strolled along the prettily named Quai aux Fleurs, I noticed beamed towers and dormer windows that have barely changed in five centuries; I could almost picture the medieval maidens sighing through the glass with longing at the lives and loves they couldn't have.

I was lucky to live in a time when women could do anything, I reminded myself — as my magazine always reminded our readers. You couldn't, however, have any*one*. The magazine was wrong on one front: it was impossible to make a man love you if he didn't.

&

At number 9–11 on the *quai* of flowers, a plaque marks the site where one of history's most passionate relationships bloomed. 'Former home of Héloïse and Abélard, 1118, rebuilt in 1849,' it reads. The medieval duo has been immortalised in wrought iron, their sculpted heads craning from each of the curlicue-covered doors, tormentingly out of reach of one another. I instinctively stretched out my hand to console Héloïse's smooth, solemn forehead, before quickly withdrawing it into my pocket, a little abashed at my show of emotion for a door. I sheepishly looked around; a middle-aged woman walking past proffered a knowing smile, as though acknowledging a fellow member of a secret society. Any Parisienne who has ever had her heart crushed well understands the power of the epic tale of Héloïse and Abélard, a love story so eternal in its emotions that it entrances to this day.

Pierre Abélard was a brilliant-minded man (and knew it), who ventured from his small village in Brittany to the big Parisian smoke in the early twelfth century, in search of expanding his inner horizons. The unerring arrogance for which he would become renowned developed early. He would endlessly question the logic of his professors' lines of theological reasoning, infuriating religious authorities. The iconoclast soon took to teaching himself, and with his dashing mix of philosophy, poetry and songs, he was a magnetic figure who attracted a loyal, adoring following.

Enter Héloïse, the teenage niece of Canon Fulbert, who agreed to board Abélard on the condition that the celebrated teacher instruct his precious ward. Héloïse was already proficient in Latin, Greek and Hebrew at a time when most women could not even read their own language. She was also as sensual as she was intelligent, and the inevitable occurred.

As Héloïse's lessons fell by the wayside, so did Abélard's classes. His students grumbled that he'd lost his mojo; at the time, scholars were expected to stay celibate to keep their minds sharp and focused. Eventually everyone knew about the clandestine couple — except Uncle Fulbert. The jig was finally up when Héloïse fell pregnant. Far from ashamed, Héloïse named her son Astrolabe, after the old tool of astronomers and astrologers — a sure declaration of her transcendent love.

The fuming uncle nagged the couple to marry. They finally agreed on the condition that it would be kept a secret. Even so, it rankled with Abélard, who wasn't much into the mundane realities of an official relationship. 'In marrying, I was destroying myself; I was casting a slur upon my own honour,' he (so gallantly) remarked in later life. It must be admitted that Héloïse — who was worried domestic life could extinguish their passion — wasn't a fan of the marital institution herself: 'If the name of wife appears more sacred and more valid, sweeter to me is ever the word friend, or, if thou be not ashamed, concubine or whore.'

To take the edge off the tension in the household, Abélard temporarily sent Héloïse off to a convent. It was the final straw for her uncle, who saw this as banishment. And so the canon plotted his ultimate revenge: one night, when Abélard was sleeping, two thugs were let into his room with the order of castration. It was a shocking act even in those tough medieval times.

Abélard, however, came to see the crime as divine punishment; he recuperated in the lap of religion, holing himself up in monasteries to refocus his mind. Having regained his physical and mental strength, the once-more celibate Abélard returned to a brilliant teaching career.

As a renowned abbess, Héloïse's career also thrived; still, she was never completely fulfilled by an existence she had not wished for herself. When the couple began corresponding fifteen years later, Héloïse was still in mourning for the loss of that more passionate parallel life. 'Why after our entry into religion, which was your decision alone, have I been so neglected and forgotten by you? … It was desire, not affection which bound you to me, the flame of lust rather than love.'

Over time, they made peace with each other, and she with her lot. But, heartbreakingly, they never saw one another again, and nobody knows what happened to Astrolabe, the cosmic love child.

While the ups and downs of Héloïse and Abélard's story make for delicious Gothic tragedy, I couldn't help wishing for a less dramatic — and more romantic — ending. For someone celebrated for his radical thinking, couldn't Abélard have found a way to coexist with Héloïse, who was unique and inspiring in every way, and who believed their love had the capacity to rise above the ho-hum of convention.

But perhaps, like so many women, Héloïse was asking too much. Her love was all-encompassing, but his love was limited in scope; hers was spiritual, which expands over time, his physical, which only fades. Men's brawn-over-brains take on love is still a dilemma women fret over (my magazine certainly wailed about it a lot), and perhaps that's why Héloïse resonates with us to this day. She speaks so eloquently of the anguish we feel when love is taken from us too soon, and too suddenly.

&

'*Bonsoir, Madame*,' trilled the waiter, as I sat myself down in a café back near my hotel.

I'd possibly been called 'Madame' before, but its significance suddenly hit me like a sucker punch. Madame is French for Mrs. Which I was decidedly not going to be any time soon. And here's the rub: Madame is also a form of address for a woman too advanced in age to be considered a Mademoiselle. While it's a courtesy — and probably one many French women appreciate — the title can be shocking for a non-Parisienne who still sees herself as very much a youthful Mademoiselle. The realisation that I was now a Madame was not going to help ameliorate my quarter-life crisis any time soon.

I ordered champagne. After all, as Napoléon philosophised, you need it as much in the good times as the bad. With the first sip, I closed my eyes and let the bubbles burst over my tongue before an intoxicating warmth whirled around my head. Then, as the initial rush dissipated, I felt my tensions begin to dissolve. You see, if you sip champagne when in a dark mood, its frothy lightness will lift you out of any miserable emotional depths. At least for a while. So I ordered a second glass.

I drank a third, promising myself it would be my last of the night, with my dinner-for-one, as the tables around me filled up with couples whose loved-up glow intensified in the luminescence of magic hour. Not that I was exactly unhappy on my own. As an only child, you learn early on to cherish your own company; your thick skin is the protective fortress you began building around yourself during idle childhood hours — the emotional equivalent of a castle for one, complete with fairy-tale turrets. This doesn't mean that you never let the drawbridge down and allow some dashing knight to make his way across the moat. But mostly you're more than happy in the ivory tower, watching the world from afar.

Walking around Île Saint-Louis that night, my senses tingling from the champagne, it did indeed seem as though I was ensconced in a kind of fairy realm. The island still looks as it did in the 1600s, when it was made over from pastoral land into a model modern city in miniature. An exquisite little metropolis of light, its bright stone buildings positively glow during the day, and shine under lamplight at night, their windows transformed into framed tableaux of ornate, chandelier-lit interiors. Everything seems suspended in time, in a shimmering bubble floating on the Seine.

Darkness had draped itself over Paris like a velvety cape, and the weight of the night felt both comforting and liberating. No longer exposed as a single woman trying to keep up appearances, I was free to be invisible, to skulk and scowl if I so wished. I imagined this is what it must have felt like back in the seventeenth century, when the fashion for going incognito saw women take to the streets holding black masks coyly over their faces.

I've always loved night-wandering around Paris, claiming the quiet footpaths as my own, breathing in the calm, clean air, and soaking up the hazy glow of the street lights designed to evoke the halo-like aura of old oil lamps. The habit might sound somewhat risky, but my ever-present paranoia about what might be around the corner (literally and figuratively) has (so far) kept me safely on track, and I've somehow developed a sixth sense for not veering into territory that might be a little dicey after dark.

Nevertheless, there are some streets in even the prettiest parts of Paris where you experience a frisson of chills, as though you're walking over a grave, and you can't help but get a sense of the shadowy secrets this city keeps. The eighteenth-century writer Restif de la Bretonne documented the dangers of his nocturnal city in his book *Parisian Nights.* Although it must be noted that Restif himself wasn't the type of guy a girl would want to bump into in a shady laneway; he was also a pornographer and a shoe fetishist, who gave the heel-obsessed condition its official name, retifism.

In the name of research, Restif roamed around the Parisian streets at a time the French call *entre chien et loup* — between dog and wolf. It's an ancient expression that refers to the period when you can no longer distinguish between the two animals — and, once upon a time, wolves were known to roam just beyond the walls of Paris, so it also suggests a time of danger. A time when the Restifs of the world would come out to prowl and prey; when the light of day no longer kept men on a leash of civility, and the nightfall allowed them to explore their wild side.

Charles Baudelaire, the Romantic poet I'd had a crush on as a teenager, was another inveterate nightwalker, often strolling the streets of this very island, where he once lived, long before syphilis and booze ravaged his features. Powerless to resist the erotic promise of a light-melting sunset, he would often be found lurking around a blackening Paris, his nostrils quivering with excitement as he sniffed out his next source of literary inspiration. Some believe the poet was a synaesthete, meaning his senses of sight, sound and smell would all whirl together. Perhaps, because his words are certainly uniquely evocative. But Paris, with her all-encompassing beauty, does this to you: heightens the senses, stirs the emotions. You feel as though you, well, *feel* things that bit more.

&

My champagne-induced sugar rush slumped, dragging my mood down with it, and a surge of sadness overwhelmed me. A long, emotionally draining day was almost over, which was a relief, yes — but it also signified time to say goodbye. Not just to Zack, but to the life I would have led with him, the me I would have grown into.

My mum had got it right, I thought. She'd met my dad when she was in her final year of school. By twenty-one she was a wife; by twenty-two, a mother; at twenty-five, she'd finished her first university degree and was on rung number one of her career. She was someone who had a plan, and made sure to stick to it. Her life was orderly and systematised and, it now hit me, exactly how I wished mine could be. I might have careered off course at varying times these past ten or so years, but I realised that lately I'd been hanging onto a subconscious hope that twenty-five would signal a turning point in life, taking me off the meandering scenic route I tended to prefer, onto a more direct life path that would get me to that place where everything came together. When I'd get married, take a promotion, grow up, all that. I suddenly wanted a plan, too.

Back in my hotel room, I called Mum and blubbered out the sad and sorry story.

'Do some deep breathing while I talk for a while, okay?' she said, when I had finally come up for air. 'You're too young to settle down, there's still the whole world to explore — which, believe it or not, consists of more than just Paris.'

'But you had done so much by my age ...'

'It was a different world. Men were different, too. They didn't get scared about growing up and moving into the next life stage as they seem to now.'

It was true. Boys just wanted to, well, be boys. The Peter Pan Syndrome. We'd also written about that particular phenomenon in the magazine.

'Then again,' Mum added, 'I don't think girls should marry young either anymore. There are so many more opportunities now, but it's also more competitive than ever. Focus on yourself and your career and where you want to go as a person. Now, it's late there, so wash your face, go to bed, and things will seem a lot better in the morning. After all, you're in Paris!'

She was right, of course; she always was. And I should totally have taken her advice about going straight to sleep.

If a fourth glass of champagne would not have been wise, a well-stocked mini bar at my disposal most certainly was not. If I were French, my well-honed sense of rationality — and commitment to quality over quantity — would have ensured that I stopped at three drinks, probably two. But I had far to go on my wishful journey to turn French by osmosis. Any Frenchness I had picked up certainly didn't yet extend into the realm of drinking habits. So I uncorked a bottle of *rouge*, and methodically made my way through it while leaning out the window, sighing tragically to the night sky. The tiled and tinned roofs of Paris were glinting in the moonlight, and I imagined with envy the scenes of romantic domesticity being played out beneath them. All I needed was a beret and a packet of Gauloises and I was starring in my own personal French melodrama.

In a way, Paris is as suited to sadness as to happiness. Just like champagne, it consoles as much as it exhilarates. Melancholy moodiness has been at home there since the brooding days of Romanticism, which idealised a world long gone. The French movement's founding *papa*, François-René de Chateaubriand, in 1802 wrote of world-weariness as *le mal du siècle*. Literally: the sickness of the century. The new world, thought the Romanticists, made people ill. And it was chic to be sick. As Baudelaire wrote, 'I can barely conceive of a type of beauty in which there is no melancholy.'

Ever since, French intellectuals and artists have excelled at pessimism. Many French seem to consider an excess of happiness to be a sign of stupidity. Because if you really thought in any great depth, you couldn't help but see the woes of the world, and that the best of times are behind us. French melancholy goes hand-in-wringing-hand with nostalgia. Which is fair enough: the French boast some spectacular past glories. But when you consistently idealise the past, the present can never live up.

In signature paradox style, however, the French do value *joie de vivre* (of course, they invented the term). They just seem happier striving for happiness than actually attaining it. Because from the giddy heights of good times, of course, there's nowhere to go but down. And perhaps melancholy and joy are simply, once again, opposite sides of the one *centime*; how would you truly know what pleasure is, unless you knew what it isn't?

The next morning, I experienced what the French call a *gueule de bois.* Wooden mouth. I've never quite got the hangover analogy. For me, the morning-after mouth is dry, sure, but the texture is more on the furry side of things. And that's just the start. My whole head feels like it's made of shattered glass, with jagged shards piercing my eyeballs. As my thoroughly disgusted body attempts to detox itself, acrid fumes ooze from the pores of my clammy skin, while my stomach churns, sending hot waves of nausea around my body.

And so, in this woeful state, I tossed and turned in my twisted, sweaty hotel sheets all morning, in and out of consciousness. The bright Parisian sunshine was glaring through the gaps in the curtains, highlighting my state of messiness, so in contrast to the prettiness of my room, and the beauty of what lay outside. I finally woke to a sensation of relief, my system having mostly purged itself of the previous night. After showering, slipping into a floral dress and painting my lips pink, I headed out into the daylight, large dark glasses firmly in place.

I wandered down a little side street, Rue le Regrattier. At the end, I looked up to find its original name etched into stone: street of the headless woman. Just above were the robed remains of a statue. I feel your pain, I thought. Turns out that the statue is not of a head-deprived woman, but of Saint Nicolas, who was hacked in half by one of the revolutionaries who ran around the streets of Paris, obliterating all signs of royalty and religion. As for the woman *sans* head, she was once the name and emblem of a tavern on this site, which no doubt served up goblets of ale that caused many a wooden mouth. My head was still throbbing. But at least I had one.

I turned onto Quai de Bourbon, which runs along the Seine on the northern side of the island. The poplar trees dotted along the riverfront soothed with their dappled shadows, and the pink geraniums bursting from the window boxes above seemed to freshen my stale senses. This was surely the ideal place to mend a broken — or at least fractured — heart.

Île Saint-Louis, for all its harmoniously balanced beauty, has certainly seen its share of emotional turmoil. At number 19, a plaque tells you that Camille Claudel lived and worked there from 1899 to 1913. 'At this date, [she] ended her brief career as an artist and began the long night of internment.' And because that doesn't sound bleak enough, it ends with a quote from a letter Camille wrote to her once paramour, fellow sculptor Auguste Rodin, in 1886: 'There is always something missing which torments me.'

The French don't say, 'I miss you.' They say, 'You are missing from me.' I had not before fully appreciated the strength of the sentiment, but it was starting to make total sense. When someone you love rips himself from you, it aches as though a very piece of you is absent; you are no longer complete.

Perhaps Camille was articulating her agony when she smashed up years' worth of sculptures in this very studio. Soon after, her family locked her in an asylum, where she would remain for the rest of her days, even against her doctor's wishes. The thought of the creations that were destroyed, as well as those that never materialised — precious works of onyx and marble cut as precisely as a flawless diamond — is enough to make your heart pang. Let alone the thought of Camille's pain as she pined her half-lived life away.

This wasn't the ending Camille's story was meant to have. Prodigiously talented, she began modelling in clay at the age of twelve. Sculpting was considered a dirty, unladylike profession, but the beautiful Camille wowed everyone with her brilliant hands, including the legendary Rodin, who took her on as an assistant, a status that was swiftly upgraded to muse and lover. He was twenty-four years her senior and married by common law to the long-suffering Rose Beuret. Madly in love with Camille, he promised to leave his wife but never did, which infused their passionate relationship with an agonising, tormenting tension — as highly and tautly tuned as the muscular expression of their works.

During the couple's most ardent years together, they each sculpted a couple in embrace, and while the similarities are striking, it's the key difference that's most telling. In Rodin's *The Kiss*, we see a man and woman hugging in a traditional manner; she is scooped beneath him, her lips raised to his as his manly physique curves protectively around her. In Camille's *Cacountala*, however, it's the man yearning upwards, on his knees in supplicant mode, begging for a kiss from his passive partner.

Camille wanted more from Rodin than he could give. She needed a man to not only adore and worship her, but hand himself over to her completely. In her later autobiographical work, *The Mature Age*, a young woman — now the one on her knees — imploringly reaches up to an older man, who is being dragged away by a harpy of an elderly woman. The message is hardly subtle. But the utter rawness of emotion behind the sculpture snatches the breath; so twisted with pain and sorrow is it, you wince just looking at it.

Passion can bring out the best in us, but it can also make us crazy, as Camille only too well found out. Lust might razzle and dazzle, but it soon crashes and burns, leaving the unwitting scarred. Love blazes for longer, but the real secret to a well-stoked relationship that glows for a lifetime is, quite simply, Like. There's perhaps good reason the French use the same word (*aimer*) for love and like. You can't genuinely love someone if you don't, deep down, like them, warts and all. You're there for the good times, but also the bad ones. Rodin couldn't leave Rose — his faithful companion of fifty years — because, when it came down to it, maybe he just liked her too much. If only Camille could have found what Rodin already had, she would have been nurtured for life. Everyone needs a Rose.

Roses are the most contradictory of flowers. From furled-up buds through to full-blown langour, they symbolise the spectrum of life — and yet they're infuriatingly short-lived, a sign of the fleeting nature of our time on earth, too. In English, we seize the moment with a chant of 'carpe diem'; the French have poet Pierre de Ronsard's famous quote in mind: 'Gather the roses of life today.'

Roses, for me, seem so emblematic of Paris, and her live-in-the-moment, stop-to-smell-the-flowers beauty. A contrast of soft ruffles and thorn-barbed stems, they nicely symbolise Parisiennes, too, also a paradox of feminine allure spiked with razor-sharp wit. No wonder then that Paris is redolent with rose-blooming florists and rose-drenched perfumes, revelling in a floral obsession that can be traced back to one of history's most seductive Parisiennes.

Several days later, I walked through the wrought-iron gates of Château de Malmaison, once the cherished estate of Emperor Napoléon's first wife.

There Joséphine loved nothing more than to potter about the fragrant gardens of her country manor house, nestled into pretty parklands a seven-mile carriage ride away from the stenches and stresses of Paris. She had a particular fondness for her roses, cultivating hundreds of varieties, enlisting painter and botanist Pierre-Joseph Redouté to catalogue them. His intricately detailed watercolours are technically precise, yet painted with such passion that the lush petals seem to want to burst from the paper. He was surely inspired by the elegant yet disarmingly voluptuous lady of the house, who grew roses not just for scientific purposes — but so she could fill her home and adorn her hair with her favourite flower. One of her more extravagant dresses was pink, covered entirely in rose petals.

I traipsed along the gravel-strewn path lined with signature rosebushes and topiary cones echoing the high-pitched roofs of the seventeenth-century château. Perfectly proportioned, it's both grand and intimate — a reflection of Joséphine herself, who treasured her private life, while graciously submitting to the public persona that destiny forced her to wear like a heavy ermine robe.

Joséphine and Napoléon ushered in the age of post-Revolutionary France, of an expanding French empire, and passing over the threshold of Malmaison — an entrance styled like a striped military pavilion — is akin to stepping into that new world order. The impeccable Joséphine hired the best architects of the day to fit out the house's interiors with the latest in neoclassical style, a design trend that complemented France's endeavours to rival history's great nations. Pompeiian frescoes decorated the walls and ceilings, mini obelisks and sphinxes added touches of Egyptian exotica, and the marble columns would have looked at home in a Roman villa belonging to a Caesar.

Malmaison also saluted a modern hero, Napoléon, who saw himself as a second Alexander the Great. Tent motifs abounded, which must have made the warrior, ever on the march of war, feel right at home. Rusty tones suggestive of the Egyptian desert reminded him of how far he had ventured. Detailing inspired by military trophies celebrated his prowess on the battlefield and stroked his healthy ego.

The personal elements of Malmaison are undeniably touching. I could well imagine Joséphine gliding over the black-and-white tiles while directing the designers in every detail. And yet … it made me cringe. This was her own personal retreat, which could have been a haven of feminine comfort; instead she turned it into a shrine to Napoléon. Then again, perhaps it wasn't fair to be so judgemental. Hers was another age, a time when a woman's survival often meant learning how to please men.

Joséphine, who came to embody sensual French femininity, was actually a self-made Parisienne. Having been born in French-ruled Martinique to a noble yet poor family, she ran wild and free on the sun-soaked island until the age of sixteen, when she was sent to France to marry. Joséphine immediately fell for her dashing Alexandre de Beauharnais, who in turn looked down his patrician nose at the unsophisticated girl before him. The marriage was not a happy one. After two children — produced despite his many long absences — the serially unfaithful Alexandre separated from his young bride, banishing her to a convent.

It was at this unlikely place that Joséphine learned the arts of feminine wiles. Her fellow boarders, high-society Parisiennes taking shelter from reality for various reasons, were some of the most graceful women she had ever encountered. She studied and emulated the way they sat, walked and talked (low and soft, diluting her Creole accent). She mimicked their style of flattering, low-cut muslin gowns and suggestively wrapped shawls; and she started to wear rouge, which gave her face a flush that managed to be both girlish and sensuous. In short, Joséphine made herself over into a Parisienne.

The seductive makeover, *malheureusement*, didn't win her back her husband: he was guillotined during the Terror years of the Revolution. But it did help her to get through those turbulent times (including an emotionally scarring stint in jail) and, as a penniless widow and mother of two, to secure some wealthy protectors. A star of the salons, she was as smart as she was enticing, the ideal French woman. No wonder Napoléon saw in her his perfect future empress.

The trouble is, when you start a relationship atop a pedestal of perfection, it's all too easy to topple off. Women's magazine tirelessly run articles on not just how to get a man, but also how to keep him — and it makes for exhausting reading. This constant pursuit of pleasing someone else comes at a cost: your own pleasure.

Joséphine soon found Napoléon increasingly hard to please. As his successes mounted, so too did his arrogance, and the dynamics of their relationship changed. While Napoléon still loved his wife, often passionately, she wasn't the Joséphine he had envisaged: one who could give him an heir. Heartbreakingly, Joséphine's need for Napoléon only intensified as his for her diminished.

It's an age-old story, of course. Man meets woman, woos her, wins her over, loses interest. Or how about this one: man trades in wife for younger model. Napoléon divorced Joséphine so that he could go in search of a fresh and fecund new empress, and his former wife retreated to her roses. Like her signature flower, she had bloomed with sensual beauty, but all too easily wilted from the ravages of life, drooping under the weight of her worries and wrinkles, and fading fertility.

While walking around her gardens one day, in one of her diaphanous muslin gowns — so ephemeral they have dissolved into the past, leaving little physical trace of the style icon for museums to showcase — Joséphine caught a chill, from which she would never recover. Perhaps it felt an apt way to go.

You can walk through the very bedroom where Joséphine lived and loved, and see the actual bed in which she took her last breath, with her desolate son by her side. The circular room was draped in red fabric to mimic a tent, again to appeal to the warrior emperor's military tastes. The canopied bed is surmounted by the imperial eagle: Napoléon's powerful presence forever hovering over Joséphine's life. I wondered what her final thoughts were. Did she ask herself if it was worth dying for this love, when there was still so much more to live for?

I blithely whiled away most of my final day in the Jardin des Tuileries, happy for no reason other than the beauty of living. The Tuileries are at their most gorgeous in the springtime, when you can laze on the green chairs scattered throughout the park, admiring the garden beds brimming with tulips and pansies, and bask in the light glowing through blossom-laden trees. The hours there seem to melt, and it's all too easy to indulge in this fluidity of time. If you stay until the last burst of sunshine, everything appears to dissolve before your eyes into golden dust, and you fully appreciate why the Tuileries were a favourite subject of Impressionist painters.

At one end of the Tuileries is the Musée de l'Orangerie, nestled into a neo-Renaissance-style pavilion that takes its name from its Second Empire life as the greenhouse that supplied the gardens with orange plants. It morphed into an Impressionism museum, then one devoted to twentieth-century art. The Orangerie well merits a visit, because eight huge panels of Claude Monet's *Water Lilies* remain.

Monet was the *père* of the Impressionists, the late nineteenth-century group of artists who portrayed life as their own optimistic eyes saw it: a celebration of colour, movement and sunlight, painted with love and joy as much as with soft, dreamy pigments. Impressionists loved the beauty of the simple life, and of nature, which is why they were drawn to pastoral scenes, but 'this giddy-fying Paris' especially enchanted.

Monet spent his final years just outside Paris, at his house in Giverny, surrounded by the gardens and ponds that so inspired him — and in turn seem to be his very art brought to life. If you can't make a day trip to Giverny, an early-morning pre-crowds stint at the Orangerie is an alternative oasis for the senses. Sitting before the entrancing *Water Lilies*, their cool tones of blue and purple glimmering with iridescence beneath the glass roof, you can't help but be lulled into a meditative mood — a zen state that is otherwise difficult to attain in a city where all senses are continually overstimulated.

Monsieur Monet would have loved that spring day in Paris, I thought, as I sat down for afternoon tea at one of the park's cafés. Ella Fitzgerald's 'April in Paris' was crooning in my head. 'Chestnuts in blossom. Holiday tables under the trees ...' And there, under the flowering chestnut trees, I nibbled on a chocolate éclair, its wispy pastry shell and whipped-cream filling so light I swore it couldn't possibly contain a single kilojoule. It was Paris in a dessert: sweet, frothy, feminine and so very satisfying.

It was approaching a respectable hour for my final Parisian flute of champagne — and this time it would be for reasons of celebration not commiseration. I walked along the Seine, pulling my pashmina around the fluttery straps of my sundress (how very à la Joséphine of me), as the crepuscular sky slowly tinted the atmosphere a moody lilac blue.

L'heure bleue is one of the most celebrated times in this city of so many lights; it's that enchanted hour suspended between day and night, a sliding-doors moment where you have the chance to drift into another world, and explore the mysteries of nocturnal Paris. You can almost hear the footsteps and sense the quivering nostrils of Baudelaire's ghost.

Another synaesthete, Jacques Guerlain, so loved the blue hour of Paris, and the new moods and aromas that bloomed with the descending darkness, that he bottled it. He, too, had been walking along the Seine one dusk, and noted how Paris turned herself into an Impressionist painting, all aglimmer in Monet-worthy blues and purples. In Guerlain L'Heure Bleue — one of the first thematic fragrances, capturing the complexities of a mood — he interpreted this vaporous quality with powdery iris. Yet the blue hour promises so much more — a lush, velvety after-dark — which is perhaps why Monsieur Guerlain soaked the base of the perfume with a heady musk, making for a *sillage* — or perfume trail — so entrancing it would have had Baudelaire's nose in absolute thrall.

My favourite place to be when Paris is awash in blue is Place Dauphine, on Île de la Cité, as its hushed otherworldliness is only enhanced when seen through such a nostalgically toned filter. (Perhaps this is why the author Colette ordered her sheets of paper in a pale-blue tone from the Papeteries Gaubert, which still sells her favourite old shade.) When you walk through the western tip of the triangular piazza, you feel as though you're stepping into Paris past. The red brick buildings trimmed in stone hark back to regional French architecture of the sixteenth century, giving Place Dauphine a rustic, village-like quality.

I sat outside — *en terrasse* — and inhaled a rosé champagne along with the aroma of the pink blooms that were bursting from the chestnut trees dotted over the triangle of a 'square' before me. Surrealist writer André Breton once named Place Dauphine the '*sexe de Paris*' due to its suggestive shape, and indeed it's a most intimate and feminine oasis.

Maybe I wasn't meant to share Paris with a guy, after all, and maybe the reason I was so drawn to this city wasn't even to meet *un homme* — it was to get to know myself. Instead of the romantic itinerary I'd devised — long since torn up — I'd had ten days of chaste solitude, walking any and every which way around town, my long-term vision distracted by the live-for-the-now beauty of the city around, and above, me. Paris is a place that trains you to look up, I thought, which seemed apt, as I felt like I'd lived much of life with my head in the proverbial clouds, that I didn't spend enough time taking careful, strategic steps, or watching for signs that scream 'Danger! Turn back!' I knew where I wanted to go, I realised, but didn't map out how best to get there. As you can imagine, it made for much time-consuming meandering and quite a few dead-ends — yet also pleasant views and surprises along the way. Which is, when you think about it, reflective of the Paris experience. There are all sorts of monumental destinations to tick off your to-do list, but no one perfect way to reach them. Paris is for walkers and wanderers, as much as for drifters and dreamers. It's the city that allows you to find your own way — and yourself.

I hadn't visited any of the usual tourist landmarks, although I noticed many couples posing with them in the background, creating their own future soft-focused memories and wall art. While it made my heart lurch a little, I was glad that Zack and I had ended things elsewhere, that he had dropped me off just outside Paris. It meant that there were no bridges that would forever remind me of a past love that went nowhere, no monuments whose grandeur would mock old aspirations. Paris remained my own escape, a haven and sanctuary, where I only had to please, and learn to love, myself.

I thought a lot about the woman I wanted to become on that trip. I wasn't sure exactly who she was, but I knew who she wasn't: someone who saw everything purely through the prism of attracting a mate. In short, the woman I thought I was writing for. Beauty, I now knew, was at least as much about feeling, as looking, good. It was about the rose-drenched fragrance that fills you with joy, the pretty lipstick that picks your confidence back up, helps you get out the door again, your head held high. The real beauty of life was in being happy with the face you showed the world, in not having to rely on too much artifice. That was how to avoid the real Impostor Syndrome.

I was growing up, I figured; maybe this twenty-five-year-old business wasn't going to be all bad. In fact, it was starting to feel quite liberating. I didn't have a plan, but I could make any plans I liked. There are many tales of Parisiennes that teach the dangers of being one half of a couple at the expense of being one whole of a person. Of course, it was now an era when we didn't need a man to live a fulfilled life. The world had drastically changed since my mother had clocked up a quarter-century; women could do almost everything — just, as Mum noted, not everything at once. There was a wealth of choice — yet another reason not to have a plan. Modern life required an open mind as much as an open road — just as I preferred to explore Paris without an itinerary. I decided I liked the meandering scenic route after all.

CHAPTER 6

BONNE VIVANTE

[bɔn] *adj* good [vivɑ̃t] *adj* living; good-time girl

In which, aged almost thirty, I learn the real secrets to *savoir-vivre.*

The job of a beauty editor is a curious one. It's as frivolous and fabulous as it sounds, yet seriously critical to the bottom line of magazines, which are propped up by the financial might of fragrance and makeup advertisers. In the same breath, a beauty editor might find herself talking psychographic segmentation with a brand's marketing team while cooing over the coral shades of a new blush collection. Many women have trouble reconciling the two-faced nature of the job — as pretty as the faces might be. But I've come to the realisation that to get your head around the sublime ridiculousness (or should that be ridiculous sublimity?) of beauty editing, you need to have the kind of insouciant outlook on life that allows you to see the little things as worthy of consideration, while keeping the big ones in perspective with a near-flippant nonchalance. In other words, you need to have a French way of thinking.

I was nearing the grand age of thirty. I had not for the first time heard it said that perhaps I was growing out of my role. My mum didn't tend to wonder out loud when I was going to get a 'real' job, but I sensed the question hovering permanently on her lips. Beautifully balmed and tinted lips, I might add. Mum relished helping me road-test beauty products, something that might have aided in her acceptance, if not understanding, of my chosen profession.

My editor had taken me aside several times to ask if I wanted to move on and up, to ascend the masthead ladder, but I stubbornly dug my kitten heels into the beauty rung. My desk might not have had a corner-window view, but I could nevertheless see Paris on the horizon. I not only received regular parcels from the global beauty capital, but my work took me there on occasion, to interview a perfumer, test out some innovative hair-colouring technique or celebrate a new lipstick range over afternoon tea. Tough gig, *non*?

But my favourite Parisian event by far was the launch of my best friend into married life. I had met Karlie in my early beauty days, when she was working in a public relations agency that specialised in makeup and skincare. We bonded over more than just lip gloss. Both newcomers to Sydney, we helped one another navigate our adopted city, the urban jungle of office politics as much as the dim-lit intrigues of after dark. Karlie rode a lipstick-red scooter in those days, and must have caused countless cases of whiplash. It was evident to all that this head-turning beauty, who carried an immaculately penned Filofax in her glamorous bags, was going places. Karlie was the first among us to get engaged — to a French-Australian, no less, with a wedding to take place in a château in the South of France. At the time I didn't think to bemoan the fact that our social group was starting to grow up. I was too damn excited, for one. And, as bridesmaid, I had the enviable task of seeing to a hens' celebration in Paris.

First on the itinerary was lunch at L'Avenue, the velvet-lined and chandelier-lit restaurant beloved by celebrities and supermodels, and the paparazzi who linger permanently on the footpath, hoping to catch their prey with blinding flashlights. Our group, however, didn't inspire a single click of a camera button, all being from the anonymous side of the glamour industry — PRs, beauty editors, a makeup artist and a fashion designer, who happily toiled behind the scenes, lenses and glossy pages. Not that we were immune to fashion's power, to the relentless pursuit of looking one's best. Anyone whose work takes them anywhere near the ever-spinning world of style — as most Parisiennes would know — eventually succumbs to its gravitational pull.

Fashionable restaurants must sometimes question the value of their stylish status, because fashion people don't really eat. It would be much healthier for profits (if not your clients' heart health) to appeal to the fat cats of the world. But L'Avenue is the kind of place that doesn't arch an eyebrow if you order a salad — hold the dressing — and proceed to play with it for an hour. Which is pretty much what we did that afternoon, swishing and swirling our leaves and tartares around our plates. We all shared a basket of *pommes frites, bien sûr* — so elegantly slim in France they look as though they couldn't possibly pose a threat to the waistline. Karlie was the only one to eye them suspiciously. Her bride diet, combined with the stress of coordinating a wedding on the other side of the world, had seen her whittle herself away to the size of a Parisian chip, plus the corset of her medieval-inspired wedding gown would not have allowed for a *soupçon* of additional weight. 'I'm going to gorge myself on the *croquembouche* cake,' she sighed, visualising the future feast in an attempt to satisfy present cravings.

French food is surprisingly light if you want it to be. It might have a heavy-handed reputation for rich creams and buttery sauces, but the so-called *nouvelle cuisine* — with its herb-tinged love of soup, seafood and fresh, colourful vegetables — is a refreshing alternative. And one that means, of course, you can easily earn yourself kilojoule credit for alcohol … which we proceeded to spend by ordering bottle after bottle of crisp sancerre. After all, wine is so good for you in France that they say *santé* (health) when clinking glasses.

'Ah, *c'est la vie*,' declared Mel, a fellow beauty editor.

'I just want to freeze this moment,' I said. 'We'll never experience anything like this again: all of us together, single, with not a care in the world but to drink wine and shop and enjoy each other's company.'

Karlie's phone beeped. 'I do have one extra care in the world,' she sighed. 'The candles we ordered for the church have apparently turned up yellow. I have to somehow track down a hundred new white ones.'

'Well, I guess shopping for French candles is a pretty fabulous problem to have,' said Janey, also a beauty editor. 'In the meantime, let's have one more toast: to ladies who French-lunch.'

The French lunch is a national treasure. When the rest of the working world started eschewing a midday break to scoff down a sandwich at their desk, the French steadfastly continued to dine out, because *le déjeuner* represents all that they hold dear. It's a chance to make a statement about working to live rather than living to work — and living to eat rather than eating to live. And it's an opportunity to indulge in conversation along with cuisine — lunch is about chewing over *quenelles* as much as the pros and cons of the latest labour strike, imbibing one another's opinions along with a carafe of house wine.

French wining and dining is such an art form that it has even won a place on UNESCO's cultural heritage list. There food is art on a gold-trimmed porcelain plate, a feast for the eyes as much as the tastebuds. It's telling that this elegance survived the Revolution, before which only the upper classes ate in style. *Liberté, égalité, gastronomie.* Everyone deserves to dine. Some of the most legendary French chefs have risen from poverty, hungry with desire to live well. Fittingly, the two biggest, Carême and Escoffier, were inspired by architecture and sculpture respectively, helping to give French food a reputation for artistic flair. It was the French who first linked culinary taste with the aesthetic kind of taste: *le goût*. You just aren't living if you're not eating fabulously.

L'Avenue is so named because it's situated on Avenue Montaigne, the *crème de la crème* of Parisian shopping strips, a grandiose street lined with immaculately tended horse chestnut trees and every designer store worth its weight in handbags. In other words, it's a dangerous place to be after a mostly liquid lunch. Luckily we had strict guidelines keeping us in check: we were shopping for Karlie, specifically for an outfit for her town hall ceremony, the civil wedding being the only legally recognised form of marriage in France. While not the scene of frothy white extravagance, it's nevertheless a traditional affair and calls for something suitably refined. We found her perfect ensemble in Valentino: a vanilla-white trouser suit, as soft as Chantilly cream. And for the finishing flourish: an ivory camellia brooch from Chanel.

'Did you ever in your wildest girlhood dreams imagine this?' I asked Karlie.

'Are you kidding — it *was* my wildest dream,' she exclaimed. 'Shopping in Paris for your French wedding is surely the very definition of every girl's fashion fantasy.'

There are many reasons Paris became the world's fashion capital. Originally, it was a nifty strategy for the Sun King, Louis XIV, to not only deck himself out in his beloved frills and finery, but also wield further power over his aristocratic subjects, to keep their minds filled with ruffles rather than rebellion. There was no serendipity about it; Parisiennes, regardless of what they might like to tell you, weren't predestined to be the world's most fashionable women.

Fashion was also the lace-trimmed handiwork of pure, cold economics: the king, together with his Minister of Finances, Jean-Baptiste Colbert, pioneered a state-supported interventionist policy to create the French luxury industry and fill the country's coffers with coins. And fashion — the jewel in the luxury crown — was indeed a golden affair. 'Fashion is to France what the gold mines of Peru are to Spain,' claimed Colbert, who reigned over this shiny new realm. Where once there was just tailor-made, *couturières* now ran fancy boutiques where women could buy off the rack, inspired by the illustrations of fashionable socialites they pored over in the burgeoning fashion press, the precursor to today's street-style snaps. All of France — and soon much of the world — wanted to dress à la parisienne.

The remarkable thing about the early French fashion industry was that it managed to be both exclusive and democratic, a contradictory allure that still holds today. Like fine dining, high fashion persisted beyond the Revolution, appealing to the middle classes who wanted to dress up in rank. Parisians of all classes have long admired things of beauty. Which is somewhat odd given their often violent history — although perhaps it's these moments of ugliness that have helped them appreciate glamour all the more. There's a deep respect for luxury in France, especially given the fact that the industry keeps so many French people in work. Paris also surely took to fashion because the city has been perfectly designed for the ritual of fashion display. Swan along Avenue Montaigne swinging several shopping bags and you'll surely agree.

I've always loved that this high-fashion street is named after the Renaissance writer Michel de Montaigne, who railed against sumptuary legislation — the fashion laws of the time that limited the ownership of the likes of brocade, lace, gold and silver to the elite. The anti-fashionista believed that the world would be a better place if only prostitutes wore 'scarlet or goldsmiths' work' and if 'abominable breeches' were done away with altogether. An armchair philosopher, Montaigne was famous for his rambling, chatty essays, in which he opined on everything from cannibalism to idleness, with a startling openness that revealed a little too much about his bodily functions. It was a style of literature way ahead of its time: inner observation to help explain the outer world. If Montaigne were alive in modern times, he would have been one of the world's leading bloggers.

In the early years of the new millennium, the digital diary known as blogging was only just picking up steam. It was a form of media largely for people who craved a connection with the outside world and needed to order and clarify their complex intimate thoughts. It was a group that didn't include me. I didn't do introspection all that well at the time. Or, more to the point, I chose not to.

'I worry that our lives are a bit superficial,' I once confessed to Janey after a few glasses of champagne at a launch one evening. We'd been listening to someone talk about her brand's new lipstick for forty-five minutes, and the mind-numbingness of it had sobered me into some sort of minor existential crisis.

'Are you superficial if you know it?' she laughed. 'I'm sure genuinely surface people don't think to that extent.'

I went home and registered for a sponsor child, cringingly aware it was merely a guilt-driven gesture, but one that would disperse some good into the world all the same. One day I'd try to do more, I assured myself before falling asleep, only to wake up and hit the beauty circuit treadmill once more.

Looking back, I think I stayed in the world of beauty for so long because, yes, it was fun and glamorous and all that, but also because of its intoxicating youthfulness. Beauty, at least in Australia, is utterly obsessed with youth; every second product that launches seems to be some anti-ageing wonder. So when you're in the thick of this, you can't help fretting about every little facial line. But for me, I think I was also fighting emotional wrinkles, those inner kinks and dints you get when life becomes complicated. So I didn't date with any serious mindfulness (think a succession of affairs so wrong to begin with they were always going to end badly). And in the same way, I didn't push my career. Perhaps, on some level, I thought that taking a promotion would require me to step up in other areas of life, too. I was, for the moment, happy to remain young at heart — and in every other way, too.

I'd once wished my life would have sorted itself out as neatly as my mother's had, but I now understood mine was its own story, and I appreciated that women no longer need live by a linear plotline and set chapters. Mum hadn't had her twenties to herself. I was more than making up for that. In many ways, my twenties were like one long hens' party. My friends and I were at the age and life stage where you can't hold too much against a girl for taking herself lightly. I knew that the various commitments of marriage and a mortgage were hovering somewhere just beyond the horizon. In the meantime, I decided to relish the moment, go with the flow of each day, and live without an agenda — except to enjoy myself — for as long as I was lucky enough to do so.

After walking north along Avenue Matignon and turning right onto Rue du Faubourg Saint-Honoré — that other vaunted Parisian fashion strip — we Parisian hens found ourselves clucking outside the presidential Élysée Palace. 'Pompadour, we salute you,' I sighed, as we peered through the lacy wrought-iron gates. The guards probably figured we were hoping for a glimpse of Jacques Chirac. In actual fact we were envisaging the ghost of the palace's much more powerful former tenant. It's another sign of the potency of fashion in France that the president's digs were most famously those of the Marquise de Pompadour, mistress of King Louis XV in the eighteenth century, and one of the country's leading taste-makers.

How Pompadour gave her flamboyant name to a 1950s male hairstyle is beyond me — as she favoured neat, rippled 'dos herself (technically called *tête de mouton*: sheep head) — but Pomp (her name has nothing to do with lowercase-p pomp, although she did love ostentation) influenced pretty much every other element of style at the time. If you've ever sipped herbal tea out of a pastel porcelain cup or quaffed champagne from an etched-crystal *coupe*, luxuriated in a gilt-edged velvet armchair or arranged peachy roses in a celadon-green vase, or brushed rose-pink blush over your powdered complexion, you have La Pomp to say *merci* to. She practically single-handedly created the rococo style, at once delicate and exuberant, which is still synonymous with French flair and femininity.

Born into a world increasingly in thrall to the thrills of fashion, the then Jeanne-Antoinette Poisson was the poster girl for the power of a makeover, rising from humble bourgeois beginnings to become the king's right-hand woman through virtue of sheer determination and strategic artifice. She was the patron saint of prettiness — as her biographer Nancy Mitford commented, 'Few people since the world began can have owned so many beautiful things' — and shopped on the luxury-laden street where she would eventually reside. It remains alive with her spirit of fabulous frivolity.

We walked past more former grand townhouses, one of which was home to another of history's glamour pusses, Pauline Bonaparte. Now the British Embassy, its throne room was once Pauline's decadent boudoir, which is deliciously ironic, as Napoléon's sister might have become a princess when she married Prince Borghese, but her behaviour was far from regal. The highly sexed socialite indulged in a series of affairs with eminent men, who were totally entranced by her unabashedly feminine wiles. At a time when the trend-setting *Merveilleuses* (marvellous women) of post-revolutionary Paris wore little more than gauzy gowns moistened with water to enhance cling factor, Pauline was the true princess of provocation. She was particularly renowned for the high esteem in which she held her bust — so much so that she had a set of gold punch cups moulded on one of her breasts, and wore such gossamer-light bodices that she may as well have walked around topless.

Diaphanous dresses are not as suited to modern Paris, I discovered, as we crossed Rue Royale, stepping over a metro grate just as a train whizzed beneath us and — *whoosh!* — a warm gust of wind blew everything up around my head, revealing little more than a g-string below. Car horns blared and my cheeks blushed to pink Pompadour proportions. Pauline wouldn't have minded but I was mortified. 'I just want a hole to open up right now,' I wailed, as everyone else fell about hysterically. Surely perishing on Paris's most fabled fashion street wouldn't be a bad way to go?

We were now on Rue Saint-Honoré, with its even higher, headier concentration of chic. This part of Paris has been the spiritual home of high French fashion since Rose Bertin, Marie Antoinette's legendary *couturière*, set up shop down the road. Post-Pompadour rococo, trimmings became less important than the actual cut of the dress, and the industry of *couture* — derived from the Latin for 'sew together' — was in the ascendant, reaching the pinnacle of *haute* when Charles Frederick Worth opened his rooms on the nearby Rue de la Paix and made a true art of the tradition of tailoring for women. Instead of designing from scratch, in consultation with a client, however, he produced a limited number of gowns every season — shown off in a precursor to today's fashion parade — that could be adapted and altered to fit each woman. He famously invented the bustle, bumping out the era of the crinoline, which meant ladies no longer had to fear their skirts swaying in the wind, revealing their pantaloons to the public — the shame of which I now could appreciate.

The haute couture market is not what it was in its 1980s heyday when thousands of women flocked to Paris to pay $40,000 for a made-to-measure dress. But couture is economically viable in one crucial way: by garnering publicity it helps sell a brand's various other products, such as perfume and lipstick. It's also the accessories that make money, which is blindingly obvious in Place Vendôme, the heart of Paris's fine jewellery industry. We turned off Rue Saint-Honoré to do a loop of the plaza, a vast space girded by a chain of seventeenth-century townhouses that were once home to the top bankers in town. Whether from glistening coins or glittering earrings, Place Vendôme has always smelt like money.

Boucheron, Cartier, Chanel, Dior, Chaumet ... We window-shopped our way around the storefronts, oohing and ahhing at the diamonds on display, dazzling brilliant cuts (originally invented for the Sun King to give him maximum sparkle power) and elegant marquise cuts (a shape commissioned by the following king, in homage to his lover Pompadour's dainty lips). Even the square itself is chiselled like a cut gem, its corners sliced off for an octagonal effect, the light bouncing off one facet to another to another.

'You know, I don't even need the ceremony,' said Janey. 'I just want the rock.'

'Well, diamonds last a lot longer than guys,' added Mel, who was belatedly going through her single-girl phase after the recent end of a long-term relationship. 'Oh my goodness, I'm so sorry, Karlie!' she suddenly exclaimed, mortified. 'What a stupid thing to say to a bride-to-be. Of course I don't mean you; you never put a foot wrong.'

Karlie smiled, deflecting any negative vibes with a casual shrug. It was true: her life was meticulously planned. She never launched into anything unless she was sure it would be a success. She reminded me of my mother in many ways: clear-headed, determined, whip-smart. Although she was marrying at a relatively young age, she was an old soul, and I had no doubt that she was following the right playbook for her.

We strolled by the Ritz Hotel, which had redefined luxury for the twentieth century. Such was the glamour of the hotel — beloved by designers and dancers, playboys and princesses, courtesans and counts — that soon after the 1898 opening its name became synonymous with swank. To put on the ritz is to live it up a notch or ten, to dress up in all your diamonds, and drink and dance the night away. (Even a soup can get its ritz on, according to the *Oxford Dictionary*, if it's garnished with 'an asparagus tip nestled in a small spoonful of lightly whipped cream'.)

By the break of the following century, however, time had worn some lustre off the Ritz, and the cool new hotel on the block (well, just back on Rue Saint-Honoré) was Costes, where we decided to head upon realising the time: 'kir o'clock', as Karlie put it. So intimidatingly glamorous is this hotel that you almost need to have a fortifying drink *before* you enter through its glossy black doors, although once you're in the lush pomegranate interior — the air scented with roses and spices, and buzzing with Costes' signature electronic lounge music — you're as at ease with the opulence as Pompadour in her palace. We slunk into the plush bar and ordered a round of bellinis from a waitress whose mix of beauty and boredom suggested that she didn't see this as her ideal day job.

'Have a look: all the waitresses could be models,' whispered Janey. 'It kind of puts you off your food!'

'Not me,' exclaimed Mel, perusing the bar snacks menu. Before she had turned beauty editor — and self-confessed gourmande — Mel was a makeup artist, and working in such proximity to beauty had normalised it for her somewhat.

I too had become accustomed to models and their freak-of-nature gorgeousness. Flocks of long-legged, long-lashed gazelles would linger for hours in the magazine office, in the hope of being cast for the next fashion shoot. I'd also interviewed many supermodels, getting so close and personal that I could attest to their perfect poreless skin. At first it depressed me no end. But I came to realise that it was simply their job to look beautiful; mine was to write. And this gave a new perspective to beauty editing for me, a realisation that my pages should try not to over-promise. Because a face mask and concealer and the right shade of red lipstick will make you look a whole lot better, sure, but you're only truly going to look like a top model if you were at the front of that particular DNA queue to begin with.

The occasional acquaintance has asked me if I worry that magazines sell unattainable glamour. It's a tough one. Because I know that some women feel inadequate in the face of the type of beauty that usually graces glossy pages. But I also know that most women like looking at beautiful things. And I do believe that women, complex creatures as we are, are smart enough to pick and choose what we take from magazines, which are not purely about beauty, but are a whole package — like women ourselves — with looks being just one element. If you're into beauty, great: read those articles and buy the mascara. If not, no problem: flip past to the career section or the food pages.

A gazelle of a waitress clattered our dinner on the table — all too eager to offload the kilojoule-laden plates, as though she was fearful of ingesting fat vicariously — before turning on her vertiginously high stilettos and strutting off. 'Somehow I don't think she's a foodie,' observed Mel, spreading a chunk of foie gras on a tartine. 'Although I wish I wasn't one myself sometimes. I'm trying to be careful because there's not much give in the dress I want to wear for the wedding.'

'You know you're practically eating pure fat, right?' Karlie asked. 'Foie gras is French for fatty liver.'

Mel froze, the pâté-laden toast hovering just below her mouth, a look of panic in her eyes. 'But I thought I was just eating protein, a kind of Parisian version of a can of tuna. I even had it for dinner last night!'

'I don't think the Parisians even have a version of canned tuna,' said Karlie, laughing. 'You have to watch this French food, it can be sneaky if you're not careful. You know, all of JF's French friends, the girls, they hardly eat meals. Perhaps a salad. And they just pick from their boyfriends' plates.'

'Oh, I thought I was being so Parisian,' sighed Mel. 'I'll go for a run tomorrow to make up for it.'

'Now that's most definitely *not* Parisian,' I said.

'I know, but I'm determined to go home looking more French. And a pot belly is not exactly the ideal accessory.'

&

Some time during our blur of bellinis, Mel talked me into being her jogging partner the next day, a pledge I desperately regretted at 8 a.m., when I was woken by a perky and persistent knock on my hotel door.

'Remind me why I agreed to this,' I puffed, ten minutes later, as we jogged towards the Seine.

'Because I can't speak French, and what happens if I meet a gorgeous Parisian but I don't understand that he's telling me he's just fallen hopelessly in love and wants me to move here with him at once?'

'I don't think French men hit on joggers. Otherwise women would be running all over the place instead of swanning about with their perfect sweat-free skin.'

Sure enough, as we turned into the Tuileries it became clear that running was not one of this city's pastimes. Women were striding (if en route to work) or strolling (if wheeling their prams over the gravel paths) or ambling (if walking their impeccably groomed dogs), but they were most definitely not sprinting, racing, jogging or anything that was technically pacier than a walk. There, more than most places in Paris, the usual mode is not much faster than that of the park's statues, figures of antiquity and ancient mythology whose stone faces wear a look of scorn for less-evolved souls who can't stop and smell the roses — or foxgloves and delphiniums, as the case might be.

'Then how do Parisians stay so goddamn skinny?' asked Mel.

'They don't eat fatty liver?' I suggested.

'Ugh, don't remind me.'

Half an hour later, Mel decided that she'd adequately cleansed her own liver, and I gratefully agreed to head back. After such a virtuous start to the day, it seemed illogical to break our fast with croissants and hot chocolate, so we stopped at the market across from our hotel for a fix of fruit (which, until now, had only appeared on our menus in the form of alcoholic grape juice and bellini mixers). As we lined up to order our punnets of berries, two elderly, dignified French ladies in front of us turned around, simultaneously looked us and our workout gear up and down, and swivelled back while shaking their perfectly coiffed, pearly heads. '*Les Américaines*,' one muttered to the other, who tut-tutted in agreement. We had evidently let the city down by airing our sweaty tracksuits in public.

Luckily, today was another designated shopping day, and we could make up for our insolent lapse in style. Better yet, it was sales time, which was fortunate, as this was one of my first trips to Paris paying with the newly introduced euro — and the city was suddenly as expensive as it looked. With an economy dominated by the forces of fashion, *les soldes* are serious business in France; the powers that be even set strict dates for the sales, which can occur only twice a year. (If they could also designate the public display of tracksuits as a fashion crime, I'm sure they would.)

I was becoming quite adept at this thing called shopping. For the past six months, I'd worked overtime to help launch Australia's first shopping magazine. It was a period when the so-called fast-fashion of the high street was picking up speed, driven by the world wide web's relentless output of red-carpet and catwalk images, yet the internet had not yet spread to e-tailing, so there was an accelerating demand for shopping information. We filled that void, jamming every page with photos of the latest dresses, shoes and lipsticks that were hitting racks and shelves that month, and letting women know in which sizes and colours they came, and the number they could call to order instantly. Of course, all magazines are shopping aids in a way (we were just more direct about it, and had a lot less white space); even the word magazine derives from the French word for a shop, *magasin*.

No self-respecting shopper can come home from Paris empty-handed — or footed; this is a city of shoes as exquisite as its cakes and jewellery, and heel heaven is Rue de Grenelle, an old and winding, whimsical street of the Left Bank that's lined with townhouses from the eighteenth century. It was an era of intense shoe mania; *Cinderella* had been published in Paris in 1697, setting off a craze for fancy slippers. An old French word for slipper is mule, and this backless, slip-on style of heeled shoe became the must-have accessory of the 1700s. Once confined to the boudoir, it was now a fetishly sexy accessory, suggestively easy to kick off. Have a close look at the floral hemlines in the Marquise de Pompadour's portraits, and chances are you'll see a minxy little mule peeking out. And to this day, you'll find at least one pair of seductively pointed mules in most Parisennes' wardrobes.

Somehow, by midday, Mel, Janey and I had racked up thirteen pairs of shoes between us, everything from chunky raffia wedges to lace-up golden sandals to that must-have mule. We had trekked as far as the jewel box of a boutique that is Christian Louboutin, where we were trying on pale-pink pumps topped with powder-soft pompoms — the kind of rococo-esque accessory with which the Marquise de Pompadour loved to adorn her hair, thereby providing inspiration for its name. And then something in my mind clicked (possibly fear of the sound of my credit card getting cut in half). 'Girls, I think we might have gone a little crazy,' I whispered when the salesman was out of earshot. 'I mean, these shoes are pretty up there on the wall like art, but do we really want to walk around with fluffy balls on our toes?'

After all, '*C'est le pompon*' is French for 'That takes the cake'. The pompom was a sign, perhaps, of our fuzzy minds, and that we needed to restore our blood sugar levels before trusting ourselves to shop any further.

Ladurée on the nearby Rue Bonaparte is another one of those dainty boutiques that you only find in Paris, but instead of delectably trimmed shoes it sells treats of the confectionery kind, such as its legendary *macaron*. The first Ladurée, over on Rue Royale (right about where I flashed my g-string for all and sundry to see) is the original, and dates back to 1862 when it was a tearoom for women, but it wasn't until 1930 that the head pastry chef struck upon the idea of sticking two almond meringue biscuits together with a creamy ganache filling. In the early 2000s, *macarons* had become the new cupcake, as food bloggers started spreading the word about Ladurée's latest pâtissier, who was revamping the treat for modern times. When Pierre Hermé left to unveil his own eponymous pâtisserie down the road on the Left Bank, the *macaron* wars were on. The battle was for pastry perfection: an eggshell-thin surface that cracks to reveal a mushy meringue-esque texture and a butter-cream or jam filling. Hermé was getting tricky with experimental flavours like Szechuan pepper and salted caramel, while Ladurée stuck to its traditionally ladylike favourites, such as rosewater and raspberry.

Ladurée is as much about satisfaction of the visual kind, its tearooms an homage to Parisian interior decoration (if the Marquise de Pompadour were alive now, she'd be a Ladurée kind of girl). We had flopped down in the blue salon upstairs, and were luxuriating amid its tasselled velvet splendour. It's Parisian moments such as these that really soothe the soul — as much as sole.

'Why did I think it was wise to go shopping in heels?' asked Mel. 'Oh, and then buy even more of them?'

'Do you know, not one of us bought a pair of flats,' I said. 'It's like we women are gluttons for punishment.'

'Not here they're not,' said Janey. 'Have you noticed how Parisiennes don't wear heels during the day?'

'They must just wear their heels out occasionally, like the way they eat foie gras,' noted Mel, ever determined to crack the codes of Parisienne style. After our lunch of club sandwiches and salads — all served on pastel porcelain, *naturellement* — we wandered down the road to what we'd heard was the city's best *pharmacie*. A world away from the Australian chemist, with its garish plastic tubs jostling for attention beneath fluorescent lighting, the French variety is both stylish and serious, selling all kinds of dermatologically tested formulations in appropriately subdued packaging, because French women shop for face creams with as much vested care and interest as they decide on their *macarons*.

Seemingly found on every corner, a Parisian chemist can easily be identified by the green neon cross alight above its doorway — or else the larger-than-life-size posters of bare female butts in the windows. 'As if I wasn't feeling like a big enough loaf after scoffing down all of those *macarons*,' said Janey, nodding towards a blown-up image of one such sleekly defined derrière.

'Have you seen how many thigh-shrinking lotions and creams there are in here?' asked Mel, after we'd spent some time fossicking around inside. 'If only they knew about this ingenious trick called running, it would save them lots of money.'

'You know, now that you say it, French magazines don't seem to go into exercise like we do,' said Janey. 'It's all detoxing pills and massage tools and leg gels. Maybe French women think they don't have to work too hard at being beautiful.'

Buying into the dream, we ended up purchasing a basket full of skin oils and lotions, and then turned our attention back to fashion, scouring the nearby Agnès B and Cacharel boutiques in search of that elusive sartorial *je ne sais quoi*.

'I never knew how hard it would be to choose a stripy navy-and-cream top,' remarked Janey later that afternoon, over a kir at Les Deux Magots. 'Who knew it could come in so many variations?'

'I never knew how many shades of white there are in the world,' said Karlie, who had joined us after her candle-seeking mission. 'I have total DMF: decision-making fatigue. Or maybe it's just plain old general fatigue — I feel like I haven't slept in weeks and my dark shadows are out of control. Hey, can we go makeup shopping?'

'Are you kidding?' I answered. 'You're in Paris with three beauty editors. *Of course* we'll take you makeup shopping.'

&

Sephora is to beauty lovers what a *confiserie* is to a French kid: a heart-fluttering, mouth-watering array of sensory overload. The first Sephora was founded on the Champs-Élysées, but we ended up in the store under the Louvre. 'Only in Paris could you sell lipstick beneath the greatest museum in the world without it seeming like a desecration,' noted Mel, Karlie's official *maquilleuse* for the big day. Switching to artist mode, she examined the varying pigments and intensities of the blushes on offer as studiously as she would have viewed the French masterpieces above, and mixed creams together on the back of her hand, palette-like, until hitting upon the perfect peachy-pink, which she blended into Karlie's cheeks. And just like that, all traces of weariness seemed magically to dissolve. 'Now that's what I call a work of art,' she declared.

Blush has long been a French woman's secret to looking in peak form, a way to mimic the healthy effects of the outdoor run for which she never goes. It's also one of those fabulous French paradoxes that something as seemingly giddily girlish as blush can, in the right hands, become a powerful weapon for a Parisienne. For the Marquise de Pompadour, rouge was the enduring symbol of her fabled charm, the very attribute that propelled her to power in the first place. She was more than just a pretty pink-flushed face; for example, she sweet-talked the king into endorsing the encyclopaedia (penned by her philosopher friends), which he had originally thought to be dangerously enlightening for his simple-minded subjects. Pompadour so believed in the life-enhancing powers of blush that she was still requesting it on her deathbed.

The painter Élisabeth Vigée Le Brun, who came into her artistic own around the time the marquise was applying rouge for the final time, ushered in the modern era of blush with her dreamy pastel portrayals of the beautiful people of Paris. Her most famous subject was the ill-fated Marie Antoinette, and the portraitist doubled as the unpopular queen's public relations minister, working hard to paint her in a soft and flattering light. Scarlet circles of blush had long been the exclusive stamp of aristocrats — with their preening, powdered ways — so a sheerer flush of cheek colour was one way to revamp the queen, make her appear naturally warm. Alas, sometimes even the greatest blush masterstroke isn't enough to save a girl.

&

Versailles is the ultimate symbol of Old France, and the glitzy majesty that came to be associated with Marie Antoinette. It was also a place of pilgrimage on our last official hens' day (we would have made Karlie wear a princess tiara if she weren't so elegant). We walked through the golden gates, over a succession of cobblestoned courtyards. A sprawl of classical magnificence from afar, the pomp ramps up with every step because, even though the scale decreases, the elaborateness of detailing climbs to dizzy heights. Standing in the final courtyard, the *cour de marbre* — a square paved geometrically in black-and-white marble — you're struck with the sensation of being on a set, a stage on which balletic glamour and operatic tragedy could unfold — and, of course, have. Columns of pink-swirled marble bolster a balcony decorated in yet more gold, glamorously framing the entrance. It was through these doors that the fourteen-year-old Austrian archduchess stepped — over the threshold into her new life as the next queen of France. And it was on the balcony above, nineteen years later, that she bowed to the angry, hungry women of Paris, pleading for calm while another mob found their way into her bedroom, slashing her bed and smashing her mirrors.

I'd visited Versailles before, and experienced the contradictory sensations of both contempt for, and envy of, the luxurious lifestyle of Marie Antoinette, whose story I thought I knew ('Let them eat cake' and all that). But her tale was extraordinarily complex, as I'd only just come to appreciate on reading Antonia Fraser's *Marie Antoinette: The Journey*. So compassionate is Fraser's take on the queen that I was in tears well before the final pages, when the author concludes that the accidental teen bride was a victim from birth, a pawn of her power-playing empress mother, an unintentional, untrained ambassador for the Franco-Austrian relationship, a misunderstood affection-seeker and pleasure-lover, a yearningly unfulfilled wife, a fiercely loving mother, and the ultimate scapegoat for the economic woes of France.

We walked down the Hall of Mirrors, the central gallery of the palace. Its inner wall is lined with seventeen arch-shaped mirrors, while sunlight streams through the arcaded windows opposite, flickering around the chandeliers before bouncing off the mirrored glass. You can almost see the reflections of spirits of partygoers past, their festooned wigs tickling the crystals suspended above as they twirl around the parquet floor in glossy ball gowns and flashing jewels. But there's an unbearable lightness to it all. With the vaulted ceiling above, heaving with gold and paintings of the glorious Sun King, living there must have felt like fluttering around in a gilded cage.

It's not until you turn into Marie Antoinette's official bedroom that you really sense the suffocating splendour, the abundance of dazzling gold and full-blown floral fabrics, magnified in mirrors, that comes so very close to the edge of crassness. The throne bed, the central feature, is as extravagant as the queen herself must have appeared. The bed is covered with gown-worthy upholstery of rich brocade woven in roses, ribbons and peacock feathers, and just like Marie Antoinette's towering wigs, up top looms a heady canopy, with a riot of golden imperial eagles and white ostrich plumes.

Feeling somewhat overwhelmed, we ventured outside for fresh air, and wandered by the lush green carpet of lawn leading down to the grand canal, every now and then taking a detour and turning into a maze of hornbeam hedges to come across a dancing fountain or a party of statues. Still, there's even a constricting formality there, an overly contrived precision to everything. It's no surprise that the word etiquette can be traced to this very spot. The story goes that the Sun King was so annoyed by guests trampling his lawn or jumping in the fountain that he had his gardener place little signs everywhere, telling people what to do — and not. In Old French, *estiquette* was the word for label, and *une etiquette* still means that, as well as the prescribed social protocol that reached peak craziness at Versailles, where only certain ranks could sit on stools or pass the king his gloves.

You can't help but breathe a sigh of relief as much as delight as you amble into the queen's private park, where she would run to escape the pressures of palace life. The gardens there are as pretty as a pastel tapestry of an English pastoral scene; Marie Antoinette favoured a landscaping style far removed from the orderly nature of typical French parks, with their neat flowerbeds and rows of trimmed hedges. Here and there is a gorgeous folly, such as the Temple of Love, its domed roof held aloft by a dozen columns encircling a statue of cupid. Over by the lake perches a pretty octagonal pavilion, known as the Belvedere, the queen's music room; its classic exterior, sweetly adorned with a garlands-of-fruit frieze, is beautifully offset by a finely detailed interior of marble mosaic flooring and floral wall motifs. You swear you hear the old harpsichord still at play. Nearby is a rugged rockery complete with grotto — the very one in which the queen was said to be found when the ravenous mob was marching to Versailles.

And then we stumbled into one of the reasons for that mob's anger towards their queen. The Hamlet was Marie Antoinette's hobby farm, inspired by her idealisation of Norman rural life: a cluster of life-size doll houses, decorated with beams and bricks, prettied up with flowering vines, and topped whimsically with thatched roofs. The queen must have felt pure unadulterated happiness when wafting through there in her soft muslin dress and sun hat, so out of touch with reality that she had no idea the rest of the world thought she was making a mockery of them.

'She just really wanted the simple life,' I reflected. 'Even if simple is a relative term.'

'An earth mother after my own heart,' said Janey, who loved the beauty world but ultimately craved living in a country cottage with a brood of babies.

'You can have your farms,' responded Karlie, having grown up on one. 'I could totally get used to living back in that palace.'

&

We met up for dinner with friends newly arrived in Paris, at a restaurant–nightclub that just happened to be located on the old site of Le Grand Mogol, the fashion boutique of Rose Bertin, Marie Antoinette's designer. More fitting still, across the road was once the opera, famed for its masked balls where the queen, liberated from the trappings of her public role, would anonymously party and flirt the night away, often until dawn was breaking.

'If Marie Antoinette were alive today, I wonder if this is the kind of place she would party at,' I wondered, looking around at the ruby-hued, moodily lit room.

'They certainly have some delicious desserts,' sighed Mel, looking longingly at the menu.

'Hey, did you know that she didn't ever say 'Let them eat cake'?' I asked. 'But the French hated her so much that they attributed it to her. The fact that they thought she *could* say it was enough.'

'All I've ever heard is how superficial and vain she was,' said someone else. 'A party girl, like the Paris Hilton of her time.'

'Oh, please,' cried Janey at the mention of the Californian heiress famous for being famous. 'She doesn't deserve the name Paris.'

'You have to read the book, it's eye-opening,' I added. 'Marie Antoinette did party, but she was young and not prepared for the role she had to take on. She reacted by rebelling, and for a while she was just this frivolous girl who liked fashion and big hair and pretty things too much.'

'Well, that doesn't sound familiar at all!' said Janey, laughing.

'Some of us are growing up and getting all married and mature,' Mel said, poking Karlie, who was already yawning, unsure if she'd make it to the dance floor in the basement bar.

'You know, Marie Antoinette did grow up,' I noted. 'She became really motherly and tried to simplify her life, but it was too late. France was already on its way to revolution and they never forgave her for being that party girl.'

'Well, I totally do,' said Janey, getting ready to disappear downstairs.

Later on, I wondered about the impact, on France, of Marie Antoinette, arguably the most famous French woman in history — even though she wasn't born French. For a while the queen *was* accepted with open arms. She played the Parisienne to perfection, her frilly dresses and festooned hairdos slavishly copied. But the forces of destiny were against Marie Antoinette, and she couldn't step up when history required it. She hadn't been brought up to be so multifaceted. The youngest of many daughters, she wasn't expected to be a wife to anyone important, and so she wasn't educated beyond dancing and harp-playing. The French might be starting to see their former queen in a more flattering light — through the sympathetic eyes of Élisabeth Vigée Le Brun or Antonia Fraser — but back then she became the symbol of what a woman shouldn't be. The French expect women to be more than just a pretty face, to have brains behind their beauty.

The French talk a lot about *savoir-vivre*, the ability to live life tastefully and a modern form of etiquette — which spoon to use when, and so on. Developed after the Revolution as a code for civil behaviour, *savoir-vivre* was a cloak of politeness to keep the rebellious tendencies of the French in check. So to-the-letter have the French defined the concept that we use their expression in English, rather than the literal translation: to know how to live.

A subset of *savoir-vivre* is *savoir-faire*, and it generally means, in French, what it does in English: know-how. You might have amazing savoir-faire when it comes to, say, making a *macaron* or applying blush. But I like to take the literal translation: to know how to do, to make. You see, what I've learned from the French is that you can't have *savoir-vivre* without *savoir-faire*. You can't *live* without *doing* something good, *making* something of yourself. You can't just be a *bon vivant*, a good liver (and I don't mean the foie gras kind). You have to be a person with a rich inner life, too, one that translates into a full outer life.

I was still in the midst of my *bonne vivante* phase, and I made no apologies for it, because I knew it wouldn't last. I hadn't been born into overt luxury and frivolity — I was simply lucky enough to have landed a job in a glamorous world, one of perfume parties and Parisian lipstick launches. But I knew that it was ephemeral, like the youthfulness my industry so loved to celebrate. I knew my parents expected me to be more, do more, and I would expand, like so many other women do, lucky as we are to live in times that have freed us from the gilded cages and corsets of the past, that allow us to write our own stories. My next chapter was around the corner. Maybe it was marriage, as it was for Karlie. Perhaps a promotion. I knew I'd have to progress in my career at some point soon. But for now, I was having too much fun to worry about it. As I might very well have proclaimed: let me eat *macarons*.

CHAPTER 7

FEMME

[fam] *nf* woman

In which, aged a third-of-a-century,
I find my place in the world.

Resting my head against the cool stone of an ancient arch, I slowly exhaled. For the first time in so long, I felt re-centred. The Cloître des Billettes, with its graceful curves and cobbled courtyard, never ceases to inspire a sense of calm, silencing the white noise in my mind. Paris's only remaining medieval cloister might be small, but the serenity is pervasive. When you step through the archway entrance, away from the overstimulations of the Marais (the crowds, the cafés, the bars, the aching hipness), you feel as though you've glided back to a time when there actually was time, to reflect and to hear your deepest thoughts. There was no better first stop for me on this soul-searching trip to Paris.

My dilemma was my future in journalism, and in New York, where I'd moved a couple of years earlier, thinking that's what I had to do in order to advance my career. But the media landscape was changing more radically than my personal horizons. Blogging was fast becoming the thing to do, with writers putting themselves front and centre, increasingly before a camera. This cult-of-self approach to media particularly suited America, and the me-me-me nature of Manhattan. It seemed as though everyone suddenly wanted to be famous, although I couldn't understand why. Celebrity status only served to shove you, warts and all, into the harsh spotlight of an insatiable press, particularly the tabloid magazines and websites that were proliferating in practically every Western country.

Except, that is, in France. I loved that the smutty trend for trash talk hadn't yet sullied the elegant dark-green newsstands of Paris. There was a tone of civility to the press that was lacking in most other Western markets. Truth was, French privacy laws prevented journalists from delving too deeply into the lives of public figures. Some complained that this reined in investigative journalism, and diluted the power of the press. But that wasn't my field. I was a beauty writer — the grittiest I got was when I dug into the issue of blackheads. And, of course, I wrote for advertisers as much as for readers. I belonged to the If You Don't Have Anything Nice to Say, Don't Say Anything school of journalism. Which I didn't mind at all. It seemed so very French, in line with a culture that believes dirty laundry, even of the designer lingerie kind, shouldn't be displayed beyond one's own secret garden, that place of shadowy retreat within every French woman.

Or, perhaps, one's inner cloister, the site of personal reflection. I, for one, preferred to work through my own issues in solitude. I've heard it said that confessional journalism best suits Protestant cultures, with their history of public confessions. Me, I was like France: Catholic, lapsed (I still believed in God; as Blaise Pascal, the seventeenth-century philosopher basically argued in his famous wager, what did I have to lose in doing so, really?), yet nonetheless still accustomed to a certain level of fear and guilt (some might say a love of suffering), along with a deep-seated sense of ritual and propriety. Part of this is that confession is a private affair: you spill all to a priest and — *voilà* — absolution. But even if you no longer make it to the confessional booth, sin feels like a subject best kept boxed in, not publicly aired and shared.

The Billettes Cloister dates to an era when France was arguably the world's most Catholic nation. Curiously Paris, having converted to Christianity well before so many others, was the first European city to de-Christianise. Not that she's as secular as you might think — signs everywhere prove the lingering influence of Paris's Catholic past. Point Zéro of France, the spot from which all distances are measured, the very heart of the nation, lies just in front of Notre-Dame Cathedral. The Panthéon, the resting place for France's greatest men (and a scattering of women), is a deconsecrated church. Some argue that the French State, with all its pampering interventionism, is the new church to which subjects dutifully submit (and pay exorbitant taxes), and that the country's beloved intellectuals are akin to clergy. The French still think in terms of good and evil, although they're often accused of leaning to pessimism, fearing the future as their ancestors once dreaded the Apocalypse. Family is the new religion — witness many French people's enduring commitment to Sunday clan lunches. In fact, the French seem to have an ingrained desire for social rituals.

Oh, and they love a show of glamour and glitz, which is surely also some kind of sacred throwback; after all, few know how to do pomp and pageantry like the Catholic Church. I've sometimes wondered if the awe-inspiring baroque beauty of Catholicism was a key reason France eschewed the Reformation — with all its gloomy black garb and angry Calvinist talk — in the first place. Some say the country lost out by banishing its labour-intensive Protestants — tradesmen and merchants — who went on to power up England's industrial age, and build America into global power-player status. The French, on the other hand, have always had a wary relationship with work and income, viewing flashy shows of material success as some sort of social sin. To this day, the French remain tight-lipped on the subject of money, whereas New Yorkers, say, have a knack for measuring your vital statistics — top of which is net income — within nanoseconds.

Did France simply give up and in by rejecting the Reformation, filing it in the too-hard basket? And also, was I giving in by not working myself to my full potential? Because I had all but decided to quit New York and move back to Sydney. America had challenged me to succeed, to climb the proverbial ladder, and I had clawed my way up several rungs, which was exhilarating at times, but mostly it was tiring. One day I woke up and realised I wanted a good life, not a hard one, even if the latter brought the success I had originally dreamed of. It wasn't because I saw success as an evil of any kind (my Catholicism is at an advanced state of lapse, remember) but it was just that I didn't see it as my right. Actually, that's wrong; it was a right — but no more than my right to a calm, tranquil life. And I alone could make the correct choice for me. I guess some people see successful as the definition of a good life, but good is such a malleable and personal notion. At the time, I craved a life that was happy, above all. I wanted to stop demanding more and more of myself — you usually end up only letting yourself down — and trust in a higher power than myself (not God so much as the universe) that everything would work out. And perhaps, yes, like France, I was taking the path of least resistance. But I couldn't shake the feeling that, rather than speed along a concrete highway of life, I would be so much happier sauntering along quieter streets, enjoying the scenery — which, for the moment, would be Parisian.

A *marais* was a swamp, or marsh, in old French, which is a rather unpromising name for a district, you have to admit. Nevertheless, this was the scene of intense aristocratic action in the seventeenth century, when nobles lavished the drained, fertile lands with mini urban châteaux. At the time, architectural style was transitioning from medieval to classic — why you might spot a Gothic turret or tower here or there — and it was in the Marais that the template for the French *hôtel particulier* (private mansion) was set in grandiose stone: a curtain wall complete with a hefty wooden door behind which was a courtyard large enough for a carriage to turn, along with said mansion and a pretty garden out back.

My rental apartment (not a chandelier-lit manor but a beam-ceilinged studio in a poky walk-up) was just down from one of the Marais' most legendary abodes, that of Pierre Beaumarchais. On the eve of the Revolution, the overachieving Beaumarchais was working as a clockmaker and music teacher at the royal court during the day, and a subversive at night, supporting the American War of Independence and donating his own money to the cause, even before France officially entered the fray. Beaumarchais also played a role in his own country's Revolution by writing, in this very mansion, *The Marriage of Figaro*, in which a valet chastises his count with the famous lines, 'Just because you are a great nobleman, you think you are a great genius — nobility, fortune, rank, position! How proud they make a man feel! What have you done to deserve such advantages? Put yourself to the trouble of being born — nothing more.' It was no less than a theatrical call to arms.

Beaumarchais was a believer in meritocracy over aristocracy, and it was this individualistic spirit that animated the new world of America, the doctrine that everyone deserved a mansion if they worked hard enough, were talented enough. On the slim island of Manhattan, this can-do attitude can still be found at its most potent concentration. I loved the fact that, there, you could become whoever you wanted to be. Still, I could not see *myself* there — nor a version of the self I wanted to become. She was back home, or perhaps she was most at home in Paris. After I'd settled into my Marais apartment that first day, I noticed that the owner had hung a large black-and-white photo of New York on the wall. I couldn't help but smile. '*La vraie vie est ailleurs*,' claimed Arthur Rimbaud, the vagabond teen poet who inspired the Symbolists. 'Real life is elsewhere.' Everyone has an *ailleurs*.

Paris might have been my personal 'elsewhere', but I had, for a time, lost my inner Parisienne. She was floundering about somewhere beneath my excess layers of American fat, a cumulative result of consuming the surfeit of sugars that lurk unexpectedly in so many American foods. I didn't just have a muffin top but, as the French would say, a *brioche* — a bulge of belly. It rose up slowly but surely, until one day I couldn't zip up my trusty LBD, my go-to frock for job interviews. As distressing as the dress episode was, there was a silver lining: it spurred me to delve deeper than skin-surface in my work, venturing beyond beauty into health journalism. Inspired as much as distraught, I eventually worked out how to eliminate toxins from my body. By the time I'd almost decided to leave New York, I had already juice-cleansed much of the city right out of my system.

The big health buzz at the time was *French Women Don't Get Fat*, the best-selling book by Mireille Guiliano that would initiate a new literary genre: lifestyle guides devoted to the secrets of Gallic chic, everything from tying scarves to keeping silhouettes trimly intact. Guiliano, the then New York-based head of Veuve Clicquot, had had her own excess-baggage issue during her first stint in the States, and learned to retrain her body à la française — it's these French time-honed health tricks that are outlined in her book. Through her, I worked out how to lure out my inner Parisienne: to shop at markets; to commit to three good meals a day, lots of them soup; to ritual-eat, sitting down at a table; to aim to feel enriched rather than stuffed after a meal; to go for quality over quantity, enhancing flavour satisfaction with fresh herbs; to nibble on a square of dark, rich cocoa, rather than gobble down a sugar-packed chocolate bar. I was searching for a more balanced life, but through Guiliano I realised you also had to have equilibrium in your body. 'The key to continued weight loss,' she writes, 'is keeping one's compensations just slightly ahead of one's indulgences.'

Believe it or not, there was actually a time when French women *did* get fat. When the Marais was coming into its fashionable own, the most stylish women around were what you could call Rubenesque, the adjective inspired by the *volupté*-loving artist. It's telling that *embonpoint*, the word once used by French and English speakers to describe plumpness — the kind seen in Peter Paul Rubens' paintings — comes from the old French for 'in good condition'. The look was all about almost spilling out of your dress with an excess of pale, pillowy skin. It was a sign that a woman could afford to eat — and eat a lot — and that she didn't have to run around town in clogs; the maximum effort her dainty satin slippers had to exert was stepping up into a gilded carriage. It was only early in the twentieth century that French women become obsessed with sleekness, remodelling their bodies into lean, mean modern machines.

I'd been attempting to convert my own body, from fat to muscle, into a slimmer model, by way of yoga. But when, on that first morning in Paris, I unrolled my yoga mat, I found that it didn't sit right — literally and figuratively. I couldn't find the floor space to lay out the mat with an appropriate Zen-like smoothness, but what ruffled me more was that yoga suddenly seemed so foreign, so out of sync with its Parisian surroundings. Yoga was my refuge from New York, but Paris, I realised, *was* my retreat. It's a place for meditating as you meander around cobbled streets or along tree-lined boulevards, for losing yourself, as much as finding yourself. But it's much more than a symbolic journey; pounding the pavement, as Guiliano notes, is the most effective form of Parisian exercise — because it doesn't seem like exercise at all.

Parisians are programmed to love walking because their city has been designed as such a stroller's delight. Relatively smooth in surface and small in size, Paris can be easily criss-crossed; there are seemingly endless ways of getting from *ah* to *bé*; and any route you choose is a picturesque one. No wonder it was the French who invented the term *flâner*, which means to walk without any particular purpose, to immerse yourself in your city. The *flâneur* himself is such a classic Parisian character and concept that the word doesn't directly translate to English — nor does the act of *flânant* feel quite as satisfactorily the same anywhere but Paris.

After exploring my inner vision in the Billettes Cloister, it was time to get back into the real world, so I set out to search for other nooks and crannies of the Marais. I soon found that there's only one thing that will hamper the happiness that is roaming the streets of Paris. Let's just go with the French word for starters, as the French language has a way of making everything seem so much nicer: *crotte de chien*. '*Merde*!' I muttered, rather aptly, as I looked down to see one of my wedge shoes in a hot brown mess. There are some 200,000 dogs who call Paris home, and it is estimated they leave sixteen tonnes' worth of souvenirs behind them every day, causing some 650 people to slip on the stuff and break a bone each year. At the very least, it's a serious risk to your footwear. Even Carrie Bradshaw had just trod her white Louboutins in Parisian canine *crotte* in the *Sex & the City* finale. I decided to look at my predicament as an auspicious sign of sorts: that it was time for a new pair of shoes.

'Are those sandals in the window made of leather?' I enquired on entering a nearby boutique.

'*Mais, oui*!' the salesman exclaimed, as though I'd queried whether the world was round.

'Oh, that's a shame — I'd rather not buy leather,' I explained. To answer the question writing itself into his furrowed brow, I added: 'I'm trying to go vegan.'

'But what is "*végétalienne*"?' the man asked, more incredulous by the second. By the time I explained that veganism eschews not only meat but any ingredient or material that can be traced back to an animal or insect, he was looking at me as though I had three heads.

'*Oh là là*,' he was muttering, as I thanked him and walked out the door. 'To not eat meat … *pas normal*!'

Just down the street, I spotted a Bensimon store, and bought myself a pair of the iconic tennis sneakers. They were so comfortably conducive to walking that I soon figured I'd earned myself kilojoule credit for afternoon tea. *La vie* was all about balance, *non*?

Parisian tearooms, or *salons de thé*, flourished in the late nineteenth century, when women began to take tea in town, in the pretty new cafés designed to mimic their own *salons* (reception rooms): walls gleaming in polished wood and ornately framed mirrors, ceilings frescoed in pastel scenes and lit by chandeliers, marble tables decorated with porcelain tea sets and plates glistening with bijou pastries. Tea is an unashamedly feminine ritual in France; delicate *infusions*, basically warm perfumed water, are particularly popular. It's also serious business: tea menus can read like wine lists, and a *sommelier du thé* might be at hand to guide you to your perfect palate match.

My favourite *salon de thé* is the Marais' Mariage Frères, with its French colonial air that harks back to the brand's heritage: the original Mariage brothers claimed to have introduced tea to France, at the court of Louis XIV — a time when commerce with the East was opening up a tantalising new world of sensory pleasures — and later generations of Mariage men traded tea in this very district.

I sank into a rattan chair beneath a burst of palm fronds, as waiters in creamy-white linen suits scurried around. Once you make a decision from the 500-plus concoctions on offer, there are all sorts of complementary cakes to choose from. I ordered a spice-infused black brew and slice of tea-tinged tarte tatin, the famous upside-down apple tart invented, albeit by chance, by the Tatin sisters. If the French adore tea for its taste of the elsewhere, their pastries are proudly patriotic, celebrating the fruits of their famed *terroir* (soil); they might sigh over the *ailleurs*, but their hearts and stomachs rarely leave home.

Terroir is a word that French people, especially Parisians, say in a somewhat dreamy tone. The concept takes them back to their literal roots, their ancestral region, and the provincial tastes of childhood. 'Tell me what you eat, and I will tell you who you are,' asserted France's original food writer, Jean Anthelme Brillat-Savarin. Most French people now live in big cities, but they crave one kind of *ailleurs* above all others: their regional homeland. That's why homey dishes like tarte tatin (and, on the savoury side of things, ratatouille) are held in such esteem, and perhaps why French chefs load up food with butter and cream, each being a direct expression of the land of a particular region. Cheese, too; think of President de Gaulle's lamentation, 'How can you be expected to govern a country that has 246 kinds of cheese?' The *terroir* of France is incredibly fertile and varied, with each region boasting its own taste and specialty, yet it's paradoxically a unifying force: all of the ingredients swirl together in one big copper pot and reduce to the rich essence of France.

French cooking is intensely nationalistic (some might say this is what has kept it stuck in a rich, saucy rut), and eating in France is not only personal, it's political. There might be 246 cheeses (in actual fact, there are many more), but they're all fiercely, profusely, fragrantly French. To eat as your ancestors did is to take a stance against globalisation, to stick up for the stubbornly small-time French farmers, still rattling around on their rusty tractors, and stick it to the American conglomerates. But eating à la française can be as fattening as doing so à la américaine, if you don't approach it in the way Parisiennes do: eat sparingly in the first place, then walk the rest off.

I was also coming to suspect that my particular personal style preference for floaty dresses had played a major part in my weight drama; my clothes had literally lost touch with my body. Parisiennes, on the other hand, seem to appreciate the figure-checking powers of a sartorial waist. Their fashion history has taught them to be wary of even such a seemingly innocent garment as a tea dress.

It was the Sun King's legendary mistress, the fabulous Marquise de Montespan — the very definition of lavish *embonpoint* — who originally championed comfortable, corset-free dressing for modern times. Such a style of dress conveniently camouflaged her weight fluctuations, caused by a ravenous appetite as much as a scandalous succession of half-royal pregnancies. Although some tut-tutted that looser gowns hinted at relaxed morals, fashion began to lighten up, the stiff and heavy satins swapped for ethereal muslins. Such *déshabillés* were mostly worn at home, when friends came around for tea, an Anglophile ritual brewed to fullest strength in the Belle Époque, when it was known as 'le five o'clock'. But the trend eventually ventured outside — one of the first examples of innerwear as outerwear, perhaps? — so there was something inherently erotic in this traditionally private dress, and provocative in its challenge to the definition of formality. By the early twentieth century, these 'tea gowns' were flimsier than ever, little more than a flurry of chiffon. But soon most French women reverted to trim tailoring; the slim silhouette was here to stay, but if the corset wasn't coming back, they had to have some way of keeping their physiques in check.

Flirtatious feminine dresses no longer indicated any flimsiness of moral fibre, but I sometimes wondered if they gave the impression that the wearer doesn't take herself so seriously. And perhaps the way I dressed was a subconscious self-sabotaging strategy, a subliminal way of telling the world I didn't want to power ahead in confident pant-clad strides. Not that I saw this as a weak thing necessarily. The reason I fell so in love with dresses was that they made me feel free — and maybe not just in the physical sense, but also in terms of expectations. Every now and then a friend would comment on my girlish wardrobe, suggesting that

I mature my style, and dress for the next job on the rung. Well, perhaps I refused to do so because, deep down, I was still working out what I wanted to do, or be, as the proverbial grown-up. And yes, if I started to get around in sleek dark jeans and neat little jackets, I'd probably look more sophisticated — and oh so Parisienne. But I'm pretty sure that I'd feel like I was simply playing dress-ups. As much as I craved the celebrated *je ne sais quoi* of a Parisienne, evolving into her lookalike was proving to be a lifelong journey.

That night, I met up with my friend Elsa, one of those enviable women whose inner Parisienne surfaced at an early age. The Sydney-based makeup artist had just moved to Paris, where she looked every bit the local: tousled hair, complexion bare save for a smudge of black kohl around the eyes, and a long and lean frame, with cigarette-slim legs, that carries off even the simplest clothes — blue jeans, a buttoned-through striped shirt — to glamorous heights. She is the incarnation of the term *au naturel*, although the French themselves probably wouldn't choose this expression. In English, it means someone who is naturally beautiful, who has no need to resort to much artifice, while in France it tends to refer to food that's free from seasoning and sauce (*quelle horreur*!). Plus, the French know that, when it comes to beauty, there's no real thing as *au naturel*. (I mean, do you really think the nation that built a multibillion-dollar industry around lipstick and perfume truly believes that beauty comes easily?)

'I feel so at home here it's a little spooky,' said Elsa. 'It's like, I don't have to explain myself anymore, what I do is accepted and even celebrated. Makeup is considered an art form, for one, but also it's serious work: you're part of one of France's largest industries.'

I confessed, with envy, that I'd been struggling to see the value of my job in recent times. 'I think what Paris reminds you,' said Elsa, after some thought, 'is that beauty is, above all, about taking care of yourself. It's the whole 'You're worth it' thing — a tagline that, of course, belongs to a Parisian brand.'

'I totally get the personal aspect,' I replied. 'It's also as though the French feel they have a social responsibility to look good.'

'That's true,' Elsa agreed. 'They're not just beautifying for themselves, but for others; it's the same for guys here. Looking good is a form of politeness in Paris. Women never run out the door in the morning dishevelled and wearing chunky trainers, then apply makeup in the train and change into work shoes at the office. They show their best face to the world the second they step outside. The footpath is a stage here.'

'I just love how the French have a way of validating so much in life, even things other cultures might dismiss as trivial. There's an acceptance here that beauty is important, or at least not unimportant.'

'Oh no, it's of utmost seriousness,' insisted Elsa with a laugh. 'Beauty is one of the self-evident joys in life, and every Parisian knows this.'

It's true. Parisians conspire, whether consciously or not, to make their city the capital of beauty, from the women walking down the street, to the chocolatiers or florists decorating their windows, to the guys in bright-green uniforms picking up rubbish, to the chefs plating up their delicious delicacies …

Our food arrived. I had ordered *une salade de chèvre chaud*, a favourite classic French meal of mine that's found on most menus (which is lucky, as it's usually the only vegetarian option). I looked down and smiled. It was the perfect mix: little square toasts topped with circular slices of gooey, honey-drizzled goat's cheese, lounging on a bed of flouncy lettuce and cushions of tomatoes, with some other coloured crudités thrown in to trick you into believing that you're eating an antioxidant-packed salad rather than hefty chunks of fat and carbohydrate. It's easy to get hooked on this dish: the contrast between cold and warm, crunchy and soft, sharp and sweet, on its healthy-but-actually-not paradox.

'You know, it's strange,' I mused. 'I can't understand why there aren't more vegetarian or vegan restaurants, or even meals on the menu. It so suits the French: their need to be in touch with their *terroir*, and their love of staying skinny.'

The French have a reputation, it must be said, for eating all kinds — and all parts — of animals, from horse steaks to duck livers to frogs' legs. They're avid meat-eaters from way back; aristocrats feasted on a veritable menagerie of food, but I've often wondered if Parisians really got their taste for zoological gastronomy during the Prussian siege of 1870, when a starving city actually did eat the entire contents of its zoo — kangaroos, elephants and all. Still, the much-vaunted nouvelle cuisine, which is at its best when brimming with organic vegetables in colour-popping hues, is to me pure Paris on a plate, the ultimate in *terroir* to table.

'I think the whole plant-food thing is starting to happen,' said Elsa. 'There's a vegan café near me, for one. Although, hilariously, the owner stands out the front smoking all day. I don't think people go vegan in this city as a health strategy.'

'In New York,' I recalled, 'there are juice bars and raw restaurants popping up on every corner.'

'Diet is more about balance here,' said Elsa. 'The French don't like to be told they can't have something, especially if it's something that gives them pleasure.'

'I certainly get that when it comes to French cheese,' I said. 'My weakness for it is all that's stopping me from going vegan.'

'What about if you included a "Paris clause" in your vegan contract,' suggested Elsa. 'So, every time you come to Paris, you can let yourself eat vegetarian — and get your year's fix of fromage in one hit.'

'That's certainly one way to get my bum in check,' I sighed. 'Gosh, this whole ageing thing, it really is your butt or your face, isn't it? I know I should start getting more serious about controlling my food intake, but I'm a little petrified that my face would shrivel up, too.'

The oft-cited mantra that, past *un certain âge*, a woman must choose between the skin on her face and the size of her butt (basically, the price of a plumped-up complexion is a well-fed, well-rounded derrière) is usually attributed to Catherine Deneuve. One of France's best-loved actresses, Deneuve was a silky slip of a woman back in her *Belle de Jour* days. Over the years, as her roles have become meatier, she has happily added some extra kilos to her frame, padding that has helped keep her complexion beautifully cushioned and satiny-smooth. Up on the high-definition big screen, she is as luminous as ever.

'Just keep unrolling that mat, you'll get there,' answered Elsa, who grew up with a yoga instructor of a mother and has spent a cumulative total of months twisted into some improbable position. 'Come to my summer solstice class with me.'

The summer solstice, which marks the longest day of the year, officially replaced the Catholic Feast of Saint John the Baptist, a bonfire-lit bonanza that itself took over from pagan midsummer festivities — so it's a neat illustration of the French cycle of worship. Lately, the solstice has been ostensibly devoted to the universal religion of music. It's the day of the Fête de la Musique, when professional and amateur performers take to the streets of Paris, while everyone else dances the night away in a sometimes primal way that is perhaps not dissimilar to the moves their idolatrous ancestors might have once busted out.

'You'll still be here on June 21st?' Elsa asked.

Suddenly my brain clicked into compute mode: I realised the date would be exactly four months after my thirty-third birthday … which would age me at exactly a third-of-a-century. I'd never heard of a third-of-a-life crisis before, but I now believed in its plausibility.

'Ohhhh,' I groaned. 'I think I'll need more than downward dog to get me through that day.'

'Don't worry,' laughed Elsa. 'We'll go out drinking and dancing, too. Remember, life's about balance — and I don't mean tree pose.'

I sat down for breakfast on the terrace of a café on Place des Vosges, a site of almost impossible loveliness. Around the square-shaped park of pruned, lined-up linden trees and lush manicured lawns, four sets of townhouses sit pretty above colonnaded arcades and beneath sloping slate roofs. The symmetry of it all, after the skinny winding streets of the Marais, makes for a surreal sensation; its colours, too — the whimsically patterned red bricks of the façades popping against the garden greens, so bright in contrast to the time-darkened stones of the rest of the district. You feel almost as though you've stumbled onto a film set, a concocted fantasy of French urban culture — which in many ways it is, having been conceived as the first city square, something that would not only beautify Paris but enhance civic life. While there's a cloister quality to the vaulted perimeters of Place des Vosges, its sun-filled scope encourages open-hearted optimism rather that a retreat into introspection. It's places like this that surely restore Parisians' faith in a harmonious world, which must be why the park is filled with humanity at all hours of the day, with people celebrating the simple beauty of breathing in life.

My hot chocolate arrived, true to old-fashioned form: dark and plush, more or less thick molten cocoa. I was no longer able to drink coffee, to my eternal chagrin; ever since my Manhattan detox, its taste and smell made me want to retch. Not that this was much of a loss in Paris, mind you, where the coffee was bafflingly woeful. Why, in a city that does almost everything with such delicious panache, could one not get a decent caffeine fix? And why, when café culture was so full of richness and life, was the *café* itself so thin and bitter? The French had perfected the fine fragranced art of tea, and they had taken hot chocolate to a place of pure decadence, but their dubious excuse for coffee made even the most fervent Francophile somewhat question the extent of this nation's exulted commitment to *bon goût*.

As I sipped my *chocolat chaud*, I looked at the buildings around me, the roofs high-pitched like natty hats. It's apt that there's an openness to Place des Vosges, as it was built at the dawn of the 1600s, what the French call the *grand siècle*, a time when Paris welcomed in the world, and became worldlier for it. Naval exploration and maritime trade brought back a universe of new aromas and flavours (chocolate, tea and coffee represented newly explored continents, and the taste of the exotic *ailleurs*) as much as a head- and world-spinning array of ideas and inspiration.

I scrawled out a few postcards, and thought about Madame de Sévigné, France's beloved letter-writer, who was born on this very square in 1626. A well-read girl who grew into a woman whose brains vied with her beauty (almond eyes, rosebud lips, creamy skin, halo of tendrils) for society's attention, she was totally of her time. Her mind buzzing with novel ways of looking at life — helped along, no doubt, by her taste for the newfangled hot drinks of the time, particularly *chocolat chaud* (which would, she swore, make 'the most unpleasant company seem good') — Madame de Sévigné really came into her own at twenty-five, when widowhood happily relieved her of a rake of a husband (he died duelling over a courtesan), and gave her the legal status of independence. She was now gloriously free to devote her time and energy to herself.

Madame de Sévigné's epistolary skills are as clear as black and white, and at first you might think what a wonderful journalist she would make in today's world. Curious from a young age, she developed impressive investigative prowess — being plugged into all sources of information, both low and high, straddling the realms of gossip and intellect — reporting the story of seventeenth-century Paris in the countless letters that survive her. It was her cherished daughter's devastating move to the South of France that prompted most of the correspondence, but you sense that Madame de Sévigné's need to write was akin to that of breathing, it came so naturally to her.

But regardless of her unique, expressive, entertaining voice, I doubt she would have taken to journalism, or even blogging. Such writing is essentially one-sided. Even when you present others' opinions, *you* are still the one choosing and editing the information. Madame de Sévigné, however, thrived on exchange — and her letters were essentially that: one half of a witty dialogue, in ink form. Her writing is so lively because it is a living thing, something that is in constant flux, one gem in a conversation continually being embellished.

Madame de Sévigné, a dazzling socialite and brilliant *raconteuse*, positively shone in the salons of the day. It was her great friend, the Italian-born Madame de Rambouillet, who invented the concept of a salon, by inviting a distinguished group of guests from the artistic, literary and social elite to her *salone*, the famed 'blue room', for conversation and canapés, to play word games over goblets of wine. Everyone came together with one aim in mind: to refine their language and redefine their culture. It worked for all: aristocrats of the time, power and wealth diminishing, were searching for a new way to distinguish themselves; women wanted to find a voice, and in turn put their feminine touch on the French language; and anyone else was just happy to be welcomed into such glamorous company. A new high society was forming, and entry was determined more democratically than ever; if you used your words elegantly and wittily enough, you were in. Conversation was a way of connecting and equalising, regardless of place in the social hierarchy, and the epoch's French writers — who to this day weave philosophical thinking into their prose — filtered the new codes of behaviour and the new style of language to the upwardly mobile people of France, who aspired to a nobility of mind and aristocracy of manners, if not access to a sumptuous salon with its silky *chaises longues*.

I've always loved that it was women who mostly hosted salons, at a time when society granted them next to no political or legal power. Being a *salonnière* was a stealthy, subversive and seductive form of authority, as only a Parisienne could appreciate. Hostesses used all their wiles and charms to attract the greatest men of the day, and then lure them into their world and way of speaking, so that French was moulded into the most feminine of languages. Music, incidentally, was the only art to not really take off in France (unless you also count the art of coffee-making). I've often thought it was because spoken French is melodic enough, all singsongy and mellifluous as it is. The fluidity of French suits conversation beautifully, flowing gracefully like a length of satin, its exquisite words strung together and presented like a jewel-encrusted necklace on a bed of velvet. No wonder so many women swoon over its sounds. I, for one, could happily listen to even a French plumber talk about blocked pipes all day long.

The French Revolution was the beginning of the end of the salon — aristocrats ultimately had to go and get a job, leaving precious little time to ponder puns — but Parisians still love to talk away, in that beautiful accent of theirs. In cafés all over town, plumbers and politicians alike come together over ideas (and, doubtless, bad coffee), in a national conversation that has been chattering on for centuries, making for a most sociable of societies. I doubted my French would ever be strong enough to partake in this particular dialogue, but I found it stimulating all the same. When at a café, I could lose myself in other tables' conversations. Even if I couldn't always follow every segue, I'd feed off the passion, the intensity and verve with which beliefs and *bons mots* were bandied about. I felt like I'd almost forgotten how to talk myself, or at least converse. I'd worked in solitude for so long, in an industry that was increasingly inward-looking, and I was living too much in my own head, not in others'. The medium of conversation might not be recorded for posterity or branded with a by-line — I'm sure Madame de Sévigné's best work was in audio, words that swirled around the salons of Paris before dissipating into thin air and memory — but I had an inkling that bantering would satisfy me much more than blogging.

After breakfast, I wandered a couple of blocks west to Musée Carnavalet, which houses an overwhelmingly expansive collection of knick-knacks from Paris past (Roman remnants, medieval shop signs, toy guillotine), all sprawled throughout two Renaissance mansions. The museum showcases the private lives of Parisians over the centuries, with interiors from long-gone buildings. Sadly, Madame de Rambouillet's blue salon didn't survive the wrecking ball of architectural evolution, but you can still wander through some of the rooms of her great friend Madame de Sévigné, a former resident of Carnavalet; she smiles down from portraits in all her embonpoint-rich glory, her cupid's-bow lips closed into a mischievous smile, her thoughts teasingly frozen to herself.

An equally beguiling Parisienne can be found reclining in another wing of the museum, in a ravishing portrait by François Gérard. Juliette Récamier was one of the *Merveilleuses* of post-Revolutionary Paris, a period known as the Empire, which gave its name to the sheer high-waisted dresses she wore to seductive perfection. The most celebrated *salonnière* of her time, indulged by her elderly banker husband, Juliette adorned her home with trend-setting furniture inspired by the idealised ancient world, and men flocked from all over town to wistfully watch her lounging about barefoot on her various sofas. In Gérard's painting, she's propped up on cushions as plump as her skin, in a pose as languid as her dress, and her charms are all too evident. You can only wonder at her conversational skills, of course, but her soft voice reportedly enthralled anyone who came into her orbit, transfixed by her angelic aura.

Juliette was commonly described as chaste, but that didn't stop her from falling for François-René de Chateaubriand, the lauded founding father of French Romanticism — if an ice-queen is going to let herself melt, it might as well be for someone worth it — and their ongoing affair was suitably torrid. Chateaubriand, incidentally, is one of the reasons writing is taken so seriously in France, a place where writing has long had an intellectual, philosophical bent. But in the years leading up to the Revolution, there was a move away from the witty works beloved by the salon set, with authors of the new *romans* (novels) addressing the wider public. Victor Hugo was inspired to illustriousness, scribbling 'Chateaubriand or nothing' in his teenage diary; countless aspiring writers have since taken up this mantra, and still do. And perhaps this is one other reason French journalists by and large strive for greater literary heights than the gutter. If you must write — an act that will indelibly link you to your ink — do so with as much style as you can muster. You can always save the juicy gossip for your conversation.

&

That afternoon, I caught up with another friend who had left Sydney for Paris, Yasmin — an astrologer who wrote the horoscope page of a magazine I once worked for. I'd long appreciated astrology as a neat way of explaining away, even justifying, personality quirks (I was Piscean, therefore had the tendency to cry more than most, drink one glass of wine too many, and wear an overabundance of ruffly feminine dresses) — and it's for this kind of zodiacal psychology that most people turn to the stars these days. But by getting to know Yasmin, I came to appreciate the old-school methodology of it all, which traces back to a time when astrology was structured by strict mathematical rules.

You might at first think there'd be little place for astrology in Paris, the home of harmonious order and rational thought. But France, of course, practically invented the paradox, and the French in fact harbour a fascination with the stars. The astrological craze was imported from the Middle East in the Middle Ages, and soon many French monarchs — including, suitably, the Sun King, Louis XIV — were hanging onto every muttering of their court astrologers. The trend reached its celestial heights in the Renaissance, when the Italian Catherine de Medici came to Paris to marry the future Henri II, bringing along her own personal astrologer. Catherine also fretted over the predictions of Nostradamus, one of which foresaw the gruesome jousting death of her husband, on the very spot where Place des Vosges would later materialise. The Age of Enlightenment and the Revolution might have attempted to usher in a new era of straight-minded seriousness, but the

French have remained curiously open to occult sciences. Mysticism is akin to a new religion for many, with some 10 million French people said to be seeing a psychic or stargazer each year. Famously, the late president François Mitterand regularly consulted celebrity astrologer (and former Chanel model) Elizabeth Teissier, often phoning twice a day to check if the stars were aligning in favour of certain political, and even military, manoeuvres.

The French yen for matters of the mystical might seem irrational to some, but at heart it's about searching for a reason. In a secular society, if you don't have religion to assuage your fears about the meaning of life, the occult offers up some alluring options. The French, perhaps, for all their rationalism and cynicism — or, at least, nonchalance — deep down want to believe in something bigger than themselves, that there's method to the madness of life, some kind of order in the whirling, chaotic universe. They might have their feet firmly on earth — their beloved *terroir* — but the French also have stars in their eyes.

'It's strange to see you so at home in Paris,' I remarked, after meeting Yasmin in a bar in Saint-Germain. 'You're the quintessential Bondi girl to me.'

Yasmin used to live right by Bondi Beach, on the sands of which you'd often find her in meditation mode, looking every bit at one with the cosmos. But what you might not at first realise is that beneath the free-flowing curls and swirling gowns there's a serious mind clicking away — precisely, mathematically — and it's perhaps this dual nature that drew her to paradoxical Paris, that made it her *ailleurs*, too.

'I love Bondi but I've also actually dreamed of living in Paris since I was fourteen, when I used to long for the smoky Left Bank jazz bars — I'd even burn Gauloise cigarettes instead of incense,' she said, laughing. 'And now it's like my body has finally caught up with my head. I did a lot of meditating on and visualising coming to Paris before it finally happened.'

A year earlier, the universe had presented Yasmin with the opportunity to live in Paris for a few weeks. She arrived on the night of a new moon, the city shining extra brightly against the barely lit sky. 'The first thing I did, after dropping my bags off, was to walk to the Eiffel Tower,' she recalled. 'That sounds really touristy, but I knew it would be the perfect conductor to send my wishes to the heavens. And so, I stood under the spire and wished.'

'To stay in Paris?'

'For Paris to become my home.'

She met Olivier a few months later and a year on, they were still inseparable.

'Ooh, sounds serious,' I sighed, after swooning over their *amour* story.

'Sure is. So, guess why I'm not drinking?' she asked with a grin.

I hadn't noticed Yasmin's baby bump hiding beneath her flowing dress (a fashion to which — like me — she was quite partial). After the requisite hugs and enquiries into her wellbeing, I had to get to the important stuff: 'But aren't you allowed to drink red wine here when you're pregnant?'

'I think I found the only gynaecologist in Paris who doesn't let you drink wine or eat cheese.'

'Nine cheese-free months sounds like a pretty good deal for what you're getting in return. I mean, you're living the dream. This is like something that only happens in books.'

'You know, people say that to me, but I was living this as a literal dream for so long, now it seems like I've actually woken up and can get on with life.'

'Get on with life — that's something I need to get onto soon ...'

'So I did your astrological chart for you earlier today ...'

Yasmin isn't just great company; she also has some neat party tricks.

'Okay, hit me. I can take it.'

'There's nothing to worry about, but you've been living a kind of chimera the past couple of years. I can see that you would have felt a bit lost, but it's starting to clear. You just need to work out how to be true to what you really want.'

What do you truly want in life? It's never a simple question, really. Especially as you're usually at your most confused when you most need the answer. At the time, I wasn't yet able to string my thoughts into a polished sound bite, but I had a few catchwords I kept going back to: home, health, happiness.

'There's nothing wrong with wanting a simple life,' said Yasmin with a smile. 'And we all need a Rousseau moment from time to time.'

It was French-speaking Swiss philosopher Jean-Jacques Rousseau who, back in the Age of Enlightenment, taught France the importance of home, of being faithful to yourself, listening to your transparent heart. The patron saint of earth mothers, he urged women to go back to nature and return to their *terroir*, and eat simple *au naturel* vegetarian food for calmer constitutions. His philosophy-laden novels waxed lyrical about the delights of rural life and sweet, spontaneous love. Rousseau had lived long enough in Parisian high society to know he didn't belong, and it was with both disdain and bitterness that he launched himself on a one-man crusade against modern civilisation, with all its airs and graces, which he claimed corrupted human beings' otherwise good selves. He was a bit of a party-pooper, in other words.

You have to pick and choose your Rousseau. The French, for instance, have obviously ignored the vegetarian bit, and of course most of them nowadays live in cities where they happily partake in the finer things in life. Then again, the French also display admirably utopian sensibilities, and Rousseau can take major credit for that (even though his talk of the common good and general will has been appropriated for evil by not a few dictators). I also have to laud his fashion eye; he might have been a committed misogynist, but his call for women to break out of corseted clothing into breezy gowns fit for a divinity has sparked many a dress trend I've happily bought into.

'Do you want me to read a goddess card for you?'

See, having an astrologer friend really does have its benefits.

Yasmin shuffled a deck of cards and placed them in front of me. I drew Aphrodite.

'Ooh nice,' she nodded. 'This is a card for a woman, not a girl.'

'In other words, it's time to grow up?'

'It's more that you need to pamper and bring out your inner goddess.'

'I think I can do that.' (I had already lined myself up a deluxe facial.)

'And you should let yourself have fun — wear a beautiful dress and go out dancing.'

'Already on it!'

&

On the evening of the summer solstice, Elsa, Yasmin and I met for dinner. Despite its traditionally French name, Chez Marianne is the multicultural Marais in a melting pot, an exuberant tasting platter of vibrant colours and flavours from *ailleurs*: eggplant caviar, hummus, tarama, stuffed peppers, felafel, and more. For all three of us, of course, Paris was our *ailleurs*. It surprised locals that we could speak French well enough in this increasingly Anglophone era. Once was a time, back when the Marais was the centre of the social universe, that French was *the* language to speak, no matter where you lived. By communicating in the words of the salons, you proved that you knew not only how to converse well, but also how to live well, because the French at the time defined civilisation, manners and style — and they conspired to perfect the French language, as almost everything else they created, into a thing of beauty: as seductive as a silken gown, as effervescent as champagne, as polished as a crystal chandelier, as delicious to roll around the mouth as velvety-thick hot chocolate.

Now, of course, the world largely communicates in English, a fact that the French have taken a while to accept — because it's a sign of not so much globalisation as Americanisation. With every visit to Paris, I've noticed more locals willing and able to speak English whenever I struggle to express myself, although admittedly, they seem considerably more eager to do so when they discover I'm not American.

'Ah, you're Australian,' exclaimed our waiter. 'It's my dream to open a restaurant in Palm Cove.'

File it under: everyone has an *ailleurs*.

'Why do you think women love Paris so much?' I asked Yasmin and Elsa. 'Apart from the obvious beauty of it.'

'One thing I think women adore about this city, and that I really love,' said Yasmin, 'is that it seems to welcome you, as a woman, with open arms, no matter who you are, or your age or your style. Paris loves women.'

I thought about my many times there: I'd skipped in the snow like my childhood girl-crush Madeline; as a teenager, I flounced around the streets like some silly baby Bardot; I'd come to Paris to commemorate the end of school and university, to prepare me for the next stages of life and help hone my sense of self; I'd had occasional flings and flirtations there, and overcome my first major heartbreak; and I'd shopped and partied way more than should be legal. But whatever role I was playing at the time, Paris provided the perfect backdrop. And now? I wondered what stop in the itinerary of life I had come to, and how Paris would redirect me from here.

Yasmin had already fallen head over heels into her next life stage, her *grand amour*, and was quickly en route to the following one: *maman*. Elsa had also just met the guy she would go on to marry. 'He's Australian and wants to go back home,' she sighed, but not wistfully, as though she'd happily resigned herself to the wisdom of destiny. 'But I'm sure I'll be back. I don't think it's a place you'll ever feel old in.'

'I'll totally be here as an old maid,' I shot back, with a laugh.

'Oh, Kat,' tutted Yasmin. 'I have absolutely no doubt you'll find someone.'

It's always reassuring when an astrologer believes that your tall, dark stranger is around the corner, but at the time I truly didn't mind when, perhaps even if, he'd turn up. I guess I'd placed myself in the hands of fate, too, or of some higher power. Sure, it would be lovely to find a life partner — my mum and dad, after all, were poster parents for marriage — but I had to find myself first (as trite as that sentiment might sound), or at least my inner woman.

The French word *femme* means both woman and wife. In my university days, I would grumble that this implied a woman's unquestioned fate was to marry, or that you weren't inherently womanly if you didn't have a rock on your ring finger. But in later years I came to look at it from another angle: being married doesn't change who you are — you are still, above all, a woman.

I had also begun to believe that you didn't even need love — in that tall, dark stranger sense — to have a great life. 'We cease loving ourselves if no one loves us,' wrote Romantic author, Germaine de Staël, but even she came to scoff at the whole 'you complete me' notion of love. Anyway,

Romanticism — a term she, incidentally, popularised — didn't at the time mean torrid, all-consuming affairs (although she did have her fair share of those); it was about living and feeling the full scale of human emotions. Realism might technically be a separate school of literature, but there was something very rational about Germaine's passionate approach to life; she was as true to her big heart as her brilliant brain, and threw herself into everything — mind, body and soul. She was as much sense as sensibility.

Germaine was a baby of the Enlightenment, sitting at the skirts of her *salonnière* mother, listening to the greatest thinkers of the time carve out and polish up new ideas. Her prodigious intelligence was evident from an early age, but there was also more to Germaine: a warmth and passion that lured people closer. She bloomed into a seductive conversationalist who delighted all in her circle, despite being considered gauche and ungainly. Her multifacetedness, too, was seen to be vulgar for a woman; a wife and a mother, a mistress and cherished friend to many, she wanted it all even though she was smart enough to know this was impossible (especially in those pre-feminist times), a thread that wove through her impressive body of essays and novels. Her awe-inspiring intellect thrived on political intrigue, and her morality-fuelled views caused her multiple banishments from her beloved Paris in the rocky years following the Revolution. 'True pleasure for me can be found only in love, Paris or power,' she said, but she never gave up on striving for all three, and so much more.

With age, I find myself more and more impressed by Germaine, inspired by her eternal liberal-minded optimism. She might never have found the mutual conjugal love she admired in her parents — I could empathise with the awe such a high standard must have struck in an only child — but she never gave up looking. And perhaps she loved the idea of love more than love itself, and who's to say which is more fulfilling? Germaine was driven by the pursuit of happiness, the promise of a better future. She was constantly in flux — life being a journey, not a destination, after all — filling her days to the brim, especially with work, something for which she never apologised. One of Germaine's biographers called her the 'first modern woman'. Not just, I think, in the proto-feminist, superwoman sense. But she was also a *femme* according to my French reading of that word — no matter whether she was married (or separated, or in a clandestine relationship ...), nothing altered her own true sense of self. Of course, being French, she could also do womanly in sartorial terms. Germaine wore flimsy muslin gowns that clung to her ample curves, and trailed a rainbow of colourful scarves — a worshipper of goddess fashion just like her best friend, Juliette Récamier.

The French, I've often been told, don't do girls' or guys' nights out. Since the days of the salon, socialising has entailed a mingling of men and women. The contrast of genders charges the atmosphere with seductive piquancy, inspiring feminine flirtatiousness and keeping men on their polished, gallant toes. It also makes for more varied, stimulating banter, one where all manner of subjects, from fashion to philosophy, are subjected to light-heartedly serious examination. As one of the earliest *salonnières* of the Marais, Mademoiselle de Scudéry, commanded: 'I want great and small things to be spoken of, so long as they are spoken of elegantly.'

While I find it admirable that French men and women are so at ease with each other, I couldn't survive without a sisterhood of sorts. This could well be because I don't have sisters of my own (and perhaps that's why Germaine, out of her many friends and lovers, found her kindred spirit in Juliette), but I do believe that, when given the dedicated time and space, women connect with each other in a soul-satisfyingly deep way. Anyway, I think Parisiennes have a secret sisterhood. These were the people, after all, who established salons in the first place to give women a voice, who perfected the art of letter-writing, and turned tea-taking into a long, languid daily ritual, all for the pleasure of relishing one another's company.

&

Nourished by our flavourful food and rich conversation, high on rosé wine and bubbly spirits, Elsa and I kicked on to celebrate the remainder of the Fête de la Musique. 'Go dance, get in touch with those inner goddesses,' urged Yasmin, before taking herself, and her own inner supreme being, home to bed.

We padded through the paved streets of the Marais, the slowly setting sun shooting its final golden rays across a lapis lazuli sky, then turned into Place des Vosges, its street lamps burning their amber glow against the coral-hued façades. At the end of one of the vaulted arcades, we stepped through a wooden door, into a hidden gem, a literal secret garden. Not many know this back way to the Hôtel de Sully, one of the Marais' grandest seventeenth-century townhouses. It takes you directly into a jewel of a garden that has been faceted into emerald-cut perfection, its four jade-green lawns edged by clipped boxwood hedges.

In front of the old orangery — one of the first in Paris, built to grow hothouse citrus fruit from Italy, the most fashionable *ailleurs* at the time — a stage had been set up, and under flashing fluorescent lights a singer from the French West Indies (there's some more serious *ailleurs* right there) was mixing electronic beats, a folksy guitar melody and a velvety voice to captivating effect, entrancing the Parisians of all ages who were swaying before him on the gravel dance floor.

France struggled to find its musical voice for centuries. Sure, it has had its homegrown superstars and some have managed to translate to international cult status — think Édith Piaf and Serge Gainsbourg. But, for the most part, the domestic success of Gallic crooners has left the rest of the world scratching its head (Johnny Hallyday, anyone?). Since the 1990s, however, a new breed of French musicians, boasting diverse ethnic backgrounds, had not only found their own voice, but had also given classic French an alluring new accent, the poetry of the French language working magic when combined with the chants of rap and hip-hop.

We joined the throng of dancing Parisians, and were soon blissfully oblivious to the light summer rain sprinkling down. The cloud-rippled sky was a swirl of orange on blue, giving a tie-dyed effect that seemed to cast a spell of the exotic over Paris. It reminded me of the world out there, so many *ailleurs*, but one in particular that was beckoning me home.

In the end, turning a third-of-a-century wasn't so much a crisis point as a turning one. I suddenly had a new direction and vision, with New York in the rear-view mirror. Paris would, as ever, be my *ailleurs*, my constant detour, and perhaps I would live there one day; but for now, it was time to get in touch again with my own *terroir*, go back to my roots. I wanted to reconnect with place as much as people, to take care to converse — I craved communication through more than the written word, even though I still had much to write in this changing world of journalism. The concept of beauty, too, was evolving for me, with age. I wanted to stop being so hard on myself — how I looked and how much I weighed, as much as what I was going to do next with my life. It was time to live in the moment, go with some kind of flow, learn to be *chez moi* in my own skin. Because no matter where you go or live on this earth, the most important home you live in, as much as the temple to worship, is the one you carry around with you.

CHAPTER 8

FEMME

[fam] *nf* wife

In which, aged thirty-six,
I find that I'll always have Paris.

You could take the girl out of Paris … but I was still there in a way, because I'd styled my Sydney apartment into my fantasy of how a Parisienne would live: musky-pink carpet, rose-crystal chandeliers, antique furniture painted in faded pastel hues, flowers and framed photos everywhere. Paris, after all, practically invented interior decoration, polishing it into a fine rococo art. It was there that boudoirs were first fashioned — the original rooms of one's own; exquisite writing tables, too, on which Parisiennes could scribble their innermost thoughts. No place loves amassing and displaying beautiful objects quite like Paris, and I've long thought this was because, in a city of classic, sometimes staid apartment buildings, interior spaces have become the realm for self-expression, places in which Parisians can retreat and truly be themselves.

So I was very much at home, living by myself in my Parisian-esque boudoir, a reflection of a contented inner existence. I'd happily taken a break from romance for the past year, choosing to nurture myself after some dismal dating experiences. And then Andy came knocking. Andy, I must preface, is an interior designer, but his idea of domestic style is as far from mine as Sydney is from Paris — he would basically be happy living in a large concrete box. I'm actually surprised he didn't run a mile on first glimpse of my pink apartment. But while we were opposites in the aesthetic sense, we somehow clicked, the feminine and masculine balancing each other out. Our relationship instantly felt easy and comfortable, like sinking into my big cushiony cream sofa — even though his ideal couch would be black, leather and sharply edged.

The sofa, incidentally, was also created in Paris, when the pioneers of the interior arts played around with new ways of bringing people together. The two-seater was initially considered a little risqué, and author Joan DeJean has noted that the term *tomber amoureux* — to fall in love — was coined around this time, perhaps as a sign of the emotional, as much as physical, impact of this new intimate furniture. To this day, however, every couple needs a good couch — it's therapy without the therapist, the ideal way to relax in one another's company, to unwind after a day, to work through various stresses. Andy and I spent many evenings ensconced in said cream sofa, taking turns to choose the night's movie. I, of course, would opt for something vintage or French. Andy would nominate a war movie, which surprised me at first, given his pacifist leanings. 'What is it about guys and war movies?' I asked. 'What is it about girls and pink?' he shot back. We eventually found something we both loved: *Casablanca*. Equally a film about war and romance, you also can't beat it for dialogue. No prizes for guessing my favourite line: 'We'll always have Paris.'

Every couple, I suspected, would also benefit from having Paris in their life, and Andy and I soon had the opportunity. I won a trip there for a fragrance article I'd written, and traded my business-class ticket for two economy ones ('You must really like him, to give up your French champagne for sparkling wine,' a colleague quipped.) We flew out the day after Christmas, wondering if it was slightly crazy to spend a fortnight in Paris in her wintry depths. But twenty-four hours later, as our taxi neared the City of Light in all her glimmering glory — set against a mauve-grey sky that seemed on the verge of dissolving in a flurry of snowflakes — we knew there was no place in the world we'd rather be.

I'd booked an apartment in the 6th arrondissement, picturing us spending evenings in toasty, cigarette-hazy basement jazz bars, even though the cool heyday of Saint-Germain was long gone, and nobody could smoke indoors anymore. But then again, Saint-Germain is so mythologised it's as much a dreamscape as streetscape. Paris, after all, is surely history's most filmed, photographed and painted city, as much fantasy as reality, which is, I think, why you often experience the sensation of time standing still, of stepping back into the past, into a frame of an old film or vintage photograph.

But scratch the classic surface, sniff down alleyways into the past, and you'll find that Paris has indeed transformed over time, the ageing *grande dame* that she is, with tidy nips and tucks or a spruce-up of paint, and sadly the occasional scarring botch job, too. A quick perusal of any postcard shop will have you yearning as much for the Paris of today as that of yesterday. I've always collected cards displaying the photographs by Eugène Atget, who recorded his beloved Paris of the early twentieth century, as the city struggled to adapt to a brutal new century. An inveterate *flâneur*, Atget was a street photographer *avant la lettre*, although unlike today's urban snaps, most of Atget's images are devoid of people. In Atget's work, it's the stones of the buildings and roads that are alive, vibrating with history and longing to be heard. Atget referred to himself as an author–producer, telling the story of Old Paris, freezing it into sentimental shades of warm sepia and cool dusky violet. He photographed not only the grand monuments and majestic parks, but also the shady nooks and decaying crannies, and you swear you can see, floating in the nebulous mist of his lens, the ghosts of Parisians past.

We were staying on Rue du Dragon, the street of the dragon, so called because it once linked to the Cour du Dragon, one of the nostalgia-filled crevices photographed by Atget. The cobbled courtyard — a passage of workshops, where coppersmiths and blacksmiths hammered out their trade — escaped Baron Haussmann's knife as he sliced through the area to make way for the nearby Rue de Rennes and Boulevard Saint-Germain, but it gradually crumbled to pieces, until a demolition warrant rang its death knell in 1934. Fortunately, most of Saint-Germain was sturdily built and well maintained, having been the stomping ground of mule-clad socialistas before the boot-wearing beatniks came along, and our building dated back to the district's early urban days, an eighteenth-century townhouse now carved up into a warren of abodes. Our apartment was jammed in a back corner, over the top two floors, the bedroom nestled into the rooftop. It was crooked and creaky yet so romantically redolent with character, and was the perfect home for a pair playing at Parisian coupledom.

On our first morning — warmed up by Café de Flore's buttery croissants and creamy hot chocolate, and layers of thermals and scarves — we wound our way towards the Seine, stopping here and there to surreptitiously lean against old coach doors in the hope that they would creak open and offer up a glance into the worlds within. When you holiday with an interior designer, you find yourself constantly peering up through windows, peeping into old keyholes cut in elaborately carved wooden gates, and discussing what wonders could be behind ivy-clad stone walls. Paris, I found, only intensified Andy's obsession, because as much as the streets are alive with cafés and lined with architectural gems, Paris is at heart an internal city — especially so in winter — reflecting those rich inner lives of her inhabitants.

We found ourselves at the Pont des Arts, the city's first steel bridge, built by Napoléon in 1803. A span of seven dainty arches, as airy and graceful as ballerina leaps, the bridge perfectly demonstrates the lightness of French design, even when working with hefty materials — it's as though some sort of engineering alchemy has transformed base metal into lace. At the time, the Pont des Arts was dealing with another weighty matter: love locks. The trend for couples to clip a padlock, scribbled with their heart-framed initials, onto the railing of the bridge before throwing the key into the waters below, had only started the year before, but already the bridge seemed to groan under the excess load. Parisians, too, groaned at the touristy trend. You see, the French prefer their amorous declarations to be — like their bridges — light and elegant. It's that ability of theirs to treat even the most substantial of subjects with breezy aplomb. Even Napoléon, that war-mongering engineer-minded soldier-turned-emperor, had a tender inner romantic who wrote gushing passion-soaked prose to his empress. A Parisian, I expect, would prefer a love letter to a love lock any day.

The passionate padlock trend, of course, seems fitting for the self-confessed city of love. But then, Paris is also the city of beauty. And this was the bridge of arts not hearts. Parisians, being rationalist romantics at core, must have sighed with relief to hear, in 2014, that the locks were threatening the structure of the historic bridge, hazardously weighing it down with all the emotional baggage. So in the end, the decision between art and heart was made for them: the authorities lopped off the locks and replaced the wire railings with glass panels. Not quite the fade-out happily-ever-after ending, but then Parisians know that love is never easy. You only need to watch a couple of French films to understand this.

Andy and I were still in the early act of our particular script, but we'd finished the awkward scenes, where you're still getting to know each other and work out if in fact you really do like each other, and we'd moved into the second act, where you can sit together for hours, often wordlessly so, just content to hang around in one another's company. The Pont des Arts is the ideal location for such scenes to take place. With its perfect panoramic views — the baroque gold-domed French Institute on one bank, the eternal Louvre on the other, the Eiffel

Tower piercing the air downstream, the islands jutting towards you upstream — and the hypnotic sounds of the Seine below, this is where you can experience one of those time-suspended sensations. It's just you, him and one wonderful world.

As heart-warming as our view was, the iciness of the air soon brought tears to our eyes, blurring the rose-tinted vision. It was time to get walking again, and briskly at that. We cut through an archway in the riverside wing of the Louvre, to Place du Carrousel. To our right was the once controversial glass pyramid in the museum's courtyard, to our left the Arc de Triomphe du Carrousel, which aligns with the more famous Parisian triumphal arc up there on the Étoile, the star-shaped 'square' at the end of the Champs-Élysées. Unlike its big sister, however, which serves as a kind of grand statement of welcome to Paris, the petite Carrousel arch, with its pink-marbled columns and tiara of statues, does little more than sit pretty in a park.

'A gateway to nowhere,' remarked Andy. 'This seems very French to me.'

The French penchant for decoration for decoration's sake, to not just paint a lily but gild it, was not quite to Andy's taste. He demanded a reason for everything, and the reason had to be more than 'It looks pretty'. I got the importance of practicality — and that architect I.M. Pei's pyramid-capped museum entrance did indeed make the Louvre experience less stressful — but I just couldn't forgive a structure any ugliness, no matter its function or effect. As for things that are all style, no substance, well perhaps I'm a little more lenient there.

Anyway, I explained to Andy, the Carrousel Arch did once serve a purpose: it was the gateway to the Palais des Tuileries, which ran between the two tips of the Louvre's wings. The Renaissance palace, built by Catherine de Medici, was destroyed in 1871, during the fiery clashes of the Paris Commune, when so much else of Old Paris was consigned to the dustbin. On the upside, the Louvre now opened out to the old palace's gardens, giving us that glorious arch-to-arch vista that is surely one of the world's most stunning urban stretches.

The Tuileries Garden bursts with joy in the warmer months, as their celebration of life's simple pleasures seems to bring out the happiest in people. But in the eerie starkness of winter, it's easy to get a sense of the world in which the so-called Black Queen lived. Catherine, a scheming power player at court, was brought up reading Machiavelli, and dark rumours of plottings and poisonings constantly swirled around her. When the park is drained of colour and the trees have been stripped back to spikes, I can well imagine Catherine cutting a foreboding figure there, her heavy black robes swishing the grounds as she paced around her parterre gardens.

To my delight, it had started to snow, and we walked glove in glove past phantoms of Old Paris loitering in the scattered green chairs. It was almost as though we were moving through one of Atget's photos of the Tuileries, images hushed of humanity and moody with melancholy. Even the sky was tinted an Atget-esque shade of purplish-brown, speckled with flecks of white. If only you could bottle up such moments, encapsulate them in a snowdome, ready to reactivate and relive with a shake.

The snowflakes fluttered down, droplets of water crystallised into elaborate jewel-like structures, and the black branches seemed to reach out for them, as though desperate for adornment. The French author Stendhal used the term *crystalisation* to describe human beings' habit of embellishing loved ones with the properties we'd ideally like them to have. Okay, so he was talking specifically about salt, but I also see an analogy with the rough diamond complex — the belief that we can polish a guy of all his faults, shine him up into a flawless gem. Perhaps Andy and I, having met in our late thirties, were old enough to know we couldn't substantially change the other, that we had to accept one another without the trappings and trimmings.

This, however, has never stopped a girl from giving a guy fashion advice. 'Are you going to buy yourself a new coat?' I asked, attempting to sound as subtle and casual as possible.

'What's wrong with this?' asked Andy, somewhat defensively, looking down at his second-hand army jacket. 'It's actually quite cool, you know.'

Granted, everyone was wearing the look back in Bondi, where Andy technically lived, but Bondi Beach is to Paris what hobo is to boho: quite another thing altogether.

'I'm not saying you should start wearing pastel cashmere and beige trench coats,' I persisted. 'But the whole Aussie casual thing doesn't always translate to Paris.'

Cue slightly moody silence. Quickly remembering Andy's need for reason and justification at all times, especially when battling an issue of aesthetics, I tried a different tack, pointing out that perhaps military fashion is culturally inappropriate in a city that has experienced the horrors of war.

Andy looked thoughtful. 'I guess war would have a different context here,' he agreed. 'Okay, you win. Let's go shopping tomorrow.'

See, relationships are about finding common ground — and victory by diplomacy over warfare.

Despite all our thermal and woollen layers, our teeth had begun to chatter, so we took shelter in a booth of the Grande Roue, the Ferris wheel at the end of the gardens. We floated above Paris thanks to modern engineering, but it seemed an invention of pure magic, and I thought about the exhilaration the Robert brothers must have felt when they launched the first hydrogen balloon, from the Tuileries, back in 1783, rising above the heads of awestruck Parisians.

The Paris skyline, of course, has greatly changed since then. Palaces have gone, arches and towers have shot up, names have been renamed, innocence lost. The Grande Roue sits by the magnificent octagonal piazza Place de la Concorde. Known as Place Louis XV before the Revolution, it was built to commemorate the king whose grandson would meet his gruesome fate there later in the century, at the bloody hands of Madame La Guillotine, when people flocked to the square not to watch balloons soar, but heads fall into baskets — so many that the streets were stained red.

France might have freed itself of despotic royal rule and hosed down this square and given it a new name (and a random Egyptian obelisk as the central focus), but no matter how high and lofty its modern ideals, there you're reminded that Paris has some serious ghosts. Concorde means harmony, and you have to wonder if the Parisian pursuit of beauty and order is so committed and intense because the alternative is just too shocking to return to.

We treated ourselves to a late, long lunch up on the Champs-Élysées, at Ladurée, the famous *salon de thé* that was fast expanding its empire, fuelled by an insatiable appetite for its multicoloured *macarons*. Although this outlet had only been open for a decade or so, it was a portal into Paris of the mid nineteenth century, a time when French interior decoration was at its most flamboyant and frivolous, when anything went as long as it was ostentatious. Dining in the restaurant upstairs, we were surrounded by a swirl of marble and tasselled brocade curtains, sitting at a glossy porcelain-plated table on velvet-upholstered, gilded chairs, with floral carpet underfoot and chandeliers above.

'Can you breathe okay?' I asked the minimalism-loving man opposite me.

'I'm only just coping,' he replied. 'I mean, it's like they simply couldn't leave any surface untouched. It's obsessive-compulsive design.'

'Well, I could happily live in a room like this.'

'The things I do for you ...'

'Oh yes, life's so tough right now!'

'But seriously, I would never have come here if not for you — this place, but also this city. I hated it for years.'

Andy had last been in Paris with a girlfriend who ended up skipping town with a mineral water millionaire.

'You should have just eaten your way out of heartbreak — that's what I did when I broke up with Zack.'

Little soothes the soul like a Parisian pastry. For dessert, Andy ordered a selection of *macarons*, and I opted for an ispahan, a giant rose *macaron* sandwiching a ring of raspberries on a bed of rose water and lychee crème. Such concoctions are pure pleasure on a plate. Sure, there's a matter of all the sweetness swirling endorphins around your system, but it's more than that: Parisian *patissiers* have a talent for delighting the eyes and nose as much as the mouth, in a way that can't help but make your heart smile.

As our sugar highs descended to earth, we wandered back down the avenue as the footpath turned a whiter shade of pale. Beneath the greying sky, the fluted lamps flared up, the bud lights quivered like fire flies in the plane trees, the Grande Roue ahead whirled like a Catherine wheel, and the Christmas market glittered like tinsel, with its string of fairy-lit chalets. We stopped to warm ourselves with roasted chestnuts and mulled wine, before walking back to Saint-Germain. The snowflakes continued to form around us, but we didn't need to embellish a thing. Life, at that moment, seemed crystallised to perfection.

&

In an attempt to rein in our spending, we dedicated the next day to stocking up our kitchen. Granted, that sounds mundane, but in Paris grocery shopping is like an exhilarating treasure hunt. There are few megamarkets in the centre of town, because authorities encourage local merchants to thrive. This means more legwork, but the thrill of the chase is pure adrenalin rush, propelling you from one specialty store to another, cherry-picking everything from juicy berries to pungent cheese.

'Let's pretend we're a Parisian couple doing our errands,' I said, attempting to wrap a tablecloth-sized scarf around my neck in that *je ne sais quoi* way of Parisiennes.

'Except I'm wearing my scruffy Bondi coat, remember,' quipped Andy, his voice ever so tinged with indignation.

'Well, best we begin with the most essential Parisian shopping item of all,' I answered. 'Fashion.'

One sleek, buttoned-through, collared-up woollen coat (and new-look Andy) later, we popped around the corner from Agnès B to buy the next items on our hitlist: salted caramel *macarons* from Pierre Hermé, followed by chocolate (priorities, people). Anyway, at Debauve & Gallais chocolate is basically a health food. Its founders back in 1800, Messieurs Debauve and Gallais, were pharmacists who extolled the wellbeing benefits of cocoa for those whose bodies are their temples. Fittingly, the marble-columned boutique is like a shrine to cocoa, its revered chocolates grandstanding on the glossy counter, just waiting to be worshipped. It would be rude not to pay tribute.

Our next place of pilgrimage was Poilâne, my favourite *boulangerie* in the whole of Paris. Bread, of course, is iconic in France; it — or lack of it — has even started a revolution. People usually picture Parisians wandering around with baguettes tucked under their stripy sleeves, but I personally can't go past Poilâne's signature whole-wheat sourdough *boule*: a large ball of *miche* with a P extravagantly twirled into its golden-brown crust that cuts into perfect slices of chewy carbohydrate goodness. I'd first discovered it in Sydney, at a French bakery that used to air-freight loaves in every week (before the term 'carbon footprint' was widely known), selling them — unsurprisingly — for an outrageous price, especially given the fact they were at least two days old.

True, Poilâne bread is made to last a week or so, and its tanginess intensifies with time, but for me there's nothing like buying it fresh. The red-brick Rue du Cherche-Midi store, which dates from 1932, even sells by the slice so you can stock up daily. I ordered ten *tranches*, salivating at the thought of the tartines I could concoct. A tartine is a slice of toasted bread with some kind of topping, but it's also so much more: a cherished French snack that conjures up jam-smothered childhood memories, it can also make for a sophisticated meal when the likes of smoked salmon, crème fraîche, capers and chives are involved.

'So, now we need our toppings,' I declared to a bemused-looking Andy. The most important being, of course, cheese. I was still technically vegan, but I'd adopted my friend Elsa's suggestion of a 'Paris clause' — one that would allow me to revert to vegetarianism whenever in Paris, a city where tofu was in short supply. They say you can live on love and air alone there. I, however, need cheese. The stinkier the better; I can sniff out a cheese shop from around the corner, and positively drool when out front. The French say window-licking instead of window-shopping and I swear whoever first came up with the term was a fellow *fromage* addict. My favourite *fromagerie* is Barthélemy on Rue de Grenelle. Its pretty façade painted with pastoral scenes makes the shop look like it has time-travelled in from a nineteenth-century French village. Inside, it's a veritable cheese tour of France. Every variety from every corner seems to be available, jostling for attention, exuding its enticing aromas like come-hither pheromones. We ordered brie tricked up with truffles, a *crottin de chavignol*, which is a nutty, crumbly type of goat's cheese, and a camembert from Normandy so runny that the rind could barely contain its exuberance.

Our next stop was the greengrocer, set up like a market stall, with sweet little baskets of berries and boxes of glossy vegetables bursting with so much pigment and vitality that you could almost believe a plant-based Parisian diet could suffice. We hovered at the avocados, gently poking their rippled skins to check for ripeness. '*Mais non, Madame*!' exclaimed the bewhiskered grocer, scurrying towards me. 'I do this for you.' He explained — in a voice mixed with honour, politeness and annoyance — that we were to let him know the fruits and vegetables we were after, and that he would then select our best options.

I later reflected on the incident, and realised that by prodding around, we had stomped on the grocer's *raison d'être*. Shopkeepers in Paris take immense pride in their place of work, which has traditionally been a second home. Small family businesses are still a dream for many, which is why specialist or niche merchants are a national treasure, protected by legislation as much as cultural respect. As a result, customers are considered guests, and you're expected to say '*bonjour*' when entering, and '*au revoir*' when leaving. Forget to greet, and you'll risk icy stares and scornful service — or worse still, rock-hard avocados.

'Shall we go *chez nous*?' I asked, once we had bought our bags of juicy clementines, crisp apples and pears, and earthy-hued root vegetables begging to be roasted, drizzled in oil and sprinkled with truffle salt.

'Aren't you forgetting things like, I don't know, toilet paper and washing powder?' asked Andy. 'You can't just live on chocolate and cheese, you know.'

Perhaps it was useful that Andy had such a practical domestic mind, after all.

&

Andy had displayed an admirable capacity for living in the light of rosy chandeliers, and nibbling dainty cakes in velvet-lined, ruffle-trimmed rooms, but at heart his ultimate design aesthetic included the adjectives 'modern' and 'minimal', not 'Belle Époque' or 'chintzy'. So, lest the feminine frivolities of this city overload his system like a surfeit of *macaron*-induced sugar, causing him to reach peak Paris too early, I suggested we venture out to the business hub La Défense, for a design detox of sorts.

La Défense — situated on the western outskirts, beyond the height restrictions that help to give inner Paris her village-like feel — was originally planned as a quasi French Manhattan, an orderly and harmonious take on an international business district. From the 1970s, however, forces of globalisation started to take hold, and the race to the top (although some say bottom) saw buildings clamour to scrape the sky. It's estimated that some 180,000 workers descend on La Défense each day. At best, you can say it serves a purpose; at worst, it's a soulless concrete jungle.

We walked along the central esplanade, a tree-averse track paved in ponderous grey, past buildings shaped every which way, some twisted, some tapered. Andy explained the feats of engineering behind the contortions but I found it difficult to even feign interest. On the cloud-dense day, the glass-and-steel creations appeared cold and sullen, and there was none of the limestone that gives central Paris its celebrated luminosity.

We walked towards the Grande Arche, the cavernous cube of an arch in the midst of it all. When you stand at its foot and peer longingly back towards Paris, you can see the original triumphal arch, perfectly aligned on the horizon kilometres away — the midpoint of an axis that stretches all the way to the pretty little pink arch at the Louvre. La Grande Arche de la Défense was one of President François Mitterand's pet projects of the 1980s; another was the glass pyramid at the Louvre. Like many past Parisian kings, Mitterand dreamed of leaving his majestic mark all over town, which explains the big shiny pomp of so many of his monuments. Andy pointed out the arch's glossy white carrera marble surface, explained how it was fashioned from four concrete frames, and noted that it was an office building as much as urban sculpture — but all that struck me was the starkness of the void.

'I'm not sure what artistic statement it's making,' I said. 'It literally has no substance.'

'But design is as much about what's there as what's not,' Andy countered. 'I mean, you don't have to cover every single space with flounces.'

Much to my relief, we were soon back on the other, frillier side of the *Périphérique*, the ring road that separates inner from outer Paris, old from new. The sun had started to shine across the ice-blue sky, the snow underfoot slowly melting to a glistening memory. Our feet were holding up, cushioned in three layers of socks snuggled into boots, so we pushed on with our architectural walking tour, to roam around Passy — a former rural village annexed and made over by Haussmann, and also the site of some seminal twentieth-century architecture.

We started at the foot of Avenue Foch, searching for the building where Andy's mother Carolyn had lived in the early 1960s. Avenue

Foch is basically the millionaires' mile of Paris. Veering off the 'grand axis' at the Arc de Triomphe, the wide chestnut-tree-lined boulevard sweeps down towards the Bois de Boulogne, the city's largest gardens. Two ribbons of lawn unfurling its full length make the avenue seem as much a park itself as a thoroughfare, and you can well envisage the glossy carriages of the Belle Époque rolling to and fro. It was once called the Avenue de l'Impératrice, in homage to Empress Eugénie, which is a rather more fitting name for such a splendid strip. Avenue Foch (named after a French Great War marshal) is at least better than Avenue Boche, its nickname during the Second World War, when the Gestapo commandeered buildings there for various operations, interrogations and much, much worse.

By the time Carolyn arrived, post-war Paris was back in party mode, in full swing of her *trente glorieuses*, the 'glorious thirty' years that saw the French economy boom — La Défense was one outcome of this — and the standard of living soar. Carolyn had been hired as the *au pair* for the youngest daughter of an *haut bourgeois* family, who lived luxuriously over an entire floor of a Haussmannian apartment building. The older brother and sister were friends with everyone who was anyone in the Parisian jetset, Brigitte Bardot included. Another party pal was heiress Christina Onassis, who lived with her father Aristotle upstairs in the penthouse, where he would go on to shack up with new wife Jackie later that decade.

At the time, of course, Jackie was Mrs Kennedy, the first lady of America. She had just come to town with her husband the president, who famously described himself as 'the man who accompanied Jackie Kennedy to Paris'. Jackie, who had studied in Paris after college, was one of those women who are innately Parisian, even if their passports state otherwise. She could speak French fluently and flawlessly, her slender frame showcased slim Chanel suits to clotheshorse perfection, and few could carry off a pillbox hat like the flip-bobbed Jackie. It was her preference for Parisian style that brought French fashion to the international mainstream. She was wearing pink Chanel when her husband was shot and she chose black Givenchy for the funeral. Less than six months later, Paris honoured her late husband by changing the name of Quai de Passy, running along the Seine, to Avenue du Président Kennedy.

I'd stayed in Passy as a teenager and delighted in the voluptuous apartment buildings there, with their grandiose domes and feminine curves, but I'd missed the more modern elements of the district's architecture (possibly because I've tended to ignore anything newish when it comes to the arts for most of my life; most of my favourite books, for instance, were penned — or plumed — centuries ago). But, as Andy explained, Passy is a place of pilgrimage for architects the world over. Peppered with examples of modern design, it stands out from the rest of classic Paris, probably because its wealthy inhabitants have by and large been powerful enough to bend building codes, or bulldoze eighteenth-century country manors and erect architectural odes to modernity in their place.

Just around the corner from the Président Kennedy train station is the famous Castel Béranger apartment building, from 1895, by Hector Guimard, the guy who designed the city's various metro entrances, all sinuous and leafy-hued. Guimard was France's leading architect of Art Nouveau style, with its feminine, flowery inspiration, which is why Castel Béranger is decorated with a swirling wrought-iron door, and various other flourishes glazed in green. Far from the uniform harmony of Haussmann's buildings, 'Castel Dérangé' (as it was known by detractors) is a mish-mash of materials, making for a mélange of colours and textures. There's something both madcap and magical about it. 'Now this kind of modern I could do,' I said.

'Except it wasn't that modern,' replied Andy. Art Nouveau means new art but as Andy explained, it wasn't anything truly groundbreaking, more a revival of the trend for decorative exterior embellishments, which is why it didn't last. 'It didn't adapt to modern times.'

The French state, I later read, sponsored the arts and crafts industry in the 1890s — protecting small business just like it does to this day — which directly led to the flowering of Art Nouveau, with its intricately carved and decorated details. But it was ultimately too much of an interior style to work out in the big bad world, when the era of mass production was looming like a huge concrete block. Paris might have been able to save her *épiciers* and *chocolatiers*, but many artisans and craftsmen didn't make it out of Atget's ghostly otherworld.

'I just don't get why Modernism must equate to minimalism,' I sighed.

'It's essentially about refinement and using new materials and building methods,' said Andy. 'Moving with the times. Heard of that concept?'

I admittedly, and happily, cling to trappings of the past — velvet sofas and crystal-adorned lamps and floral-etched crystal glasses that have a familiarity, even if they haven't been in the family for generations, because they seem to transport you back into the comfort of a known time, not forward into an unknown future. I'd fashioned my apartment into a time capsule of sorts. Every time I walked through my door, I felt like I'd retreated into a rose-carpeted cocoon. I'm sure a Freudian analyst would have something to say about a subliminal urge to go back to the womb. But for me, it was more about creating a sanctuary. A home, I've long felt, should be a shrine to a life, to a family, filled with objects that hold memories, make your heart smile, remind you of your place in the world. And I think that's why I mistrust Modernism. It wipes the slate clean, which begs the questions: Why do you want to forget the past? What have you got to hide?

Swiss-French architect Le Corbusier, who hit his career stride in the 1920s, was the father of Modernism, with his love of concrete and geometric forms. His name fills me with horror, quite frankly, for his (thankfully unsuccessful) plans to raze the Marais and construct a grid of superhighways and sixty-storey glass towers. For Andy, however, as for most architect types, he was nothing short of genius. One of Le Corbusier's pioneering works, the Villa La Roche, in Passy, is open for public visits; tucked down the end of a quiet lane, where the unsuspecting would be little prepared for what lies ahead. Built in the early 1920s for a banker who required a suitable showcase for his Cubist art collection, Villa La Roche is essentially a white cube — concrete rendered ivory — with a whole lot of space within, around and through which units of rooms are geometrically arranged. The walls are bare, the furniture barely there. Again, it's about what's not there as much as what is — the very definition of minimal.

'Now, this is my dream home,' declared Andy.

'This is my nightmare,' I thought to myself.

If we were ever going to end up living together, we were headed for some interesting décor discussions, which we mulled over that evening at Kong, a restaurant perched on top of an inner-city Haussmannian building that looks every bit like a glass spaceship, and its décor like something from the canteen of an intergalactic cruising spaceship of the future. It was the vision of the interior and industrial designer Philippe Starck, who shot to fame when Mitterand commissioned him in the early 1980s to furnish a private apartment at the Élysée Palace; ever since, he's made a career out of his 'philosophy of the less'.

'There's a way you can meld modern and romantic,' insisted Andy. 'Look at these seats.' We were sitting on Starck's now-famous Ghost chairs, his clear plastic rework of the classic Louis XV armchair, its rococo silhouette streamlined, yet still seductive. True, it was kind of old but new, feminine but masculine … 'Kind of like us in a chair,' I pointed out.

After a blur of cocktails, we decided to sober ourselves up with a late-night stroll, and headed down the Rue de Rivoli. By the time we'd reached the Hôtel de Ville, or town hall, the glacial air had cleared our heads, but the scene had a misty quality to it nevertheless. When you look over to the town hall you can't help but recall Robert Doisneau's famous black-and-white photograph *The Kiss*. Taken in 1950, for a *Life* Magazine special on 'Love in Paris', the iconic image shows a couple pausing in front of a café for a heart-stopping embrace that seems to freeze everything around them, so that little else matters but that natural expression of affection. Few photographs so exquisitely capture the spontaneity of emotion that Paris can induce.

Not everything, however, is what it seems. *The Kiss*, which appears to be a quintessential example of documentary street photography, was set up (although at least the models were an actual couple). *C'est la vie*, as the French might say with a nonchalant shrug, as rational as they are romantic. The fairy-tale castle of a building, too, while we're here, is a remake. The original sixteenth-century town hall went up in flames around the same time the Tuileries Palace perished, but the authorities decided to immediately rebuild such an historic institution and symbol of civic power, and retain its elaborate Renaissance château allure, with its turreted roofline and sculpture-encrusted façade.

The town hall was dramatically illuminated to Gothic effect that night, evocative of all the grotesque drama that has played out on the square before it. Once named Place de Grève (river bank), in reference to its Seine-side location, this was where unemployed labourers and potential employers met to negotiate daily work, transactions that could all too easily descend into rowdiness — which is how *grève* came to assume its more common contemporary definition of 'strike'. For centuries, this was also the scene of public executions, and crowds flocked to cheer as supposed sorceresses and various other villains were burned at the stake, broken on the wheel or decapitated by guillotine.

Like so many places in Paris, however, it's difficult to reconcile the then and now, a gruesome past and a beautiful present. We stood by the flood-lit ice-skating rink, watching black-clad, beret-topped couples glide by, holding gloved hands and occasionally stopping to kiss, as though in their own personal Doisneau shoot. It was picture-perfect, like a scene from a movie. However, we decided against joining in; skating after several martinis hardly seemed a wise move, especially on a site where blades have already inflicted their fair share of damage.

Early on the last day of the year, only hours before we crossed over into 2009, Andy and I set out for Pont Neuf, a bridge that also passes from old to new. Completed in 1606, it was the first stone bridge in Paris, paving the way for a novel, yet classic and enduring, architectural tone, and it was also the first structure to connect both banks. But it brought the city together in other aspects, by featuring wide footpaths — another first — that allowed for Parisians of all walks of life — aristocrats to acrobats, preachers to prostitutes, booksellers to bootblacks — to mingle. Alcoves running down the length of each side, instead of the usual strips of houses, enabled couples to coo admiringly at the riverscape, as they still do to this day.

We turned at the equestrian statue of King Henri IV, and descended a narrow flight of stairs to the Square du Vert-Galant, a term that doesn't directly translate into English, but more or less means 'Old Charmer', in homage to Henri himself, who was quite the ladies' man: of such rugged masculinity that he was forgiven his stale-smelling skin and bad breath, said to reek of goat and garlic respectively. Within the cobbled 'square', which takes the tapered shape of the tip of the Île de la Cité, is a triangular garden, one of the city's loveliest spots. In spring, its whimsical mix of trees — maples and walnuts, hornbeams and horse chestnuts, silver lindens and lilacs — come vibrantly and fragrantly alive. Winter doesn't quite do the park justice, although it does have an alluring, shadowy Atget-ness to it. At the very end of the island, a delightful weeping willow spreads its canopy of leaves like a filigree parasol. I've spent countless hours sitting in its shade, admiring the view as though on the prow of a boat, anchored to my happy place.

Too cold to linger, too weary to walk any longer, we bought tickets for a river tour. A suited attendant was on hand to greet us cordially and help us on board, his Gallic gallantry as much innate as a requirement of his job. Gallantry has major history in this city. Henri IV, that old Vert-Galant, and a poetry-citing, chivalry-minded Renaissance man, might have got the party started, but it was his grandson, Louis XIV, the Sun King, who refined it to a true art form. A dashing twenty-three-year-old when crowned, Louis was partial to dancing, and to surrounding himself with beautiful people and pleasant conversation. *Galant* originally meant courteous, and Louis' style of *galanterie* was a continuation of the courtly ways of knights and troubadours: flawlessly cultivated manners, unerring politeness to others, especially social inferiors — women included. A stickler for etiquette, Louis was nevertheless willing to bend rigid court rules if it meant stopping a lady from slipping on the parquet floor, or allowing a pregnant woman to sit in his regal presence.

It was all well and good in theory, but over time the aristocrats became blasé in the gilded cage of Versailles, and gallantry degenerated into debauchery: a pursuit of pleasure over politeness, a game of seduction rather than a way of life. Then came the raucous Regency, the era that redefined gallantry for the eighteenth century. The fun-loving Philippe II, Duke of Orléans, acted as regent for the future Louis XV for only eight years, but he made the most of his time in power. Philippe was a work-hard-play-harder type of guy, who turned the Palais-Royal — his Parisian headquarters — into a party palace every evening, hosting all-night candle-lit suppers for a flurry of rouged actresses and free-thinking friends. He was the very epitome of libertine — liberated in mind, body and soul.

We floated under the Pont des Arts, dotted with couples whose arms were interlinked as tightly as the glistening padlocks beside them. Passion in Paris is now a very public affair, with unabashed displays of affection, because gender relations, at least in the realm of love, are balanced; men and women equally hold the keys to their own locks. But for a long time, gallantry was a man's world. A *femme galante* wasn't gallant in the default sense — she was an 'easy women', many rungs down the ladder of social acceptability. And pity the man who tumbled to her level, like the Chevalier des Grieux from the cautionary 1731 novel *Manon Lescaut.*

Our boat passed by Quai Voltaire, which pays tribute to the famed intellectual, who was very much a ladies' man, but more a student of the earlier, gentlemanly school of gallantry (in his 1764 *Philosophical Dictionary*, Voltaire practically tut-tutted that a modern gallant had a certain 'impudence and effrontery'). The embankment is one of my favourite riverside strips, because its beautiful buildings — classic stone Paris at her grandest, atop wood-fronted ground-floor shops selling artwork and antiques — belie the kind of behind-doors goings-on that would have had François Boucher (the rococo artist whose work doubled as the Libertines' preferred soft-core porn of his day) in ecstasy.

For starters, there were all the nude muses whom Pradier sculpted, Ingres painted and Baudelaire swooned over. Also, along there lived five blush-cheeked beauties, the celebrated de Mailly-Nesle sisters, four of whom became mistress to King Louis XV — a man who graduated with honours from the later school of gallantry. The king's obsession with the sisters was eventually curbed by his head mistress Madame de Pompadour, although his irrepressible libertine spirit saw him continue through a succession of flings, including one with Marie-Louise O'Murphy, who shot to notoriety when Boucher painted her sprawled naked on a sinful sofa.

There's not much left of the old Hôtel de Mailly-Nesle, although its 'gold room', in which the king and a sister often nestled, is still somewhere up in the Rue de Beaune wing, looking over Le Voltaire, a restaurant that dates back to the same era. Le Voltaire, incidentally, is famous for its *oeuf mayo* — a plate of crudités and mayonnaise-smothered hard-boiled eggs — which is somewhat fitting, seeing as the yolky sauce was concocted in honour of Duc de Richelieu, the scheming friend of the king and the Mailly-Nesle sisters, after his prowess during the Battle of Port Mahon.

The duke was a rake of the first order. In his time, he would have been labelled a *roué*, a man so dissolute that he deserved to be strung to the wheel (*la roue*) — and not the Ferris variety, but the kind once installed on the Place de Grève. His countless liaisons involved an affair with the Mailly-Nesle sisters' mother — who fought her sister-in-law in a duel over him — and his devious seduction strategies included dressing as a chambermaid and lurking in underground passages. Little wonder the duke was the inspiration for the Vicomte de Valmont, the scheming, manipulating libertine antihero of the novel *Dangerous Liaisons*, which was the Parisian *succès de scandale* of 1782.

Our boat cruised as far as the Eiffel Tower, before turning to head back upstream. Andy and I had sat happily in silence most of the ride, soaking in the scenery as much as one another's presence. It's the calm, quiet moments that speak volumes in relationships, those times when you don't feel a desperate need to fill in the blank spaces; you're not fretting over what he might be thinking, because you can read his mind like an open book — and it's not a book of the *Dangerous Liaisons* variety.

I'd met my fair share of latter-day Valmonts in the party town that is Sydney. It was part of the reason I'd been on a self-imposed dating hiatus. I was no Madame de Tourvel, mind you, but I was no game-player either. If a relationship wasn't going to be smooth sailing from the start, I wasn't interested in hopping on board.

In the *bouquinistes* you can often find reproductions of the *Carte de Tendre*, or the *Map of Tenderness*. The illustration, famous in France, was first published in *Clélie*, a 1650s romance in ten volumes, by Madeleine de Scudéry, one of the leading *salonnières* of the era. These were the early days of gallantry when men, inspired by their courtly king, would delicately air-kiss the gloved hands of ladies in salons, where etiquette required immaculate manners at all times. Gallantry was a genius invention for aristocratic males: politeness to inferiors appeared to rebalance inequality, yet in reality it kept those very inferiors happily in their place. Everyone won. Some say that gallantry is why feminism has never truly taken off in France; women already feel special enough.

Mademoiselle de Scudéry was the star of a circle of aristocratic, intelligent women known as the *Précieuses*. They were content to luxuriate in their femininity, in their contrast to men, to be treated as delicate gems, to wear flouncy dresses and speak in frilly prose (for which they were mercilessly ridiculed by the press), but in their own way they were early feminists, because they saw their difference as strength. Highly self-aware (as much EQ as IQ), many *Précieuses* authored books (determined to control their own life plotline as much as possible), they discussed the radical notion that a female brain could be as switched-on as a man's, and they believed that love should be an equally balanced affair.

The *Map of Tenderness* was a joint project of the *Précieuses* and no doubt designing it made for hours of fun and gossip over tea and cake. But for all its whimsy, the map is surprisingly rational. I mean, it charts a course to true love — a practical guide for surely one of the rockiest quests in life. For the *Précieuses*, *l'amour* was above all about *la tendresse*, of which there are three types, and three respective routes. To arrive at Tenderness Upon Recognition, a man can make his way to a woman's heart with a long journey through towns like Small Cares and Friendship. Tenderness Upon Esteem, on the other hand, can be reached via the villages of Love Letters, Generosity and Goodness. But the shortest journey to love is to breeze down the River of Inclination, from New Friendship direct to Tenderness Upon Inclination, a town spread equally across the two banks. Because if you're each inclined towards the other, love comes together easily and quickly. You don't even need to buy flowers. A Parisian jaunt might help things along, though.

'I think we live well together,' said Andy, out of the blue.

'Even in my pink apartment?'

'I was just thinking about how nice it's been to start afresh in a way, over here. I mean, maybe we should think about finding a place of our own, something that suits both of us, when we're back in Sydney.'

'Does that seem a bit quick?' I asked, even though it didn't feel so.

'Well, we're practically living together already … And we're not getting any younger.'

'Make a girl feel good, why don't you!'

'No … I just meant that maybe we should talk about the long-term soon …' Andy looked a little flustered.

'You're not trying to propose, are you?' I teased.

'Well, no … Maybe. I mean, I just think we should talk about it soon.'

I reached for his hand and grinned. 'Yep, we should.'

People tend to assume I'm a misty-eyed romantic, given said pink apartment and my adoration of floral dresses, to which I was clinging even now, albeit worn over thermals, skivvies and boots. But in reality, I've grown into a realist over time, and it had been years since I'd fantasised about a wedding proposal. I decided, some time in my late twenties, that I didn't want the traditional down-on-knees, will-you-marry-me affair. I needed to play an equal part in the scene that would so drastically alter my life direction, to have an equal voice in that discussion.

The French don't have a 'heart-to-heart' conversation; for them it's a *tête-à-tête* — a head-to-head. And that makes so much sense to me. In love, you need to think clearly, make sure you're headed in the right direction. Because ultimately it's as simple as this: are you both equally inclined? If so, hop on that boat to Tenderness.

&

Andy and I had both had our fill of rowdy New Year's Eve celebrations followed by fuzzy mornings-after, and we wanted to kick off a fresh year with a clear head. A *nouveau départ*, say the French, which translates as 'new beginning', although it literally means 'new departure'. Which seemed much more apt, because we'd reached an age where you can't start all over again, wipe the slate squeaky-clean. You are the sum total of your years and experience, and you lug around with you various backpacks and totes stuffed heavy with emotion. Maybe in your twenties you can voyage around the world unburdened by hang-ups and cumbersome suitcases, but comes an age when you no longer travel light. Still, new adventures — and departures — are an opportunity to repack your bags, to lighten the emotional load by leaving a few fears or paranoias behind.

It felt only right to mark our new year in a way only possible in this city: by the Eiffel Tower. After a cosy dinner at a low-key local restaurant, we wished our fellow dinners (elderly couples who smiled at us with nostalgia, and made us feel happily young in turn) *une bonne année* and set off along the Seine. The ripples in the river danced by the lights of the dinner cruise boats, flashing garnet and gold, and up to our left, the windows of apartment buildings beamed bright, glamorous glimpses into soirées where men in black and women in red linked arms and clinked *coupe* glasses. The whole world was partying and then there was us, forging ahead towards our *nouveau départ*, a little emotional luggage on hand, a bottle of champagne in my handbag. We popped it just as the tower erupted into a similar frenzy of golden sparkle, and time once again seemed to shimmer suspended, like a bubble in a glass or a glitter particle in a snowdome, in a moment of perfect, scintillating sweetness.

Towards the end of our stay, after a fortnight of playing at Parisian domesticity, we were randomly invited to a cocktail party, and so had the chance to see how couples there really lived. I spent the afternoon fretting about a hostess gift. I'd read to never take flowers (this necessitates the hassle of her having to, one, locate a vase in which to then, two, arrange them), nor alcohol (too presumptuous, as she would have already carefully selected her *vins*) and that chocolate was a sure bet — as long as it was the just-so brand. (I was far from literate in the hidden codes of the language of Parisian *chocolaterie*, so after taking a deliciously dizzying chocolate-tasting tour of Saint-Germain, I ended up back at Debauve & Gallais for a gift box.) I'd also heard to never, ever arrive on time to a soirée; fifteen minutes after the official start is, apparently, the actual start. I spent the extra time anxiously tying and retying my scarves (the indoor one and the outdoor one), and working myself into a state of literal knots. I still had, I realised, much to learn about Parisian ways.

In the end, the nerves were unnecessary. The party turned out to be peopled with more expatriates than locals, which somehow made it feel familiar, and diluted the formality a more French affair might have had. Our hostess — a glamorous Parisienne swathed in satin and Shalimar — took our gift (with a nod that I decided to interpret as impressed) and led us to a couple in the corner: Lizzie, an Australian, working in advertising, and Aaron, an American, in the wine industry. We soon discovered they had met only a few months before, and had just moved in together.

'It's so nice to finally feel like this is home,' Lizzie said. 'We spent hours scouring the flea markets and furnishing our apartment to be like the perfect blend of us.'

'Where did you buy?' I asked, trying to contain my envy.

'Oh, we're just renting,' she answered. Most Parisians do, she added, explaining that the laws favour tenants in France, and the French have an obsession with keeping their household debt low. 'It gives them more freedom to live their lives.'

'After all, the English word mortgage comes from the French words for death and pledge,' pointed out Aaron. 'It's seen here as a life sentence.'

'That cherished *liberté* of theirs,' I said.

'Are they really so free though?' asked Andy. 'I mean, it seems like a very constrained society.'

'The French are fascinating,' said Aaron. 'They look quite conservative for the most part, and there are all of these codes of behaviour that take ages to learn. But at the same time, there's a rebellious streak to them, too. They don't like to be told what to do.'

'They like to bring out their rock & roll side from time to time,' added Lizzie. 'You know, break the speed limit, smoke, have affairs.'

'Is it really just a myth about the French and their endless affairs?' asked Andy.

'There's definitely more of an openness to relationships here,' said Lizzie. 'I mean, it's not uncommon for partners who have kids to not be married.'

'But it's the city of *l'amour*,' I said, in mock horror.

'Yes, but the French don't believe a ring makes a relationship last,' she replied. 'Wedding rings feel like locks to them, like the trashy ones on the Pont des Arts. Not romantic, but restraining.'

'Does that mean I'm saved the cost of an engagement ring?' Andy asked me with a laugh.

'So, I know I'm pretty modern when it comes to matrimony …' I was saying to Andy on our last evening in Paris. Earlier that day, I'd explained why I could never change my surname, 'even if your surname was fabulous and French, and I could be Mrs de la Belle, or the like.' 'But I do think diamonds are a lovely way to celebrate an engagement.' We were circling Place Vendôme, peering into the windows at the *haute joaillerie* on display, just as I had done several years before, back when the thought of commitment left me cold. Andy looked a little pale under the black sky, glittering with its own galaxy of gemstones. 'Don't worry,' I added.

'I have simple tastes when it comes to jewellery. Cocktails, on the other hand, are another matter.'

We walked over to the Hôtel Ritz, under the gleaming-white balloon awnings and up the red-carpeted stairs, into the golden-aired foyer, along the famous vitrine-lined shopping corridor dating back to 1913, right down to Bar Hemingway at the Rue Cambon end. Ernest Hemingway, it must be noted, could be found in many a watering hole around the world, but the Ritz was one of his most cherished, which is why the hotel honoured him in this way. He actually drank across the way, in what was the old Cambon Bar, but the cosy Bar Hemingway, with its wooden walls, amber lighting and various Papa paraphernalia, best retains his spirit. With spirit being the operative word, we ordered two martinis, and tried not to wince at the twenty-five-euros-a-pop prices.

The bartender brought over our cocktails, mine garnished with a full-blown lilac rose (Hemingway was as much a lover of women as wine). 'We do this for all our ladies,' he explained. 'Depending on how long you stay, you can leave with your own bouquet.'

So we settled in for the night, working on our floral arrangement. It was one of those gorgeous, glamorous evenings you can only have in Paris, that paradoxical place, where thorns lurk beneath the rosy, fragrant surface, where there's a dark, shadowy flipside to the city of sparkle, a city that has experienced as much misery as joy. The Ritz, too, has had its ups and downs. As Andy explained, the top German soldiers commandeered the hotel during the Second World War, partying with collaborationists until the Allies marched down the Champs-Élysées to liberate the city — while Hemingway and his friends took it upon themselves to emancipate the Ritz, or at least its cellars.

We marvelled that so much of Paris remains intact, given all she has been through, all those bloody revolutions and sieges. Perhaps the closest the city came to annihilation was towards the end of 1944, when Hitler realised he was about to lose his grip on Paris, and eventually the war. Bombs were placed under major landmarks, but a certain General von Cholitz, who didn't want to go down in history as the guy who burned the world's most beautiful city to the ground, managed to stall the demolition plans in time for the Allies to take over.

'Just imagine,' said Andy. 'If that had happened, your precious Paris might now be full of Le Corbusier.'

'Never,' I responded. 'In Paris, beauty always wins out. It's just not the place for such ugliness as concrete cubes or, I don't know, old green army jackets.'

'That old thing? Don't worry. I'm not even taking it home.'

We managed to sweet-talk the man at check-in not to charge us for excess baggage. We'd been attempting to help the French economy and the sales were on — how could we not have shopped? But in many ways, our bags were a lot lighter than I'd expected. Andy had abandoned that jacket, for one. And I'd resisted the floral folding screen I'd rhapsodised over at the Porte de Vanves flea market. ('Remember, we're going to move in together, into neutral territory,' said Andy. 'You promised no more pink sparkle!')

My emotional bags felt lighter, too. I no longer had to be fiercely independent, an only child going it alone. I could share the load of life. The word fiancée — in French as in English — comes from the Latin for trust. And when you completely trust your partner, it's the most liberating of sensations. You're free to keep being yourself, which is what, at my age, I above all craved. Because I might soon marry, but as the French know, a wife is first and foremost still a woman.

On the flight home (on which, to our joy, we were upgraded to business class), I took a sip of champagne only to find it acidify to sour on my tongue. 'How odd,' I thought to myself. 'I can never not drink champagne.' And then a sudden flash: 'Unless ...'

Sure enough, the future Noah was on his way. As Andy said, when we found out for sure: 'We'll always have Paris.'

CHAPTER 9

SUPERFEMME

[sypɛRfam] *nf* superwoman

In which, aged almost forty,
I gain a new perspective on *la vie*.

We eventually got around to organising a wedding, not so much out of a sense of duty or necessity (we already had a baby and a mortgage, both of which felt binding enough), but because it seemed like a lovely thing to do. And it was; marriage, too, although I soon realised I'm not a naturally inclined spouse, with an innate passion for domestic management. Or perhaps as a side effect of marrying later in life I was less mouldable to my new role in life.

My industry, even more so than the institution of matrimony, favoured youth, those with unfettered schedules and enough bright-eyed, bushy-tailed energy to devote to the issue of looking the part and getting ahead. I'd seen many women in my world drop out altogether after moving into motherhood, having decided to reprioritise and rethink their careers. On the other hand, there were those who wanted it all and somehow managed it. These were the two opposing roles that seemed available for someone newly in my life stage: earth mother and superwoman. Many would have thought me perfectly primed to assume the tie-dyed mantle of the former (I practised yoga and ate my weight in lentils daily), but in actual fact I secretly craved the heroic red cape of the latter. Work had defined me for so long, and I was good at my job. Now it felt like I had a new gig, one at which I wasn't particularly adept. I spent many afternoons listlessly pushing the pram around our local park, tears blurring my vision. I couldn't see where I was going, in all senses.

Of course, I did end up back on the work treadmill, and got better at juggling the various curve balls life threw my way. But I was constantly plagued with the fear that I wasn't a particularly wonderful mother. The more I read about parenting, the more I realised there was to learn, and the more I felt I fell short. I was totally aware of the phenomenon of mother guilt, but being able to theorise my emotions didn't allay the reality of them. Still, it didn't stop me from wanting to add to the family.

When a miscarriage put those plans temporarily on hold, life suddenly seemed in free fall, less in control than ever. I felt sick with a hollowing heartache and gut-wrenching guilt; it wasn't a joyful time. 'I think you need to treat yourself to a trip to Paris,' said Andy out of the blue one morning. I'd booked my ticket by lunchtime.

&

The Faubourg Saint-Germain, in the 7th arrondissement, on Paris's Left Bank, is a rarefied world unto itself. A *faubourg* is a suburb, although the word derives from the French for 'false' and 'borough', and it really is like a town within a town, where you feel almost as though you've stepped into a parallel Paris. There's nothing faux about this bourg, though. This is where serious money and power dwell, with Hermès Kelly handbags at every ten paces.

The district flourished in the eighteenth century, when wealthy Parisians abandoned a *démodé* and densely packed Marais for the fresh lands and air to the west of the city. Old Paris was a hodge-podge of people, with aristocrats, shopkeepers, workers and servants living in the same buildings, stratified vertically according to social importance. But as Paris boomed, the city sprawled out, and developed horizontally so that well-to-do types could live without their style being cramped, in grand urban châteaux. Most of these mansions now belong to the government and various foreign embassies, but the area still has a sense of neighbourhood, even if not of the usual picket-fence variety.

I'd chosen to stay there for the vicarious thrill of living somewhere a little la-de-da, but I think, also, I didn't want to simply be a visitor, checking into an obviously touristy part of town. I needed to actually play at being someone else for a couple of weeks, to remove myself completely from the mindset of my usual existence, and its associated stresses. My mother had cleared her diary to come along with me. 'We can pretend we're a Parisian mother and daughter,' she said. 'If we're going to play the part convincingly,' I told her, 'you know you're going to have to finally buy yourself the Chanel jacket you've been talking about for years.'

Our taxi swept along the Seine, glinting in the springtime sunshine, past the National Assembly — whose pre-parliamentary (and pre-colonnaded) life was as the Palais Bourbon, a palace so sumptuous it set the tone for the area — before curving around to Boulevard Saint-Germain, its bristling plane trees filtering through a soft aureate light. We turned off to snake our way around a series of narrow streets, all solemnly lined in beige buildings punctuated by wooden doors painted navy, maroon and jade, the deep hues adding a sense of mystique to what lay behind. On reaching our address, we saw a time-stained stone façade hung with mottled shutters. But we knew Paris well enough by now not to judge a book by its cover. Even the dustiest of jackets can open to reveal flashes of brilliance. Sure enough, once we'd made our way through the black-and-white tiled foyer and chugged up in the wrought-iron lift, we stepped back into the halcyon heyday of Faubourg Saint-Germain, into rooms filled with upholstered Louis XV chairs and dollhouse-pretty tables, the walls covered in paintings of pastoral landscapes, the marble mantelpiece heaving with Chinoiserie and the herringbone floors decorated with Persian rugs.

Paris is a city of hidden delights, a place that only gradually reveals herself to true, and patient, lovers. At first, her discreet ways can prove frustrating. Mansions with high walls and thick doors steadfastly keep the world out and shutter-clad buildings close their gaze to outsiders, just as many locals assiduously avoid eye contact. But I've often wondered if this public wariness, this reticence to connect with strangers, harks back to the Revolution, when you couldn't trust even your neighbour. Parisians, especially in the Faubourg Saint-Germain, kept their heads down and jewels locked up. Being stealthy about their wealth was a life and death matter, so it's little surprise that they instilled a sense of secrecy, a fear of opening up and showing off, in following generations.

Despite having practically invented the luxury industry, the French have a reputation for disdaining money, especially talking about it. It's considered a private matter, one to remain behind closed doors, where it tends to take the form of beautiful objects — just as their ancestors preferred precious metals moulded not into currency, but golden candlesticks and silver coffee pots, items that would hold their value as much as adorn their home. I've always adored this about the French: their preference for filling their homes with treasures rather than their coffers with coins. I've long believed that there's little point having a bulging bank account if the price is a scant existence. At that moment, I was more money-challenged than I'd been in years (a Sydney mortgage and childcare costs will do that), but I'd nevertheless rarely felt richer. As much as the adjustment to my new role of wife and mother had its challenges, I cherished our home, filling it with love, and some pretty furniture, too. Interior riches, in France, equate with inner richness. It's this redefinition of wealth — from the financial to the material and emotional realms — that, I believe, most inspires Francophiles, this rethink of what it means to live a good life.

Around the corner from our apartment, just down from Hôtel Matignon, the opulent mansion now home to the French prime minister, is the building in which American author Edith Wharton resided in the early twentieth century. She was the first in a succession of famous Francophiles to make Paris her home. In her previous life, Wharton had chronicled the showy lifestyles of high society in turn-of-the-twentieth-century New York. Influenced by sociologist Thorstein Veblen, who coined the term 'conspicuous consumption', Wharton gently derided status-seeking behaviour, and the motivating forces of greed and vanity. She was well placed to know about living luxuriously, having been born into the very family that inspired the expression 'Keeping up with the Joneses'. There's no snappy translation of that expression in French, and the concept is not as well defined either, possibly because there's not the same history of *consommation ostentatoire*. The French are, by and large, less flashy, which is probably why Wharton felt so at home in Paris. 'Their thoughts are not occupied with money-making in itself, as an end worth living for, but only with the idea of having money enough to be sure of not losing their situation in life,' wrote Wharton in her delightful 1919 essay *French Ways and Their Meaning*, where she also astutely observed, 'There is nothing like a revolution for making people conservative.'

It's easy enough to imagine the author, with her tailored skirt-suits and ribbon-trimmed hats, striding around the *faubourg*. She had quickly fallen in love with her new city, and was inspired by the Parisians' time-honoured pursuit of pleasure and beauty, as much as their natural stylishness. 'French people "have taste" as naturally as they breathe: it is not regarded as an accomplishment, like playing the flute,' she gushed in awe. And she saw that taste on display at every turn of her head, whether she was out stocking up on gloves or admiring the sculptures at Musée Rodin down the road: 'The artistic integrity of the French has led them to feel from the beginning that there is no difference in kind between the curve of a woman's hat-brim and the curve of a Rodin marble.'

Accessories and art would have to wait a while. Mum and I needed to tend to a more mundane type of taste, and buy groceries. We set out past sparkle-filled antique dealers and bottle shops, designer baby wear boutiques and luxury stationery stores, headily scented *chocolateries* and *fromageries*, eventually reaching the crème de la crème of 7th arrondissement shopping: Le Bon Marché. The first true department store, Le Bon Marché is a shrine to style, where everything seems to be bathed in a golden light, courtesy of the domed glass ceiling above. But it's the food hall next door, La Grande Épicerie, that is the true temple of good taste. We delighted to see olives in colours we didn't even know they came in, bijou bread rolls threaded on sticks, platters of artfully designed hors d'oeuvres, and fruit tarts as glossy and intricate as Cartier brooches. While many Parisians prefer to shop at specialist stores, it's at La Grande Épicerie that the French philosophy of food as a way of life is on dazzling display, and you appreciate that food should be as much a feast for the eyes as the tastebuds, almost too pretty to eat. Only almost …

Back in the apartment, we set the dining table with our various treats, arranged around a ribbon-tied basket of purple hyacinths we had picked up on the way home (for it did already feel like that: *chez nous*), and popped open a bottle of Ruinart Rosé. 'May all our pain be champagne,' I toasted, raising my cut-crystal *coupe*, and soon remembered how lovely life looks through Parisian rosé-tinted glasses.

Nestled above the old stables of the Saint-Germain-des-Prés Abbey is the Musée Delacroix, where the Romantic painter lived and worked in the mid nineteenth century. For an artist celebrated for his larger-than-life masterpieces — sweeping scenes of death and drama — a visit there is a remarkably intimate experience. Scoot up the narrow, glossy wooden staircase, just as Delacroix did before you, and you enter what was once his cosy home, complete with furniture and trinkets. From there, you can amble out the back door to his former studio, which overlooks an oasis of a garden, lovingly planned by Delacroix himself. It's a lesson in perspective, in more ways than one. Everything seems on a human scale. The paintings, even those inspired by religion or literature, somehow have greater authenticity for the compactness of their size. Delacroix himself seems more real, too. One piece of art was telling: a watercolour of three flowers — poppy, pansy and anemone. It was both whimsical and studied, proof that Delacroix — the guy who gave us the overpoweringly iconic *Liberty Leading the People* — saw beauty in the little everyday things, as much as the big momentous ones.

We walked back out through the cobbled entrance, the old stone archway leading onto Place de Furstenberg, surely Paris's quaintest square. The four towering paulownia trees on the island in the middle — surrounding an ornate lamppost grandly holding aloft five globes — were in bloom, and cast a lacy lavender veil overhead. Some of their flowers were floating to the ground, the corollas shaped like long sweeping skirts, rippled at the hem, just as Mrs Wharton might once have worn. In the film adaptation of her 1920 book *The Age of Innocence*, the final, Parisian scene takes place in this very square. Daniel Day-Lewis's Newland Archer, now an old man, decides against visiting Countess Ellen Olenska, the love of his life who got away many years before, leaving him to a socially acceptable, yet passionless, marriage. He slowly walks away, stooped with sadness — perhaps Wharton's punishment for not having followed his heart. She was, when she wrote this, well and truly an honorary and spiritual Parisienne, so it's not surprising she was won over to the cause of living in the moment. Like Delacroix, she knew that true romanticism was not about grandiose, splashy statements but to be found in life's little pleasures, in stopping to smell the roses right under your nose.

We turned a few corners and ended up at Café de Flore, one of those classic institutions you end up visiting over and over when in

Paris. Wharton would surely have approved of its timeless, time-honed traditions, having lauded France for its 'instinctive recoil from the new, the untasted, the untested', the 'preciousness of long accumulations of experience'. She doesn't seem to have frequented the café herself, despite the fact that it was a favourite haunt of writers by the late nineteenth century. Its most famous literary clients, of course, were Jean-Paul Sartre and Simone de Beauvoir, those fearless philosophers, social rebels and lifetime companions. Unlike the Flore, they were intent on trying the new, the untasted and the untested, doing their darnedest to prove that the freedom of their beloved existentialism could extend to relationships, too. Their unconventional love life was surely exciting at the time, but looking back, it's somewhat feeble that such an awesome woman allowed her partner to live up to a tired old libertine cliché. Sure, she was allowed to have affairs, too (why, thanks JP), but her heart was never anywhere near as much in it.

We sat inside, at a table near where the power couple sometimes scribbled and pondered away for hours on end. The red moleskin banquettes and the golden Art Deco mirrors and lighting are still there, and the warm intimacy still makes for the ideal environment in which to shine a light on your own inner self, and reflect on the meaning of life and love. The colour therapy also seemed to influence our lunch: gazpacho, tomato salad and a bottle of rosé.

'Did you feel a little let down by Simone de Beauvoir's views on relationships?' I asked Mum, who was avidly reading the French philosopher in her early twenties, as she was settling down with my father. Surely de Beauvoir's feminist interpretation of the patriarchal system Mum was about to enter must have been somewhat confusing.

'You know, I do remember feeling disappointed. Her relationship with Sartre seemed so contrived. Freedom and equality don't have to mean the right to see other people. What might have been radical was if they'd found a way to make marriage work for modern times.'

I observed that she and Dad had done pretty well with the experiment of modern marriage. 'The key, for me, is to rethink freedom,' Mum said, after a few thoughtful moments. 'I don't believe it's about complete independence; any relationship has strings attached but that doesn't have to be a negative thing. It's about how long those strings are. Your father and I have always kept busy, and kept up our own interests, which has given us room to breathe. Your partner should encourage you to be the person you want to be.'

'You know, part of me wonders if it's ideal to find your life partner at a young age. You're less set in your ways so you can both grow in the same direction.'

My mother nodded. 'It's a good theory. But it's not easy to know who's right for you when you're young. Your father and I were lucky. I'm sure if I'd married anyone else, I'd be divorced by now. There weren't many men in those days who would have been happy to let me have the career I've had.'

I'd recently read that divorce rates in France were even higher than those in Australia (which were daunting enough). This surprised me for some reason. Perhaps my idealism of the French automatically paints them as happier than the rest of the world.

'Modern marriage, where both partners work and share chores equally, doesn't suit a lot of guys — I suspect traditional French men, too,' mused Mum. 'Remember, feminism didn't evolve here to the extent it did in Australia, and perhaps men are clinging to the old head-of-the-household notion. Although a lot of macho Australian types would still be adjusting, too — luckily, your father was always happy to do his share of cooking and child-rearing.'

'I guess I'd assumed that French marriages were much more relaxed. They don't have the big overwhelming white weddings that we do, mostly just their small civil ceremonies.'

'Well, civil marriage is still an institution,' Mum noted. 'And don't forget that the French have a history of rebelling against institutions.'

But then, of course, the French also have a history of falling back into neat line, revering harmony and order. Perhaps then, they want freedom, but within certain limits — romance, within reason. While divorce might have been on the rise, so too were the so-called PACS, the civil unions introduced for gay couples, but taken to with gusto by straight duos, too. A French civil union is straightforward to establish, and to dissolve; while you're in it, you enjoy most of the financial and legal benefits that marriage would confer. This might not sound romantic, but maybe it's the modern type of marriage that balances the dual nature of the French: their reverence for tradition and their yearning for freedom. Because, remember, they don't need a huge romantic wedding, some spectacle worthy of a Delacroix canvas. They love the small and intimate, as the painter did himself. Because life's not about the big picture so much as the smaller details: the simple pleasures of the everyday, of smelling the roses, of sitting down with loved ones and eating juicy tomatoes or drinking sweet, silky rosé.

&

For a city of people who seek pleasure in all things, beauty is, not surprisingly, of utmost importance there, and it was in Saint-Germain that the obsession with living well, in every way, arguably originated. Saint-Germain, by the way, has none of next door's *faubourg*-ness about it. For me, it's the very essence of urban Paris, distilled, because it has housed such a cross-section of Parisians over the centuries, from pupils to preachers, philosophers to fashion designers, authors to artists. It was where Parisian shopping as we know it took form, back in medieval times at the Saint-Germain fair, and it was where coffee was first served in public, helping to energise conversation and enlighten pre-revolutionary minds.

It was also there, in the seventeenth century, that the various arts institutions were established, including the Académie d'Architecture, which set in stone, literally, the city's new classically inspired style. Around the same time, height restrictions were imposed, and the traditional pitched gable roof was banned, leading the way for the elegant mansard roof to become a quintessential emblem of Paris forevermore. Saint-Germain is home to some of the city's most whimsical rooflines, slanted every which way, dormer windows jutting out, others embedded like cut stones. Just as every Parisienne seems to know how to carry off a beret, adding her own touch — angled this way or that, accessorised with a brooch perhaps — so, too, does a Parisian building wear its crown with particular panache.

The Academy of Architecture eventually merged with those of painting, sculpture and music, and, as a school, came together under one (ironically rather flat) roof, the École des Beaux-Arts, which is located on Rue Bonaparte. 'I love how the French say beautiful arts, not fine arts,' I remarked to Mum, as we stopped by the gate, which has welcomed the likes of Delacroix, Ingres and Degas, watching the new generation of scruffy-faced guys and messy-haired girls pass by. 'It must remind creatives that their purpose is to beautify their environment, not be too crazy or irreverent.'

I pointed out, just to the right, an old church that was not quite what it seemed. The ornate façade, in actual fact, was tacked on later, having been ripped off the Château d'Anet, to the west of Paris. If you look amid the tiers of columns, you'll see the interlinked initials H and D, the insignia of King Henri II and his mistress, Diane de Poitiers, one of the most celebrated beauties in French history. And here's where the story gets juicier: the church behind these bold declarations of love was commissioned by Henri's daughter Marguerite (of *La Reine Margot* fame), who lived on this site in the early 1600s. No, the princess didn't have Diane's château destroyed as payback for breaking the heart of her mother (Catherine de Medici, who was hopelessly, unrequitedly in love with her husband). Rather, it is one of those quirky twists of only-in-Paris history. Before the city's premier fine arts school moved in, this was the site of the Museum of French Monuments, established to house various treasures displaced during the Revolution — one of which turned out to be a frontispiece from Diane's old château. You couldn't make this up.

This one slice of Paris alone serves up everything I love about this city: the history is so deliciously rich, it has more layers than a *mille-feuille* pastry, and the stories are so intricately interwoven over time that if they were threads, they would create a tapestry to rival the finest Gobelins. Nothing is what it seems — and it's usually more wonderful. No matter where you turn, you're always two degrees, possibly one, away from a story so fabulous it should be made into a movie. Paris might have mostly been built by men, but Parisiennes are her soul and spirit, infusing every stone with their stories.

Most of Marguerite's palace — once spread sumptuously over the old fields (*prés*) of Saint-Germain — has long gone, but her presence gave the district a megawatt jolt of vitality, making it the place to be. One of the first of the glamour-set to build there, in 1608, Marguerite filled her home with music, parties, ballet, fashion and conversation. Her life, up to this point, had followed the plotline of a Gothic novel: a passionate, sensual, gorgeous heroine born into a diabolical family who abused her in most ways imaginable. Married against her wishes, the naturally free spirit spent much of her life on the run — or held in captivity, like a caged exotic bird. When, finally, she was free to live back in her beloved Paris as an independent woman, she thrived. One of Marguerite's favourite poets was friend Pierre de Ronsard, he of the mantra 'Gather the roses of life today' — and she was determined to make the most of the rest of her days, taking time to both gather those roses, and smell them, too.

But even before Marguerite had set a dainty-slippered foot on the fields of the Left Bank, her father's lover, Diane de Poitiers, another connoisseur of all things beautiful, had fallen for its charms. Her city residence could be found a few blocks away from where Marguerite would settle, in the Cour de Rohan, a picture-perfect cluster of three ivy-dripping, bloom-bursting courtyards. The space is locked these days, theoretically for the use of private residents only, but loiter a little and you'll eventually be able to slip through one of the swinging grille gates. Then, wander over the cobbles, through to the middle courtyard, and look up — you'll see a red brick building, patterned with cream stones and topped with a high-pitched black-slate roof, giving off a pretty provincial air, which is further enhanced by the tumble and jumble of flowering plants. So romantic is the scene that you almost expect Diane to poke her lovely head out and sing for the gorgeousness of her life. When Henri built this love nest for his mistress, in 1550, it was a new look for the medieval city — yet to be standardised in pale stone — and it gives you an idea of the exquisite tastes of Madame de Poitiers.

Diane was, stylistically, light years ahead of her era. When other women were wearing splashy gem-encrusted gowns in bright jewel hues, Diane stuck to black and white, which beautifully set off her luminous complexion. Unlike her contemporaries, she didn't paint or powder her face. Her secret to flawless skin and rosy cheeks was a zealous wellbeing routine that involved plunging herself in cold baths every morning, drinking gallons of broth, taking regular exercise, and having early nights. Her discipline paid off; she was acknowledged as the most beautiful woman in the realm — if not the life of the party. But Diane had reason to work hard at her beauty routine: she was twenty years older than the king. She might have appeared the poster girl for ageing gracefully, but the abounding rumours about magic potions were partly true. In 2009, forensic experts examining her newly discovered bones found excessively high levels of gold and mercury, evidence that Diane regularly ingested a liquid gold brew of some kind, doubtless in the belief that it would ignite a glow from within.

Parisian women, I've come to learn, no longer resort to drastic measures in the pursuit of physical beauty, but some of their other anti-ageing tricks are remarkably Diane-esque: they regularly visit spas for the rejuvenating properties of fresh mineral-rich water; they walk as much as possible; they consume soup like it's going out of fashion … Generally, they look after themselves, and don't overdo things. There's a commonly held French view that feeling great is the most effective way to look your best, all through life. This doesn't, however, mean they don't zealously fight the hands of time. Any visit to a *pharmacie* — jam-packed with bottles of vitamin-powered potions and beautiful Parisiennes alike — will attest to this. But a good skincare ritual, according to French women, is as much about a pampering excuse as the antioxidant powers. Beauty is not pain in France. Commitment and self-control, sure. But pain, *non*.

From my numerous interviews with Paris-based beauty experts, I've also gauged that French women aren't as scared of ageing as Australian women seem to be. *La beauté n'a pas d'âge* (Beauty doesn't have an age) is a common French expression, and there's something so glamorous about the idea of *une femme d'un certain âge*, also a familiar phrase, and one that just doesn't have the same *je ne sais quoi* in English.

'Have you noticed how many women here don't look as though they've had work done?' I commented to Mum, as we approached the 7th arrondissement, an area in which you might expect to see skin as smooth and timeless as Hermès silk.

'I definitely don't feel as old as I sometimes do in Sydney,' remarked Mum, 'where you can feel out of date for not doing botox.' Now, my mother is no slouch in the complexion department — her facialist is programmed into her phone on speed-dial, and her beauty cabinet puts even mine to shame. But Mum has, with every year and new wrinkle, adhered fast to her no-knives-no-needles policy, no matter how much such invasive procedures come to be commonly considered just another component of skincare.

'I much prefer the *au naturel* way in which French women age,' added Mum. But this, I've come to discover, is not quite true. France loves to have the rest of the world think its women don't succumb to plastic surgery, that the facial exercising that comes with French vowel pronunciation is firming enough, and that everything else can be fixed with a good haircut. Truth is, while facelifts might be falling from favour, as they are in many countries, zaps and jabs (both fillers and freezers) are reported to be as common there as anywhere else. After all, it was a French man who invented the term plastic surgery, in 1798 (inspired by the Greek word for moulding: *plastikos*). A little over a century later, a French woman, plastic surgeon Suzanne Noël, would become the pioneer of the 'mini-lift', a less-is-more approach that has become the bedrock of anti-ageing philosophy in France.

'I feel like, in Sydney, there's this pressure to be ageless — it's hard to tell if some women are thirty or fifty,' I said. 'Here, it's more about looking good for your age than not your age at all. Coco Chanel once said something like, nature gives you the face you have at twenty, life shapes the face you have at thirty, but at fifty you have the face you deserve. But that's not necessarily the case anymore, because there are so many tricks for cheating nature.'

I was, at that point, at a beauty crossroads. I'd gone as far as creams and serums alone would take me — and I could continue on that road to natural ageing, but it was fast going downhill, with potholes and bumps to boot. Or, I could take a sharp right and hit the superhighway of anti-ageing — with its smooth, new surface, yet regular, and exorbitantly priced, toll stations. I'd ignored the turn-offs to it for years, but as life became busier, its various stresses mapping themselves out on my face, I was increasingly favouring the short-cut high-tech approach to looking my best.

'But beauty has never been an even playing field,' shrugged Mum. 'Just like life, really. And as with life, you have to pick your battles. You can't have it all, at least not at the same time, and you'll never be happy until you accept this. So beauty, for me, is a case of, which battles do I really need to fight? And right now, I don't have time or energy to add anything extra to my beauty routine, without it taking away from my other routines, like seeing friends or reading or working.'

Only my mother could look at beauty as an issue of opportunity cost. But then again, beauty is very much about economics, something of which Suzanne Noël was well aware. The surgeon was also a fierce suffragist, which isn't so remarkable in itself (after all, only in paradoxical Paris can femininity and feminism not be mutually exclusive), nor should it shock that she didn't challenge what could be perceived as a patriarchal definition of beauty in the first place (there were too many other fights for women to take on at the time, such as the right to vote). What's really fascinating is that Noël's motivating factor was her resolute belief that women would better compete in the workplace if they looked younger and fresher. In this, her pragmatism was radically innovative; over a century later, studies prove that the beautiful are more highly paid and regularly promoted. Life was full of battles for Noël, too, and beauty, for her, was a potent weapon — so why not use it?

French women, of course, also know that they're supporting a major local industry every time they swipe on a Lancôme lipstick or massage in a Guerlain cream. Beauty, which has many definitions in Paris, is, above all, big business. And let's not forget that the French economy is boosted by the worldwide myth that Parisiennes, of all ages, are the most elegant earthlings of all, beauty lore that can be traced back to the days of Diane de Poitiers. Four hundred years on from the original *femme d'un certain âge*, another woman famous for wearing black and white, Coco Chanel, would further embellish the myth of eternally beautiful Parisiennes. 'You can be gorgeous at thirty, charming at forty,' she proclaimed, 'and irresistible for the rest of your life.'

&

'What would be the possibility of the ability to have my omelette served without the presence of ham?' We were ordering breakfast at a local café and I realised that, in overcompensation for my rusty French, my language had not only reverted to textbook formality, but in trying to be so proper and polite, it had ascended to the realm of the abstract.

But I love French for its abstractions — its reverence for notions such as liberty, love, pleasure, grandeur. It's an idealistic language, one refined in the seventeenth century, the time of classicism, and like the architecture of that period, it so stylishly and neatly packages up the often messy human condition. No wonder French was the language of diplomacy for so long; it has both a simplicity and grandiosity to it. The nitty-gritty has been abstracted away, leaving it clean, calm, ordered and harmonious — and a touch mysterious. Some say that French is too impersonal, detached, vague and lofty, that it hovers too high above reality and talks too nonchalantly, a little about a lot, rather than drilling down into details. But the French love to talk for the sake of talking. Dialogue is not about winning a debate, it's about relishing language, rolling it around the tongue. Perhaps their abstract language allows the French to best deal with life — and who's to say that generalising your outlook isn't the best way to get your head around the complications of the modern world?

Take beauty, for instance. It's technically an abstract noun, although in Australia — or Sydney, at least — it's becoming increasingly concrete: detailed, a cookie-cutter mould in which to pour yourself. Beauty here is subject to continual redefinition, influenced by trends rather than a classic ideal. But, as I see it, beauty remains an abstract concept in France. There's no set, must-try beauty look at any one time. Instead, beauty is malleable, and can be individualised. It's about, simply and yet grandly, looking your best.

Denis Diderot, the philosopher star of the Enlightenment, wrote that ideal beauty was found in abstraction, taking away what is not beautiful rather than selecting what is. Which is precisely what good grooming is about in France: playing down the negative, subtly accentuating the positives. (It's not for no reason that in English we use the French-inspired expression *jolie laide* — pretty ugly — which demonstrates that culture's belief that anyone can be attractive by virtue of making an effort.) Diderot, of course, was referring to a grander kind of art than makeup; but then, this nicely illustrates the point that beauty is a bigger picture in

France. Its definition is wider — encompassing art, food, architecture and more — and perhaps this helps to keep facial beauty in perspective. The business of makeup, skincare and fragrance might have appropriated the designation of beauty, but really, most French industries could be rolled together under this (ruffle-trimmed) umbrella term, such is the national commitment to aesthetics as much as abstractions.

I had just read the best-selling book *The Elegance of the Hedgehog*. It's an exquisitely written, philosophically powered work of literary art that is so very French, reflecting as it does on the nature of such abstract notions as beauty, art and pleasure. Set in a chichi apartment on the well-to-do Rue de Grenelle, also in the 7th, one of its heroines is Renée, the concierge, who conforms to clichés (stout, dense, unkempt) because life is easier for her that way. In reality, however, Renée's shopping bags hide gastronomic treats beneath the turnips, and when she's not cleaning handrails she's ensconced in her back room listening to classical music, reading Tolstoy, savouring white tea and almond tuiles, and musing on the meaning of life. Beneath the hedgehog-like spikiness is a graceful soul who revels in a glorious inner life. Renée proves she has it within to groom herself to physical elegance, but by this time we already see her as a beautiful woman. So, while grooming — abstracting the blemishes — is one definition of beauty in France, it's by no means the only one.

As a beauty writer, I love France's abstract perspective on the subject in which I'm meant to be an expert. Beauty is all around, in all guises in this world, just as there are so many things to see and do and be. As much as I'd long been content to let my job define me, I was coming to realise that my title was in itself too narrow a definition, just as beauty itself should never be boxed in — no matter how prettily packaged.

&

Mum and I set off down Rue de Grenelle, for a day of research. I'd been commissioned to write an article on Parisian perfumeries — Paris and perfume being two of my favourite subjects swirled together in a bow-tied bottle. What I've always loved about classic French fragrance is that, just as certain scents can plunge you back into a specific moment in your past, it offers up an intriguing clue into the psyche of Parisian women, an olfactory subliminal message in a bottle. And there's a fascinating paradox (yet another one!) to Parisian perfume. You might expect it to be exquisitely beautiful — and at first sniff, it usually is — but inhale a little deeper, wait for things to develop, for the diaphanous top notes to dissolve, to undress and reveal their base, and you sense the force of the perfume's true character. It's the inverse of the hedgehog: elegance outside, spikes within; a leather-and-lace lingerie set worn under a classic outfit of blue jeans and white shirt.

Our first stop was the boutique Maître Parfumeur et Gantier — Master Perfumer and Glove Maker — so named in tribute to the original French perfumers, who were also tanners, specialising in leather accessories that had been scented to camouflage the stench of the urine-steeped tanning process. Catherine de Medici, while not considered a beauty, was a stylish trendsetter nonetheless, and fragranced gloves were just one of the phenomena for which she took credit. The 'black queen' had brought with her from Florence a personal perfumer, who conveniently doubled as a poison-maker. His Eau de le Reine, concocted in her honour, fell into the former category of work (fortunately, for both of them). A citrus-based, rosemary-infused perfume water, it must have reminded Catherine of home, and she would have splashed it on partly out of nostalgia, but mostly necessity; scent was, at the time, the only way to mask body odour — both your own and everyone else's. Fancy gloves aside, Parisians reeked. Diane de Poitiers' obsessive commitment to cleanliness was a rarity. Parisians, for the most part, viewed washing as unnecessary at best, unhygienic at worst. It wasn't until the early twentieth century that bathing (and bathrooms) became a regular occurrence in Paris.

It's all relative, of course. And Paris, back then, also stank, so perhaps Parisians' noses were partly inured to noxious smells. Nevertheless, the city was said to be the rankest in all of Europe, with piles of garbage rotting by the side of sewage-streaming roads, until well into the seventeenth century. And when the stink really hit the fan, all Parisians could do was douse themselves in yet more perfume — something that would hold well, that would be adequately heady to mask the funky skin beneath the frilly finery, and oomphy enough to build a protective olfactory shield around the wearer. Not even Queen Catherine's poisoner-slash-perfumer could have formulated a brew as potent as the scents chosen for the job — because black magic has nothing on animalic fragrance.

Animalic? you say … Look, there's no poetic way to spin this, so here goes: musk comes from a gland situated in the nether regions of the musk deer; similarly, civet is a secretion produced in the perineal glands of the catlike animal of the same name; castoreum is what beavers, like civets, use to mark their territory; and ambergris is a faecal mass expelled from the sperm whale. Not for the faint-hearted, in short.

Heavy animalic fragrances went out of fashion after the Revolution, when perfume had a stench about it of aristocratic airs and libertine licentiousness. But animalic notes eventually pawed their way back into perfume bottles — interestingly, particularly once Parisians had started bathing regularly. Was it a subconscious strategy to reconnect with their olfactory heritage, to put back some of the grit that washing had cleansed away? There's a particularly vivid scene in Patrick Süskind's *Perfume*, in which the antihero Grenouille, who has no odour of his own, concocts a human scent for himself, using extracts of cat poo, vinegar, decomposed cheese, rancid sardines and rotten egg, to name a few ingredients, along with castoreum and civet. In a similar way, I imagine modern perfumers finding a somewhat perverse pleasure in lacing their fragrances' base layers with such base ingredients. But it's more than an in-joke. Perfumers know that a few animalic drops not only help to prolong a perfume's power — creating that so-Parisian sillage, the scent trail wafting behind a woman like a long silken scarf — they also imbue fragrance with warmth, depth and sensuality. That's why most classic Parisian scents feature animalic notes (albeit, thankfully, in synthetic form these days) somewhere in the base of their bouquet of beautiful floral or gourmand notes.

Not that most brands will admit to it, mind you. A major fragrance company once threatened to pull its advertising from a magazine I worked for when it heard I was planning to include its top-selling scent in a feature on animalic fragrance. Dirty-edged perfumes are the French fragrance industry's dirty little secret, which I find fascinatingly ironic. Here we are, dousing ourselves in bestial secretions (unwittingly or not), when perfume is meant to be a sign of civilisation, one of the things that separate us from beasts.

If animalic notes are French fragrance's little secret, then French love's *petit secret* is adultery. The aroma of dirty lingerie, so to speak, has long lingered, despite a concerted effort by the nineteenth century to clean things up — with perfume as much as with relationships.

Mum and I had spent much of the day in Musée d'Orsay, and were walking along the *quais*, stopping by the *bouquinistes* to flick through their piles of vintage books. I bought myself a few French classics, including Gustave Flaubert's *Madame Bovary*, the ultimate cautionary tale against adultery. (Read not too much into this, please. I was mostly taken by the illustration of a French woman wearing a beribboned bonnet and furtive look on her lovely pale face.)

We'd only just been admiring Madame herself, in a way. One of the first sculptures you see as you walk into the light-drenched central vault of the Musée d'Orsay is James Pradier's *Sappho*, a marble rendition of the lyric poetess of Ancient Greece. There's a mesmerising swirl of emotions in her stillness, like the ripples of her draped dress, and the meditative melancholy of her finely chiselled features transfixes you to your spot. The model was Pradier's lover, the beautiful Louise Colet, also a prize-winning poetess, and it was in his studio, just down the road on Quai Voltaire, that Colet met, and embarked on a passionate affair with, the up-and-coming author Gustave Flaubert. Like the future Emma Bovary, she was a gushing romantic who had married to escape provincial life but cherished bigger dreams. Flaubert, on the other hand, was very much a realist and, in *Madame Bovary*, he warned of the dangers of living in a fantasy world. Colet was a perfect muse — and also provided literature with one of its steamiest scenes by throwing herself on Flaubert during a bouncing curtain-drawn carriage ride around the Bois de Boulogne.

Flaubert was put on trial for obscenity but, in reality, the women were always punished in matters of adultery. In researching *Madame Bovary*, Flaubert had also taken inspiration from another mistress, Louise Pradier, who had been thrown out of home by her husband (yes, the sculptor James; these were socially incestuous times) for an earlier dalliance, losing her children along with most else. No matter that Pradier was a serial cheater himself; men were expected to have affairs (if discreetly). Women, however, were severely punished for transgressing any boundaries of feminine propriety — as Emma Bovary did, unforgivably neglecting her kind, if boorish, husband and young daughter for the pursuit of impossible dreams.

Hanging along several of the *bouquiniste* sheds were fashion plates ripped from old magazines, the very type that Emma sighs over. Magazines have long been accused of distorting women's expectations of reality, but there's a certain type of personality that lives beyond the realms of life's probabilities. There's a French word for it: *bovarysme*. It's the syndrome whereby you live life as though you're in a romance novel, in continual denial of reality, which will only eventually fall short, crashing irrevocably down.

Another *bouquiniste* favourite is *La Princesse de Clèves*, the best-seller of 1678. Considered the first psychological novel — Edith Wharton wrote that it kicked off modern fiction — its author Madame de Lafayette, like Flaubert, argued for reason over romance, sense over sentiments. Set in the royal court late in the reign of King Henri II — his wife Catherine and mistress Diane are also characters — *La Princesse* tells the fictional story of a beautiful, virtuous girl who's thrown into a world of intrigue and affairs. Determined to honour her new and adoring husband, whom she respects but doesn't love, the princess is mortified to find that she has fallen passionately in lust for the ladies' man Duc de Nemours.

No matter how many times I read *La Princesse*, I can't help shaking my head that (spoiler alert!) she ends up resisting the dashing Nemours, even when the death of her husband leaves her fancy-free. But once I overcome my initial annoyance at the lack of a they-all-lived-happily-ever-after ending, I find the book actually leaves a refreshing aftertaste. And I think that's because we all know that life, really, isn't a simple love story. It's hard work; marriage, too. 'You need to put effort into being a spouse, just like you do with any other role in life,' my mother once told me. When the honeymoon is over, it's just the two of you, trying to make sense of the new world order, pay the bills and maybe raise some babies. You have to balance the romance with some hard-nosed realism for a successful partnership, it's not something to be taken lightly. Affairs, to me, seem an easy way out, shortsighted escapism, to a place of no good. So that's why it's novel to see a romantic heroine thinking with her head, not just her heart, to be reminded that there are other grand abstract notions to live by, such as trust and respect. And perhaps that's why something written almost 350 years ago has resonance today, and is still studied by French students. It's a cool, calm and collected counterpoint to the messiness that can ensue when love unravels. And every French person knows that the opposite of order is chaos. Just, hopefully, neither option nowadays need entail driving your husband to a miserable death, or retiring to a nunnery.

In translating *La Princesse,* English author — and devoted Francophile — Nancy Mitford wondered, in her introduction, at the 'curious shrinking from happiness' of the novel's heroine. Wharton, too, had evidently felt a certain exasperation at the 'story of hopeless love and mute renunciation'. But the princess was not simply denying herself joy; she was also protecting herself from future misery, from eventually being abandoned by a libertine lover. And that's an interesting take on the pursuit of pleasure; surely it's as much about seeking bliss as avoiding its flipside: sorrow. Anyway, Mitford knew all about keeping her emotions in check. At the age of forty-something, she moved to Paris to follow the *amour* of her life, who turned out to be the textbook French philanderer, the very type the princess was worried Nemours would reveal himself to be. But like the princess, Nancy refused to let herself fall apart. A stickler for decorum, she put on a brave face, lipstick too, and lived as elegantly as possible. Her residence of many years was not far from where Mum and I were staying, and Nancy led a glamorous existence in the *faubourg,* partying it up in Dior at night, writing her enchanting biographies and elegant, witty novels during the day. She chose, very consciously, to make peace with her lot, to not let love, with all its potential clutter and confusion, ruffle the rest of her very full, quite beautiful, life. Wharton, incidentally, also suffered through a tumultuous *amour fou* in her early Paris years, only to have to pull herself, and her frayed emotions, back together. So perhaps, by the time she wrote *The Age of Innocence*, she was somewhat philosophical about passion, and sympathetic to such a character as Newland Archer, who ultimately chose head over heart. Wharton knew firsthand that some pairings weren't meant to be.

Dinner that evening was at the home of Mum's friend Sophie, who had moved from Sydney to Paris two decades earlier. Whenever I'm in town, I check in on Sophie, and have long been enthralled by her increasingly glamorous existence. She has lived in a succession of apartments, each one a little bigger and grander, filled with ever more gilt-edged antiques and elaborate lamps. Having worked her way up to a position as a top executive for an advertising agency, Sophie had moulded herself into the quintessential Parisienne (as Edith Wharton, Nancy Mitford and many others have shown, some of the best Parisiennes weren't even born French), a stylish women of *un certain âge* as you can only find in this city.

We arrived at her latest abode — this time in Saint-Germain — punched in the digicode at the street entrance, and made our way upstairs, in what was once a private mansion. Sophie was waiting by her door, in a little black dress and Christian Louboutins, very much the lady of the *manoir*. She greeted us with requisite double-kisses, and gratefully accepted the bottle of champagne and bouquet of flowers we had brought by way of congratulations. Sophie had just celebrated her French citizenship and I couldn't help feeling a little *verte* with envy, especially as we made our way inside, which was both cosy and intimate, and styled to home-magazine perfection. Sophie, too, manages to be both warm and grandiose. Her favourite word is amazing — which she adores so much she makes the most of it: 'ahhhhmayyyzing' — and her life seems to embody this, with its frenzy of friends, socialising and jet-setting.

Every time I visit Sophie, I experience — in addition to the mild pang of jealousy — an odd spine-shivering sensation that is not so much the 'already-seen' of déjà vu as the 'could-see' if I were able to peer into a parallel universe. I can't help but wonder if this might have been my life had I stayed in Paris any of those earlier times. When you're young, your 'what ifs' are future possibilities, countless tickets to new and exotic destinations. After a certain age, the 'what ifs' have mostly expired, like wistful sighs, and it's with no little regret that you sometimes wonder where those journeys might have taken you. *Bovarysme* is in part about the lure of Paris, which has, for centuries, for so many women, represented the very essence of civilisation, the epitome of a good life. Just as Emma traces her fingers dreamily over a map of Paris, I have often walked around the city on Google Street View. But I decided a while back that I wanted to keep my feet firmly on my native soil, that I wasn't going to flit off like some character in a Romantic (or a chick-lit) novel. I've very much chosen to be happy with life at home.

'Riddle me this,' I said to Sophie, after mentioning my day's literary purchases. 'If two of the greatest French classics are cautionary tales about the dangers of affairs, why do the French have a reputation as a nation of adulterers?'

'It's in their genes,' Sophie replied. Adultery in France has centuries of court culture behind it, from the torrid love affairs of troubadours to the glamorous mistresses at Versailles to the libertine aristocrats with too much time on their wandering hands. After the Revolution, when laws made divorce near impossible, adultery became something of a new form of social rebellion, and was a particular pastime of bored bourgeois men. These days, however, adultery seems to be the domain mainly of politicians — which doesn't bother the French voters, not so much because they believe in free love but in the sanctity of private life.

'No, seriously,' Sophie added, 'you do get your cheaters everywhere, as in any country, but the committed adulterers tend to be those in a certain social milieu. Like my neighbour. He has his official family, with his three legitimate children, then his long-term mistress, who lives with their daughter across the river, and he's also now apparently seeing a third woman. You have to be wealthy to live like this!'

'And stressed,' noted Mum.

'I don't know how his heart keeps up! He's always scurrying in and out, fatigue etched all over his face.'

'And he's never been found out?' I asked, incredulous.

'I actually think they all know about each other, but just pretend not to.'

'I guess that's one way to preserve the status quo,' I remarked.

'You've hit the nail on the head. The French like to think they're passionate creatures but, in reality, they're very discreet. It's all about keeping up appearances.'

&

In sartorial terms, the French way to keep up discreet, chic appearances is to wear a neat, tailored jacket — preferably signed Chanel. It took Parisiennes until the 1960s to co-opt men's trousers, but man-style jackets have been in their repertoire for much longer. From the seventeenth century, aristocratic women would pair nipped-in styles with long skirts for riding outfits, and by the turn of the twentieth century, the look had become commonplace on city streets. But it was Coco Chanel who brought *la veste* into the modern age, making it wonderfully wearable with her cardigan style of 1925 and then, in 1954, her trim, tailored tweed version. One of the staples of contemporary fashion — up there with white shirts and blue jeans — Chanel's short collarless jacket is the very definition of classic; it overrides all fashion fads, just as it can be worn with anything, by anyone, at any age.

Generally, Parisian women don't follow the ups-and-downs of fashionable hemlines, or ride the rollercoaster of runway trends. They prefer to look steadily, consistently stylish. If the fashion one season is elegant, *bon*; if not, forget it. A Parisienne will especially not wear something that accentuates what she sees as her weaknesses — which is why Parisian style suits all in its sleek simplicity. Remember, beauty here is in abstraction. Coco Chanel, she who insisted that the definition of elegance is refusal, knew this better than anyone.

Chanel was responsible for many trends that stayed the course to become wardrobe classics. There was the little black dress, for one, and the Breton striped shirt (inspired by the fishermen tops Chanel saw when holidaying in Deauville) that has become a signifier of Francophilia the world over. But for my mum, it was 'Buy a Chanel jacket' that she added to her bucket-list years ago.

Because today was Chanel Day, we started off with breakfast at Angelina, the designer's favourite café, and even managed to score her old table (No.10 — which somehow seems a little askew). We slowly savoured our hot chocolate, rich as dark velvet, and tried to picture Mademoiselle herself in this very spot. The café has barely changed in the past century or so, with its murals of Mediterranean scenes casting a sunny glow. While

Chanel did love her seaside holidays (and the souvenir tans), Angelina seems rather lavish in style for someone who dressed so simply. But then, here's where Chanel was quintessentially Parisian: her surface might have been austere (save for a touch of faux jewellery), like the façade of her building (with a pretty window box here or there), but when it came to interiors, she loved to glitz things up.

Instead of shopping at the iconic Rue Cambon store, as originally planned, we set off for the 16th arrondissement, the spiritual home of the Parisian bourgeoisie with their, doubtless, plush interiors and, according to Sophie, the go-to for designer vintage stores.

Sure enough, we soon struck Chanel jacket heaven. The saleswoman — dressed in a monochrome suit, her pearly-white hair twisted into an elegant bun — led us to an entire rack devoted to the fashion subgenre. There was almost every colour of the rainbow, along with the classic blacks, creams and navies, and each model ever-so-slightly hinted at its vintage, from the boxy pastels of the 1960s to the cool, clean pales of the noughties. Mum found herself drawn to a black one, adorned with gold-coin buttons. While it had the same sleekness as all the others, with the celebrated skinny sleeves and the genius gold chain weighing down its hemline, it somehow seemed a little sturdier, perhaps in the shoulders.

'Zissss is from zeeee eighties,' explained the doyenne of the boutique.

'Of course it is!' I exclaimed, giggling.

My mother hit her career stride in the 1980s, when shoulder-padded suits provided the armour in which women could battle it out with men in the workplace. It was a cape of a kind for the new generation of superwomen and made them feel empowered.

'Well, I like it,' huffed Mum, not a little indignantly. French women might have a national signature fashion look, but for the rest of the world, there's a theory that we tend to settle on a personal style by reverting to the fashions in which we came of age, which helped to define us at such a formative time. That's why, I think, Mum feels so at ease in a suit, even a structured one.

'It's surprisingly comfortable,' Mum commented to Madame Doyenne.

'Oh oui, zay always are wiz Chanel,' she purred, and added: 'Iz almost like wearrrring a tracksuit.' Although I was pretty sure that Madame had never worn sweat pants in her entire life.

Mum and I took the jacket out that night, to hear Vivaldi's *Four Seasons* at Sainte-Chapelle, one of the true jewels in the tiara of Paris. Dating to the thirteenth century, this Gothic treasure was built as a reliquary for what was said to be the crown of thorns. And that's why you have the sensation of stepping into a jewellery box as you walk into the upper chapel, with its gem-coloured glass sparkling to the heavens. We took our seats and looked up to watch the setting sun's final rays pierce prismatic shafts through the stained glass, and transform the rose window (surely the most exquisite portrayal possible of the apocalypse) into a kaleidoscopic, almost psychedelic, flower. As the chapel darkened to a moody sapphire-blue, and the golden flickers of the candelabras intensified, we waited for the musicians to spring into action. And then suddenly: da dum dum dum dada daaa! My heart leapt to my mouth, my throat tightened and tears pricked my eyes.

Now, I'm no music connoisseur, but something about the strains of Vivaldi had pushed a button, down there under layers of denial, and triggered an emotional cascade. Often I cry for the beauty of a moment — the happy (more than sad) moments in a film, a movingly worded passage in a book, even (embarrassingly) advertisements for tissues that feature fluffy ducklings — but this was more than that. Reacting to extreme beauty, I think, is your body's way of countering and releasing past sorrows. I realised that I hadn't adequately mourned the soul I'd lost in miscarrying, who was now perhaps floating around up there somewhere, amid the divine lights and angelic tunes. I'm not the most dedicated Catholic girl around, but I take solace from religion when I need to. And sitting in this ancient chapel, former home to the crown of thorns — a perverted symbol of majesty that became one of suffering but also nobility — while listening to the sounds of spring, the season of hope and rebirth, was a painfully yet exquisitely healing experience. Such transcendent incidents refresh your perspective on life. You're reminded that pleasure always follows pain, as spring does winter.

Just as Cole Porter crooned, I love Paris in any season — but spring is when the city really sings, bursting into a stirring symphony of blooms. Mum and I were sitting in the Tuileries, on a pair of chairs in the shade of a Judas tree, a profusion of musk-pink blossoms, by a flowerbed of red and purple tulips. It was May Day, officially Labour Day, but traditionally the day of *le muguet* or lily of the valley. You see, even labourers stop to smell the flowers in Paris.

We'd brought along a basket of magazines, but I found I preferred the real-life vignettes playing out before us. This park, after all, has a picturesque history of people-watching. Once the private gardens of Catherine de Medici, they were later fancied up (that is, made more French than Italian) and then opened to the public, with one caveat: you had to be stylishly dressed to gain entry. The original women's magazines appeared around this time, and their fashion illustrators would often come to the Tuileries to find inspiration in the ornamented women parading around in their new ensembles, turning them into fashion plates delectable enough to adorn chocolate boxes. These were the watercolours that rose-tinted Emma

Bovary's dreams, and can be now bought along the Seine. They were the original street-style snaps. Perhaps this is one reason Parisiennes don't leave the house looking anything but impeccable. Their city has long been used as a photo set, on which everyone is expected to look picture-perfect.

I watched a Parisian mother (jeans, white shirt, requisite scarf) wheel an old-fashioned pram along the gravel path, her two older children skipping behind, the girl in a floral smock, the boy in a striped T-shirt and neat navy shorts, giggling as they blew bubbles at each other. It was as though an advertisement (brief: effortlessly stylish Parisienne with adorably shiny-haired children) had come to life.

'She makes motherhood look so easy,' I sighed.

'By all accounts, motherhood *is* easier here,' Mum responded.

This does indeed seem to be true. All mothers in France have access to family allowance, and the government funds maternity leave and childcare centres, making it more feasible for women to get back to work, or at least find some balance in their hectic lives. It's simpler, in other words, to be a *superfemme* in Paris than a superwoman in Sydney, where maternity leave depends on the generosity of your company, and the exorbitantly expensive daycare options are few and far between.

Still, I don't get the sense that Parisiennes put as much pressure on themselves to be so super. Perhaps this is because feminism panned out differently there. French women, by and large, haven't felt the burning desire to prove to men that they can be just like them but also a whole lot more. It's okay to be different. And it's also okay to cut a few corners in the process.

I had just read leading feminist author Elisabeth Badinter's *The Conflict: Woman and Mother*, in which she commends the tradition of French *maternité* for its 'part-time' approach to motherhood. French women, she notes, have an unapologetic history of putting themselves first, which can be traced back to the seventeenth century, when *mamans* sent their newborns off to wet nurses so that they could quickly pick their old lives back up. Badinter is firmly in the guilt-free camp of parenting, and advocates anything that will better slot motherhood into a busy life, be that formula milk, disposable nappies, pre-packaged food or full-time daycare. The best mother, according to Badinter, is the one who knows she is, above all, her own woman.

Badinter's book is a rallying cry for women to resist the call of naturalism, the myth of the idealised earth mother, with its pressures to breastfeed, cook organic lentil stew and the like. The father of all earth mothers was Jean-Jacques Rousseau. Having lost his mum at a young age, he held firm views on motherhood, which he placed high up on a rustic wooden pedestal. In his eyes, women had been put on this bucolic earth to raise lots of bouncing, breastfed babies. Badinter has little time for Rousseau, unsurprisingly, calling him — and the naturalist movement — manipulative.

The earth mother cult was alive and well in Sydney. I had tried for a while to become her. I even washed and dried cloth nappies every day. In the end, I had to go back to full-time work, which necessitated adding formula into the breastfeeding mix, and admitting that life would be a hell of a lot easier if we started using supermarket nappies. I made the decision not to give into mother guilt soon after throwing off my earth mother rags. But I also knew that the superwoman cape didn't suit me either. I still wanted to try to juggle as much in life as possible, but I was open to dropping a few balls along the way. I knew I had to be more lenient on myself if we were one day going to throw in an extra ball to juggle: another baby.

I'd only ever pictured myself with daughters, for some reason. So early in my first pregnancy, I had naturally, and openly, hoped for a girl. When I discovered I was in fact having a boy, I was told some of the oddest things. A supposed close friend exclaimed, 'Sucked in.' A neighbour, a mother of girls, said, 'You know, I was convinced I was having boys and wanted to die.' And then there were the apparently consolatory comments. 'Well, you'll still be the princess in the family' was one. And another common response: 'At least you won't have to deal with any of that weird rivalry mums and daughters have.' That last one surprised me the most, because I've always had such a good relationship with my mum — which is perhaps why I originally dreamed of having a girl, so we could replicate the rapport.

Of course, I'd heard some shocking mother–daughter tales — although, granted, few compared to that of Catherine de Medici, who was said to be the *mère* of all horror mothers to Marguerite, the most robust and spirited of her seven surviving children. Catherine beat her daughter ragged for falling in love with a man who didn't fit in with her power-hungry plans, then forced her to marry against her will. Worse yet, she turned the wedding celebrations into one of French history's darkest moments: the massacre of Saint Bartholomew's Day, in which thousands of Protestants — including Marguerite's new husband's friends — were butchered throughout Paris.

I thought about the troubled pair as we exited the gardens, walking through the ghost of Catherine's Tuileries Palace, towards the Louvre courtyard, where much of the carnage took place. The Louvre has changed almost beyond recognition since then, continually rebuilt, mostly along classical Italianate lines. During the Renaissance years, Italy, not France, was the global style capital. King François I, a passionate Italophile, handpicked the heiress Catherine for his son for her rich dowry as much as her à la mode nationality. (The king also, incidentally, invited a certain Leonardo da Vinci to France, and bought his painting *Mona Lisa*, which would one day become the star attraction of his former abode.) When

Catherine arrived at the royal court of the Louvre, she brought with her many new trends — in addition to perfume, there were the fork, pasta, artichokes and handkerchiefs — as well as a commitment to making her mark on her new city through architecture. But like the Palais des Tuileries, most of the buildings she commissioned have disappeared.

'It makes you reflect on the transitory nature of power, doesn't it?' commented Mum.

My mother was technically retired, but she had taken on a number of board jobs that, effectively, kept her toiling away full-time. Mum was unabashed in the pride she felt for a job well done, but was nevertheless philosophical about the importance of work. Having operated in politics for many years, she knew that what could be achieved one year could be all too easily dismantled the next — and so she ensured that her career was never so all-encompassing that it took away from her overall enjoyment of life.

'You know, Catherine saw most of her children die, and her plans come to nothing,' I said. 'I wonder if she might have been happier, in the end, if she'd not worked so hard, and spent more time with her children, especially Marguerite.'

'No doubt,' nodded Mum.

For our final Parisian dinner, we celebrated (and part commiserated) at Lapérouse, a seventeenth-century Seine-side townhouse that was transformed into a plush restaurant in the Belle Époque. The kind of place that could only be conjured into reality in Paris, Lapérouse is an opulence of red velvet, burnished gold and gleaming wood, and has long been notorious for its sequence of moodily lit *salons privés*. There politicians would wine and dine their courtesans and mistresses, who verified the authenticity of their gifts of diamonds by scratching the stones across the mirrors, which are still there today — complete with original etchings. If only these walls could talk!

We wound up a narrow set of stairs into the main dining room, its walls adorned with golden lamps and pastoral frescoes, and its floral-trimmed ceilings suspended low, over what were once the servant rooms. So fine and exquisite is everything that you feel like you're in a vintage dollhouse, and you half expect the food not to be real. Fortunately, it is. I ate a salad of crisp pale-green lettuce fluttered in pecorino cheese and truffles, and Mum opted for sole meunière, the classic fried fish dish that Julia Child first ate on moving to France, inspiring her to learn the ways of *la cuisine française*, and in turn spread the *amour* to the rest of the world.

Mum was one of the many new brides who bought Julia's *Mastering the Art of French Cooking*, in the early 1970s. I can still picture, and smell, the Saturday-evening dinner parties she and Dad would host. I'd greet their glamorous friends — the ladies in lurex, the men in paisley shirts — in my pyjamas, before being sent to my bedroom, where I would strain to hear the chardonnay-fuelled conversation and inhale the aromas of *duck à l'orange* and apple tart. But Mum's stint as a gourmande fizzled out when her career sapped her of the energy necessary for perfecting *boeuf bourgignon*. Meals in our house soon became platters of tomatoes, olives and cheese, anything we could quickly throw together at the end of the day. 'Something's gotta give,' Mum once said with a shrug. I'm sure Madame Badinter would approve, even if Mrs Child (and Monsieur Rousseau) would not.

Julia, incidentally, celebrated her fortieth birthday at Lapérouse, in 1952, after having moved to Paris four years earlier. The city transformed her in many ways, teaching her how to savour every moment ('Life is the proper binge,' she claimed) and fill her world to the brim with happiness, even amid her personal sorrows. The way I see it, Julia had an inner Parisienne just waiting to wriggle out. All it took was one bite of sole meunière. For others, it might be a whiff of musk-based perfume or the slinky feel of a Chanel jacket's silk lining.

'*La vie est faite de petits bonheurs*' is a French phrase I love. It means: life is made from small joys; enjoy the little things, in other words. It's another reminder for the French to live not just by the day but also by the moment, to sit down for lunch and relish it, to stop and smell those flowers. Remember, even Delacroix took time away from the big picture, to observe the little ones, to paint those delicate blooms. A still life, after all, is one way to still life, to slow it down.

When I was pregnant, I was given a book called something like *Meditation for Mothers*. It warned me that I would soon have little time for yoga, or anything else much fun while I was at it. I'd have to find calmness in such moments as washing cups. This depressed me no end. And then I had Noah, and life did indeed hit the fast-forward button. But that fortnight in Paris reminded me that I didn't have to stare at dirty crockery to still my mind. I could still look for, and find, small moments of beauty in life. And as beauty is best when abstract, you can find it all around you: by playing soul-inspiring music, relishing a plate of ripe tomatoes, or staring at the simple yet extraordinary elegance of a flower. That sounds very Rousseau of me, I admit, but I was far from being a patchouli-sniffing earth mother. At the same time, I knew that I didn't have to be her alter ego either, the superwoman. I didn't have to prove heroic feats of juggling motherhood and career. I didn't have to wear a cape. Although perhaps I would add a Chanel jacket to my own bucket-list.

CHAPTER 10

MAMAN

[mamɑ̃] *nf* mummy, mum

In which, aged forty-something,
I pass on my love of Paris.

If I couldn't have another Paris baby, I could at least bring him up à la française. When I was pregnant with Otto (*oui*, another *garçon*!), I came across *French Children Don't Throw Food* by Pamela Druckerman, and promptly tossed out all previous parenting books to make this my baby-rearing bible. It wasn't that I felt we'd got parenting that wrong the first time around, it's that we'd been warned a second child doesn't so much double the complexity of life as quintuple it, and that we would ultimately have to choose between order and chaos — and who better to know about this duality of choice than the French, right?

When it comes to parenting, the French opt for structure over spontaneity — the so-called *cadre*, or frame, of childhood. According to Druckerman, an American who has raised three children in Paris, French babies become civilised little beings — who sleep through, eat everything, accept being told *non*, and generally know their place in the world — in a matter of months.

'You don't need to read that book,' scoffed a French colleague. 'I can tell you why we all turn out the way we do: we were petrified of our parents.' While French parents are said to be less strict these days, most still believe that, by exerting some tough *amour* early on, their children will grow into upright citizens who conform to society with elegant ease, which generally makes for a more harmonious life.

Andy and I had been somewhat, let's say, *laissez-faire* with Noah, determined not to let a baby, no matter how cute, control our lives. But all the improvisation — and the freedom to stay out late with friends while Noah snoozed under the table — came at a price: by the age of two, he took hours to settle to sleep, and instead of meals he asked for platters of hors d'oeuvres, as though he was still down the road at the local bar.

Visualising Otto-to-be as a perfect French-style child with an innate talent for sleeping and eating, I stocked up on Sophie La Girafe paraphernalia and Petit Bateau striped onesies. Curiously, I didn't think to suggest names such as Louis or Gabriel. Andy and I came across the option of Otto early on in the pregnancy, and it just stuck. When said Otto finally reared his determined head in the world, he did indeed seem to suit his name. My father, however, was horrified, explaining that a certain Otto von Bismarck laid siege to Paris in 1870, shelling citizens before strutting a victory march down the Champs-Élysées. 'I doubt Paris will welcome another Otto with open arms,' he argued. (The name Otto, in fact, has been so *démodé* for decades that I drew blanks when checking its symbolism with French acquaintances, prompting us to go ahead with the palindrome.)

The *bébé* experiment went partly to plan (Otto ate almost everything on offer from four months), but also partly awry (he never took our nos all that seriously). I realised that, ideally, a baby would best fit the pattern of a perfect French child if he actually lived in the country where every other child was wearing the same stripes. Try convincing an Australian kid that he must eat blue-cheese tartine when everyone around him is munching on crustless Vegemite sandwiches; it's not easy. We finally had the chance to take the boys to France when Dad decided to celebrate his seventieth birthday in Paris. Noah and Otto, six and four at the time, had heard me talk about Paris incessantly, and were stoked. Before we flew out, I asked them what they were expecting. 'Chocolate croissants for breakfast every day?' said Otto, hopefully. 'The best place in the world,' replied Noah.

&

We began our journey at the Happiest Place on Earth. Disneyland had opened just outside Paris in 1992, to the expected Gallic grumblings of

American cultural imperialism. Still, it eventually became the number one tourist destination in Europe — ahead of the Eiffel Tower and the Louvre, which must have offended French sensibilities no end. I'd betrayed my inner Parisienne by having already visited Disneyland several times. Sure, I could see that the olde-worlde Main Street USA, with its candy-box cuteness, was still as American as apple pie — not as *française* as tarte tatin — but the park had been Frenchified somewhat, I reasoned: you could buy *croques-monsieurs* along with burgers, Chip & Dale had been renamed Tic & Tac (for no apparent purpose beyond sounding more French) and, really, France is the original home of *Sleeping Beauty* and *Cinderella*, both stories having been penned by Charles Perrault over 300 years ago, when much of what we now know as America was in fact called New France.

My unabashed adoration of Disneyland began when I was four years old, when my parents took me to the original theme park in Los Angeles. I can still recall it in technicolor memory: Alice in Wonderland in her sky-blue dress, the orange fur of Pluto as he enveloped me in a big bear hug, the pastel-pink turrets of the castle with their golden trim. Disneyland infused me with a sense of wonder about life (not to mention a penchant for pretty sparkly things) that lingered for years. And this was the magical wand of a baton I was hoping to pass on to my boys — although I didn't kid myself it would be pink and glittery.

But before we could enter, we had to deal with wands of another kind — the metal detectors now ubiquitous at major French attractions, following a year in which Paris had been rocked by terrorism. It was a sign, for me, that the world has lost some of its own wonder. Fortunately, the boys were still at the age when they believe that life is magical. Watching them skip down Main Street in their Mickey Mouse ears, towards the fantastical castle up ahead, filled me with an emotion I couldn't quite put a finger on at the time. I now realise it was the joy of watching them live their own future, happy, technicolor memories.

Taking two energetic yet jet-lagged young boys to Disneyland in peak tourist season comes with its own special challenges. 'We're at the Happiest Place on Earth and we're having Fun!' I'd enthuse-slash-demand over the three days we were there. They weren't always convinced. After snaking along a slow-moving queue for sixty minutes, we boarded a barge for the *Pirates of the Caribbean* ride, where we glided by a series of creaky-looking characters. 'Wow,' cooed the boys on cue, but you have to wonder how long Disney can stay so low-tech in a digital world where children conjure up all sorts of technological wizardry at the press of an iPad button.

On the final day we lunched back in the hotel, in a restaurant where Mickey, Minnie, Donald and Daisy wandered from table to table. By now, the boys were taking it all in their stride, totally unfazed to find life-size rodents and ducks among their dining companions. '*Bonjour, Madame*,' Noah greeted Minnie as we walked in. I'd given him some fundamental French-language lessons on the aeroplane, but stressed the most important of all: 'Being polite gets you far in life,' I said. 'And the French expect you to always says "*bonjour*" to them.'

The French are sticklers for civility, especially in children who are taught the importance of '*bonjour*' from the get-go. Inspired by my French baby book, I'd long nagged my sons to be courteous to adults. 'How do I say "I am Noah" in French,' Noah asked me on the first day of our holiday. He proceeded to announce '*Bonjour, je m'appelle Noah*' to anyone in earshot. I was still trying to teach him the codes regarding which strangers you addressed, and which not, but in Disneyland, heightened politeness seemed to suit the surroundings. '*Enchanté*,' would be the invariable response; when the French want to say 'Nice to meet you' they literally say 'Enchanted', like some spellbound character from a

Perrault tale. I've always loved this about the French — who doesn't want to be enchanting, after all?

Driving into the French capital was somewhat of a reality check. Before reaching the fairyland that is central Paris, we had to make our way through the outer suburbs. These are not the picket-fence-style suburbs of Australia, mind you. In Paris, it's mostly the wealthy who live centrally, while everyone else dwells beyond the *Périphérique* highway that rings the city, separating the haves from the have-nots. Each city has its socio-economic issues, of course, but there's something about the contrast of classes in Paris that makes things seem all the more jarring, where people often refer to the suburbs as ghettoes, a description that seems sadly apt.

As we turned off the *Périph* to head towards the 5th arrondissement, the grey, grim buildings began to transform into gleaming bright ones. Paris was doing what she has always done best: cast a magical spell over visitors. Locals might moan about the Disneyfication of their city, that it's little more than a historic tourist park with its set itinerary of rides (Seine cruise), sights (*Mona Lisa*) and thrills (Eiffel Tower climb). But what's the world to do? France could surely not have built such an beguiling city and expected us to resist its lure. Parisians, after all, know the power of beauty more than anyone.

We noticed, however, that the boulevards were not quite up to squeaky-clean Main Street standards, and remembered that the city had just experienced a spate of demonstrations and garbage strikes. The French were up in arms over a labour law President Hollande was about to push through, one that aimed to decrease unemployment by making it easier to hire, fire, and alter working hours — with the ultimate aim of creating a more flexible labour market to better suit global times. The French had long been suspicious of globalisation — which they view more or less as Americanisation — and it's one issue that will get their inner revolutionaries back out on the streets. The French also love their rituals, and demonstrating is a serious social rite. Plus, there's a passion to a protest, not to mention the tradition of historical romance; demonstrating connects Parisians to their beloved streets as much as to their riotous ancestors.

But what I most love about the French style of strike — something that is usually anarchistic by definition — is that it's actually quite conservative, because these days the French by and large protest not to change society, but to keep the status quo intact. French strikes promote harmony, in other words, which is so utterly paradoxical in the most Parisian way. But the French are evidently content with their cosseted way of life. They're not quite living in Disneyland, as a trek through the outer suburbs will prove, but generally the French state looks after its citizens admirably well. Liberalists might say that France needs to get with the times, that it lives in the past, but like Disneyland, there's a quaint loveliness to its pursuit of happiness above all else.

After dropping off our bags in our apartment, we headed to the Luxembourg Garden for a late-afternoon stroll, taking the northern entrance and passing by the side of the Palais du Luxembourg, the current seat of the French Senate. It was originally built for Florentine Marie de Medici, Henri IV's second queen, who nostalgically requested an Italianate palazzo, but ended up with something more like a typical French château, complete with formal gardens à la française, too. She at least got her grotto, although this has also been Frenchified over time. Now the Medici Fountain, the grotto sits at the head of a long basin of water that is shaded by plane trees, garlanded by ivy and dotted with urns of vibrant flowers. It's one of the most whimsical of oases around. If you weren't charged with keeping two lively boys entertained, you'd pull up a signature green chair and soak in the serenity.

The perennially popular Luxembourg Garden was teeming on that blue-skied day. Couples sunned themselves by the octagonal pond, students lolled about drinking rosé on the emerald carpets of lawn edged with rows of pruned trees, and nannies weaved after their wards, circling the lace-trimmed bandstand and zig-zagging the grove of horse chestnuts, whose wonderfully lush leaves contrasted with the austerity of the gravel ground. Almost every one of the scattered chairs had been claimed, and their owners gazed dreamily over the flower-filled *parterres*, with nothing better to do than simply watch the world go by.

I expressed envy of the lucky souls whose lives allowed them to laze around Parisian gardens all day long. Dad, pragmatic as ever, pointed out that perhaps they were simply out of work, the unemployment rate being at double digits at the time. Although in Dad's view, a higher joblessness rate is perhaps preferable to a lower one that disguises the fact the many people are underemployed — as is the case in Australia. It wouldn't surprise me if the French felt the same, as I see them as such dual-natured, all-or-nothing people who like clear-cut options. Either you have a job or you don't — it's *noir* or *blanc*, *oui* or *non* …

'NO!'

Otto — whose favourite line, along with the word no, seemed to be '*Je m'appelle Poo-Poo*' — was doing his best portrayal of the opposite of a well-mannered French boy. (Ms Druckerman would have failed me then and there.) He had dug his heels into the gravel foreground of an ice-cream stand, protesting at his grandmother's refusal to buy him a treat. 'You've had enough junk at Disneyland and it's time to eat good food like a nice French child,' she explained patiently.

'NO!!!'

Otto doesn't say no like most English-speaking children do — so it sounds like an 'oh', which almost seems to accept eventual defeat then and there. Oh no, Otto expresses denial with an almost Gallic accent, pronouncing his no like the French *non* so it's vehemently thrust forward, through an insolent pout, and thrown down at the feet of the offending adult like a particularly weighty gauntlet. Not that, I've been told, French kids actually utter the word *non* all that often. French adults, on the other hand, love to say *non*, like the disobedient children they never were, making up for lost time and lost *nons*. You might hear a *non* when you pass the ice-cream lady a fifty-euro bill and she shakes her head, even though it's 4 p.m. on a summer's day and you know for sure she would have change. Or the *non* could charge out of the moustache-topped mouth of one of the park's *gardiens*, as he runs towards you waggling his finger when you try to move some of the green chairs around. *Non* is a power play. As the authors Julie Barlow and Jean-Benoît Nadeau have pointed out, *non* is the everyday French person's right to refuse, a privilege hard won during the French Revolution after centuries of subservience to the aristocracy. When a Parisian isn't taking to the streets, he or she can still make a stand against the world in a small way, simply by saying *non*. It's the particular default position of Parisians in the service-based industry, but if you're polite and persistent, you can work around it. But maybe *non*.

With Otto, distraction was a much more effective method than logic, anger or even punishment. 'Let's go find the carousel,' trilled my mother, and the scowl melted from his face like ice cream in the sunshine. The carousel had been the boys' favourite ride at Disneyland, which surprised me, given its floral femininity, as well as the fact that nothing much happens on a merry-go-round; you literally go around in circles, and don't actually get anywhere, which doesn't tend to suit my boys' easily bored personalities. But then again, there aren't too many opportunities in life to just sit still and enjoy the scenery around you. So perhaps in this way the carousel, as a loop of suspended time, stills a restless mind, and I was more than happy to indulge the newfound passion if it entailed a lesson in living in the moment.

The merry-go-round at the Luxembourg Garden has not been Disneyfied (Paris purists will be happy to hear), but remains in its own cycle of time suspension, close to its late seventeenth-century state: a troop of creaky horses, along with some random wooden wildlife, cranking around under their bottle-green circus-tent top. The riders on the outer circle of animals take a small spear from the operator, who then stands by, holding a ring dispenser; as the kids approach, they must focus and aim their stick to try to detach and claim a ring.

It's all great for hand–eye coordination and various other buzzwords of twenty-first-century paediatric occupational therapy, but the exercise goes back to the ancient tradition of jousting, the star attraction of medieval tournaments. These knight games began in France around the same time that the myth of Sir Lancelot — passionate lover, brave fighter and all-round dreamboat — captured society's imagination as the epitome of chivalry, the knightly code encompassing courage and courtesy. Inspired knights would compete at tournaments in all their finery to thrill the maidens. Jousting — where two knights on horseback would charge at one another at full speed, and each try to unhorse the other with his lance — could be a brutal affair, and was ultimately banned by Catherine de Medici, after her adored husband King Henri II was killed in the combat game. Tournaments were eventually replaced, in the seventeenth century, by a less violent, more elaborate version of equine extravaganza, known as *un carrousel.* Almost an equestrian ballet, a carousel was an intricately coordinated pageant of a parade, with horses and their riders elaborately dressed. Games included ring tilting (a non-combat take on jousting), and the prototypes of today's merry-go-rounds were rudimentary devices that enabled young nobles to perfect their tilting skills. *Voilà* — now you know.

Young French men might no longer jump through hoops — or spear rings — to impress the ladies, but their ancestors were the first Europeans to foster a culture of love, to create codes of conduct for wooing women, and the chivalry gene lives on in many modern French men, who can kiss a female hand like few other nationalities. Australian men aren't, by and large, known for their chivalry, and they might blame this on some kind of mutant DNA, but I am a big believer in nurture over nature, and have spent countless hours talking to my sons about chivalry, reading them the stories of King Arthur and Sir Lancelot (the PC version), buying embroidered velvet costumes fit for a knight. To my chagrin (and to the amusement of Andy, who is of the boys-will-be-boys school of thought), I eventually realised that my sons wanted to play knights purely to get their hands on a sword. When their grandfather announced he was, in fact, a knight, having just been awarded a papal knighthood by the Vatican for legal work in the Catholic Church, they were most impressed — until discovering this kind of knighthood does not come with armoury of any kind. I tried to explain that the strongest men in fact don't need a weapon, that manners and kindness are the way to win in life. For the moment, it's an ongoing conversation.

As the boys ran amok in the playground, I spent some time observing the other kids at play, and what struck me was not just how those with

French accents tended to be less raucous (I already knew that would be so), but how the French girls were not kitted out like pink princesses or frothy ballerinas, as their Australian sisters so often are. *Les filles* in fact dress rather simply (albeit stylishly) overall — as do the *garçons* — and I find this curious in a place that is the spiritual capital of fairy tales, as well as ballet.

Then again, French history has given women some kick-ass icons. Think Sainte Geneviève, Joan of Arc, George Sand, Marie Curie, Simone de Beauvoir. My personal favourite is twelfth-century duchess Eleanor of Aquitaine — partly because one of my French ancestors, the Comte de Borde, swore to serve and protect her on her father's deathbed; partly because she was the original power woman, and a feminine-but-feminist icon for modern French mothers who also balance the demands of large families and full-time careers, all the while looking impossibly elegant.

The beautiful, spirited, independent and strong-willed Eleanor was the catch of her age, with a huge expanse of rich feudal land to her name. She married the King of France, Louis VII, but soon tired of their spark-free relationship, and divorced him to unite with the future King of England, Henry II. The double-queen had ten children in all, but motherhood hardly slowed her down; she was constantly on the move to maintain order in the realm — except for the decade in which Henry locked her up, that is (theirs was a passionate but somewhat complex relationship). Eleanor came into her own in her sixties, and for the next twenty years proved herself an impressive leader, strategist and negotiator at a time when it was rare for women to have even a whisper of a public voice.

Eleanor graced France with some much-needed femininity in brutal times. Born to a high-cultured family, she had grown up in a magnificent Aquitainian court that worshipped love, beauty and elegance, and was a hub for poets and artists. She inspired reams of romantic literature herself, and her daughter Marie of Champagne was the patron of writer Chrétien de Troyes, who was responsible for the romantic refashioning of Lancelot's story into a handbook of chivalry. Eleanor not only shaped the psyche of Western Europe but also its history and politics. Her blood has flowed through generations of European royals, right through to Queen Elizabeth II.

There's an exquisite series of statues in the Luxembourg Garden, along the two terraces overlooking the main pond, depicting twenty French queens and famous women. The intricate marble drapings and detailings give a wonderful lesson in French fashion history, to say the least, but I always feel the absence of the formidable, incomparable Eleanor, who would surely have been the most gracefully frocked of all the *femmes*. Then again, Eleanor did abandon Paris for London, which would probably be an unforgivable transgression even today.

We tempted the boys away from the playground with the promise of dinner, and made our way through a stand of yet more chestnut trees, over what was once the backyard of Marie de Medici, who was, appropriately, granted statuary immortality. Her son, the young King Louis XIII, would play there with his dogs, long before other Parisian children discovered the gardens as their own kingdom of pony rides and puppet shows.

'En garde!' yelled Otto, grabbing a stick from the ground and assuming battle position before us, every bit the mini musketeer.

It was Louis XIII who, in 1622, founded *les Mousquetaires*, the troupe of musket-wielding soldiers made famous by Romantic novelist Alexandre Dumas, père over 200 years later. Not that Monsieur Dumas exactly imbued the musketeers myth with much romance; his men were brawlers of the first order, with a warped sense of honour that was both strong yet delicate, so that the slightest slur triggered a reflex physical response. The behaviour was probably closer to fact than fiction; by the seventeenth century fighting had gone professional. Where once there was a warrior caste of snazzily dressed knights — usually upwardly mobile minor nobles who were wealthy enough to buy their own warhorse and equipment — a centralised army now welcomed any man born with the battling gene. Little surprise then that old-fashioned chivalry, the gem-encrusted badge of honour once worn by every self-respecting knight, started to go the way of heavy medieval armoury. The musketeers, drawn from the lower ranks of nobility, were particularly renowned for their boisterous, hot-blooded ways, always ready to draw a sword in this golden age of duelling (even though Louis had officially outlawed such street violence). Such is the enduring legend of the musketeers that Hollywood seems to make a blockbuster of their story every twenty years, for a new generation of impressionable boys.

'You can't fight it — no pun intended,' said Andy with a shrug, when I once complained about this glamourisation of combat dressed up in historical garb, the musketeer cult selling the idea that boys best bond through thuggery. 'It's like girls and princess stories — it's institutionalised.'

We walked up Rue Servandoni, which Dumas makes D'Artagnan's street of residence. You can almost hear the click-clack of his buckled boots scooting over the cobbles — fanned out in peacock-tail patterns — as he rushes off to the latest neighbourhood scuffle. The real-life musketeers would have seen a similar 6th arrondissement to the one we do today, because so much of it dates to the seventeenth century, the so-called *grand siècle* that witnessed Paris emerge as the world's eminent political and cultural power.

&

Le Procope, our dinner destination, was a product of that great century, arguably the social centre of the Age of Enlightenment. It was a time when the pen became mightier than the sword, as Parisians philosophised about how to live well in civil society. The legendary café is now a restaurant, themed to play to the tourist crowd: mirrored walls and sparkling chandeliers, glass cabinets displaying books and busts, a marble-topped table at which Voltaire himself apparently worked. But who could blame the restaurant for boasting of such a grand history?

The Disneyfication of Le Procope doesn't extend to the menu, which is as French as onion soup, just one of the options along with other Gallic gastronomic delights such as snails, pig's snout, foie gras and calf's head. It was the boys' first Parisian meal and I braced myself when Noah was presented with the kids' option: *steak haché* (minced meat) so raw it deserved tartare status. Otto dug into his, of course, while Noah stared suspiciously at the plate before him.

'This is what Parisian kids eat,' explained his grandmother.

'I was built in Paris, you know,' declared Noah suddenly, much to my mortification. His father had shared this knowledge with him just before the holiday and, even though Noah didn't really know what the euphemism meant, he seemed rather chuffed about the fact.

'Just eat,' I said quickly, before any awkward questions might be asked.

And surprisingly, he picked up his cutlery and did just that. Not with any huge enthusiasm, mind you, but still.

'Oh my gosh,' Andy whispered in surprise. 'He's acting like a French child!'

The French haven't always been civilised when it comes to dining. The fork, for instance, only gained widespread acceptance in the seventeenth century, although the Sun King, who set the template for elegant living, insisted on using his hands as utensils. While France would soon claim the silken mantle of global cultural leader, many of the ingredients for its rich brew of civilisation originated in the East. The coffee first poured from silver pots into china cups at Le Procope, for instance, came from Turkey, but the French had long been enticed by Eastern delights. Eleanor, for one, marvelled at the feasts of exquisitely spiced fare eaten with forks from silver plates, celebrated in banquet rooms carpeted in rose petals, when in Constantinople in the mid twelfth century. She was on crusade to the Holy Land, with her first husband, the piously dull French king. As a sensual southerner, Eleanor no doubt craved an exotic escape from the bleakness of Paris, no City of Light at the time. And anyway, adventure was in her blood. Her grandfather, William of Aquitaine, had also been a crusader, and his time abroad inspired him to such lyrical ecstasy that he has gone down in history as the first of the troubadours, those poet-singers of Southern France who gave us the concept of courtly love.

The crusades, for all their horrific violence, actually helped to illuminate life in Western Europe, just emerging from its so-called Dark Ages. Amid the series of holy wars, there was time for Westerners to appreciate the cultures of the East. The Islamic world was then the capital of maths, medicine and science, which stimulated the minds of Europeans, who were also agog at the splendour of the lifestyle they saw. Trade flourished to satisfy a growing Western appetite for spices and sugar, sumptuous silks and precious stones, rosewater and aromatic incense, intricate glassware and colourful cushions.

It's bittersweet to think of the beauty among the brutality. This contrast between elegance and ugliness is so often seen in French history. William of Aquitaine, arguably the founding father of romantic love, was in reality a thug of a man who would think nothing of kidnapping a woman who took his fancy. Knights, those flag-bearers of chivalry, had a day job, after all, and it was to kill. Then came the Age of Enlightenment, the celebrated summit of civilisation — that tumbled downhill into the horrors of the French Revolution, and a period so bloodthirsty it would give the world the word terrorism. And perhaps that's why Parisians, to this day, are ever ready to take to the streets in defiant protest, to say *non* after being brought up to acquiescently nod their little heads. Paris is a place where the red of passion and anger never seems too far from the elegant limestone-beige surface.

The army museum is not usually high on my Paris itinerary. In fact, it had never before even made the list. But when you're the tour guide for two young boys who often dream of being knights when they grow up, a visit there becomes somewhat inevitable. The museum is located within Les Invalides, so named because it was built, in 1671, as a home for old and infirm soldiers. This explains the austere bureaucratic sprawl of the complex. As for the reason behind the glamour of the elaborate church dome in the middle, so seemingly at odds with its surrounds, there's no definitive official one — but perhaps being Parisian is enough to have accorded it special status.

Before we'd reached the entrance of Les Invalides, we'd already walked past half a dozen soldiers, bulked up in camouflage, fingers lightly poised on the triggers of their assault rifles (their chic berets as jarring as a golden dome on a staid barracks-like building). Sadly, these officers were not part of a roving live exhibit.

'Why do the soldiers have such big guns?' asked Noah. 'Are there baddies even in Paris?' I took a deep breath. The boys had only heard that Paris is the place where all good things happen: chocolate-flavoured breakfasts, *macarons* in every colour of the rainbow, and parks filled with ponies. I decided to go for elusive over explanatory. 'They're just making sure we're extra safe,' I said, feigning nonchalance.

However, it's a jittery kind of secure that you feel every time you see such a soldier. Officially in State of Emergency mode, Parisian streets were saturated with combat troops trained to take on the world's toughest war zones. 'It feels kind of odd going to an army museum that celebrates the history of war, when war seems to be on its footsteps,' muttered Andy as we walked inside.

France had been officially at war — against terrorism and radical Islam, according to the then French prime minister — for over a year, since January 2015, when two masked gunmen forced their way into the Paris office of the satirical magazine *Charlie Hebdo*, and assassinated the editor and other staffers attending the weekly editorial meeting. The killers were radicalised French Muslims, carrying through Islamic State's threat to punish the magazine for its depictions of the Prophet Muhammad.

France and Islam have a fraught history. The old Arabic term for crusaders is *ifranj*, or Franks, as the French were the main players in the various crusades launched between 1095 and 1291. Not surprisingly, some identities have claimed that the current hostility is simply the latest holy war in a long line of many. It makes for an effective sound bite and recruiting strategy, but many historians insist this is a false interpretation of the facts. A visit to the army museum proves that the world has immeasurably changed since the time of the crusades. In the exhibition rooms — once infirmaries where countless men died from agonising injuries — uniforms are on show, sanitised of gore stains and savage rips, but precious little remains of crusader armoury, which has simply disintegrated into history.

Even so, it wouldn't hold up a mirror to today's war. For one, it's a battle where most combatants don't look like soldiers. On one side, there are the stealth fighters, wearing civilian garb and an angry scowl; on the other, regular Parisians, clad in dresses or jeans, out drinking wine *en terrasse*, their defences completely down on a Friday night. When homegrown terrorists once again struck Paris, in November 2015, shooting random targets at a music concert and various nearby restaurants and bars, the world changed forever. War no longer has a uniform.

We walked over Pont Alexandre III, the most flamboyantly exuberant of all Parisian bridges, its pillars topped with gilded Pegasuses, garlands of nymphs and cherubs, and the most voluptuous lampposts in town. It crosses the narrow gap between glamorous and gaudy, and it's this tongue-in-chic that has made the much-loved bridge a star of many movies. The sense of theatricality continues as you head towards the Champs-Élysées, past the Grand Palais and Petit Palais, their ornamentation overscaled so that you can't help but feel awed, like a child staring up at a cartoonish Disney palace.

'Pipi!' yelled Otto suddenly, somewhat shattering the sweet illusion of my moment. The boys found the French children's word for urine so hysterical that they'd shout it out at random moments. You can imagine my dismay. But this time Otto had good reason for the outburst, so we raced over the Champs-Élysées to find a public toilet. 'Will there be a Madame Pipi there?' asked Noah. He and his brother would also roll around in hysterics at the unofficial French term for a (usually female) public washroom attendant — true to the cliché of boys and their love of toilet humour.

'Guys, just say, "*Bonjour Madame*,"' I said sternly. 'I don't actually know if the ladies who work in bathrooms like being called Madame Pipi and I don't want you upsetting anyone.' I often use the potential effects of an action on other people to explain why my boys shouldn't carry out said action in the first place, but bribery is often more effective, so for good measure I threw in: 'And if you're nice to her, and say "*bonjour*" and "*merci*," we'll go get ice cream.'

After the *Charlie Hebdo* massacre, five per cent of the French population took to the streets in solidarity, and to take a stand for the right to free speech. Many Parisians raised pencils as a symbolic statement, and on social media thousands around the world shared a quote often attributed to that ultimate Enlightenment man Voltaire: 'I disapprove of what you say, but I will defend to the death your right to say it.' To this day, I'm torn. As someone who works with words, I'm supposed to inherently support unbounded freedom of expression. But I also believe in the importance of empathy and civility. We teach our children to be well mannered, to not be hurtful to others — so to then allow them to grow into adults who will say anything regardless of the consequences, well this just doesn't sit right with me. Just because you have the right to be a bigot, do you really need to bandy that right around? Then again, I would never want to suggest that someone, by causing offence, deserves physical retribution. We all need to learn to grow a thick skin in life, another lesson we teach our kids. *Charlie Hebdo* didn't take its pencil only to Islam; it actually more frequently satirised Catholicism, although politicians have by far been the most common objects of derision. Before the masthead became a household name and catchcry for libertarians, the usual response to the magazine was more shoulder-shrugging than eyebrow-raising. It was simply part of the newsstand mix; you could buy it or leave it. As Voltaire himself knew, one result of democracy is debate, with a mix of views, some ugly — but in the end, they're just words. Harsh they might be, but they don't hurt as much as swords, the old-fashioned way to inflict pain or defend your beliefs.

Satire has a long history in Paris, going back to the seventeenth century, when wits proved that the pen was much mightier than the outlawed sword. Parisians, stifled under autocratic royal rule, found an outlet for their frustrations by writing, reading or sharing satirical verses. More recently, illustrators ridiculed the powers-that-be in an autocratically presidential France by sharpening cartoons into a counter-culture art form — of which *Charlie Hebdo* became a leading example. Unless you grow up in this country, you probably can't fully appreciate the paradoxical pleasures of these very French cartoons, with their equal parts cynicism and joviality. We saw satire come to life as an impromptu street performance later in the week. Andy and I were at a bar one evening when several other customers *en terrasse* popped on masks — photos of politicians' faces, Hollande's included — and proceeded to act skits on the footpath, interacting with passers-by to the general hilarity of the crowd. I file it all in the 'Only in France' folder, along with escargots and nymph-laden bridges.

Cones in hand, we walked through the Jardin des Champs-Élysées, which was bristling with nattily dressed French children who probably don't require bribery of ice cream to induce good behaviour. Perhaps, however, this lovely park is where the seeds are sown for future Parisian rebels. One of its star attractions is a tree-bordered puppet theatre that, since 1818, has been telling the story of Guignol, the marionette famous for taking a stick to the police. Watching Guignol beat up the pompous gendarme puppet, while an audience of usually demure children duly cheered on raucously, was somewhat illuminating.

The Jardin des Champs-Élysées was mapped out in 1667, the year when Paris was lit up by almost three thousand lanterns — sparking its moniker and mythology as the capital of light — and when the city got its first serious police chief. His wide-ranging powers ran the spectrum from prettying street paving to stamping out ugly violence, and his iron-fist-velvet-glove style earned both respect and resentment. To this day, the Parisians have a love–hate relationship with their ever-present police force, which is still highly centralised and all-powerful. But, as every Parisian parent knows, sometimes you need to be told *non* to be kept in line.

Later in the week, we took a day trip to Parc Astérix, the theme park that celebrates the iconic French comic books. First published in 1961, the series has sold hundreds of millions of copies worldwide. I accounted for many of its Australian sales back in the 1980s, although I'm not sure what exactly appealed, as I was what you'd call a girlie-girl, predisposed to prefer stories of Disney princesses to battles between Gaulish tribes and Roman soldiers.

Asterix Park, as you can imagine, is no Disneyland. There are no little girls wearing tiaras and taffeta, for one, and there's a glaring absence of American accents. This is very much a fun park for French kids, who'd rather spin around in cauldrons than teacups, and who like their magic courtesy of Druids, not fairy godmothers. Big kids visit, too, for the whirl of rollercoasters, and what strikes you is that, in this idealised world of Old Gaul, the new French who are there present a fresh face for modern times, a face that comes in many different colours.

The *Asterix* books are often seen as a symbol of France's resistance culture — resistance against globalisation, modernisation, multiculturalism and change of any kind. So how could such an old-fashioned hero speak to kids today? Perhaps the diminutive Asterix, with his stash of magic potion, represents the naughty child we all secretly wish we could be, the one who can punch above his weight and stick it to the big guys.

&

Planning to spend a sunny morning in the Tuileries, we headed for its entrance on Rue de Rivoli, just near the tip of the Louvre, so that I could show the boys the golden statue of my other Gallic childhood icon. Joan of Arc is up there with Eleanor of Aquitaine when it comes to fierce sense of self and all-round girl power, and she's the counter-example I proffer whenever the boys insist that only men can be knights. *Dieu merci* for Jeanne, French mothers of girls must sometimes say, Thank God for Joan. And he did thank her, actually, by way of canonisation.

I noticed a French flag wrapped around a leg of Saint Joan's horse. It was probably tied there after a Euro Cup celebration, but it reminded me that the fifteenth-century warrior had become somewhat of a figurehead for French nationalism of late, embraced by far-right political party the National Front, which had been gaining mainstream ground in recent years. Its leader, Marine Le Pen, had positioned herself as a modern-day Joan, fighting the system, the European Union, immigration, the world in general. If she could ride right back into good old Asterix times, she no doubt would.

We wandered into the park, past the funfair that sets up in the Tuileries for the summer. The boys had had their fix of flashing-light rides for now, so we guided them to the nearby pond for the more simple pleasure of sailing model boats. We found the famous Alain, the man with the rickety trolley of wooden yachts with sun-faded pastel sails, and hired a couple of his lovingly carved boats — some of which date back decades — for two euros a pop. He placed them delicately in the water, and gave Noah and Otto each a stick for steering their sailboats around à l'ancienne, the old-fashioned way. The rest of us sat nearby on metal chairs, expecting the boys to get bored well before the end of their allotted twenty minutes. Instead, they seemed to fall into a meditative trance, almost hypnotised by the slow swirl of their activity.

'Ah, for the good old days,' said Andy. 'When kids had fun for hours on end with little more than a stick.'

The concept of the good old days had taken hold in the political and popular cultural discourse in recent times. My father always pointed out that they weren't really that good in the first place. Still, the modern era of globalisation seemed to scare many, in France as in other Western countries, who reacted by yearning for the supposed simplicity of the past, for a time when borders were more defined, and identity more clear-cut. France, until recently, had not been considered an overly patriotic nation. Proud, sure. But jingoistic, not so much. One theory is that this shirking from displays of flag-waving can be traced back to the Second World War, which showed France the horrors that nationalities can inflict upon one another.

The fabric of French society has dramatically rewoven itself since the war, with new threads of colour and patterns of religious belief. Up to ten per cent of the population of this traditionally Catholic country is now Muslim, one consequence of the collapse of France's colonial empire, which saw many Muslim Algerians flee to France during that country's war of independence. The demographic trend reached a tipping point in 2004, when the government updated its laws on *laïcité* — the concept of secularism formulated in the late nineteenth century to curb the powers of Catholicism — to outlaw, in schools, such symbols of religious affiliation as the Islamic veil, which is a particular pet peeve of the National Front. Nationalists are often accused of racism, but it's not so much a race as a very specific religion they mostly take issue with.

For lunch, we'd booked at a new brasserie in the renovated Les Halles complex, the old food markets site dubbed the belly of Paris by author Émile Zola. True to the sauce-laden heritage of French cuisine, Champeaux serves up such Gallic staples as vols-au-vent, soufflés and escargots, which Andy ordered to the boys' disgust as much as fascination.

'Eww, slimy snotty snails,' they yelled, falling about laughing, when the waiter placed Andy's plate in front of him.

'When am I going to get my perfect French children?' I sighed, looking a little longingly at the next table. A Parisian couple, on one side, was sharing a charcuterie spread and bottle of burgundy, while their three sons sat opposite, playing quietly with toy soldiers as they neatly made their way through their steak-frites. My sons, meanwhile, were squirming around in their seats, faces scrunched up, pretending to be snails. I ordered another glass of wine.

The French love their escargots so much they eat almost a billion of the slugs each year, but the country's tastes are slowly inclining to the exotic, with couscous consistently voted one of France's most popular dishes. You really sense the spicy melting pot that is modern France at Les Halles, which sits atop a station that sees several RER regional train lines constantly transport Parisians from *extra muros* to *intra muros*, giving a multicultural flavour to the inner city.

It's places like this where you feel that social change is not just inevitable, it's actually happening. Still, some believe that France won't truly be multicultural until it accepts people's differences. The official immigration policy is assimilation, which basically requires wearing a conventional French identity along with your stripy top.

'I'd be so honoured to have the chance to live here,' I reflected. 'I'd probably end up acting more French than Catherine Deneuve.'

'Well, that would be easy for a Francophile like yourself,' pointed out Dad. 'Also, you're Catholic, albeit shockingly lapsed, so it would be fairly seamless to meld your world outlook with that of France, which is Catholic in so many ways, despite officially being a secular state.'

Many French citizens say that they simply don't feel French. The problem with assimilation is that its opposite is ghettoisation, as it's all too easy to see in the outer suburbs of Paris, where so many disenfranchised youth live in a perpetual state of poverty and resentment. The various Paris attacks might be forcing France to admit to a social problem, one it has denied for so long. Not out of maliciousness or neglect, I believe. France simply doesn't have the cold, hard statistics to make such a case. The French state is not legally allowed to collect personal information about ethnicity and religion, which has been the case since the end of the Second World War, in order that the types of atrocities carried out by the Vichy government against French Jews can never occur again. So this belief that everyone can and should be equal, even if it has proved tricky to enact in practice, and even if it is going to require a rethink for modern times, comes, I believe, from a good place.

&

All French children are expected to learn the French language to grammatical perfection. School is the factory for moulding, polishing and turning out ideal citizens. The curriculum is standardised across the country, so that everyone is literally on the same neatly lined and penned page when it comes to thinking à la française. Just as school kids are dished up three-course cuisine at the canteen, they're also taught to appreciate culture from a young age. On many a museum visit, I've watched school groups listen intently to curators speak about the brush stroke techniques of Impressionism or the marvels of sculpting in marble. Kids are encouraged to make a regular activity of museums, which are free for students under the age of twenty-six.

We decided to spend the rest of the afternoon at the nearby Centre Georges Pompidou, France's National Museum of Modern Art. 'Pompipoo!' yelled Otto, over and over, like some crazed mantra, all the way there. 'It looks like a big Meccano building,' remarked Noah, adding: 'Actually, I think I'd rather go back to the apartment and play with my Lego.' I sighed once more. This wasn't boding well as a highly cultural experience.

But Pompidou was never meant to be taken seriously, which explains the irreverent inside-out architecture: the colour-coded ducts and pipes and plexiglass tubes of people movers hanging off a metal framework that would look more at home in an oil refinery. The museum opened in 1977, which is not generally a high point in the history of architecture. What's more, time hasn't softened Parisians' general disdain for the design, so at odds with the usual classically minded allure of the city's monuments. Still, it's one of the most visited of the city's museums, proof perhaps that Paris can be as open to modernity as history.

After only an hour, we admitted defeat in our mission to instil in the boys a love of contemporary art — they were more interested in racing along the escalator tubes than perusing the actual exhibitions — and we set off for home. Before long Notre-Dame loomed over us, and we stopped to try out a history lesson. Noah had only just started studying history at school, and was having trouble grasping the concept. 'You mean they're all dead?' he'd ask, eyes welling, whenever we'd speak to him about, say, the gladiators of Ancient Rome or the kings and queens of Versailles. 'Are they in heaven?'

Noah had also begun to take Catholicism classes. To our disappointment our local public school didn't offer general religion as a subject, but required students to identify with one faith, and we had decided to go along with the Catholic concept of heaven. To Noah, the world was a rainbow-filled bubble, and we wanted the dream-state of innocence and wonder to last as long as possible. But heaven, as lovely as we made it sound, was something we preferred him not to dwell on too much, which is why, when his budgie died, she didn't go to the place with the gilded gates and marshmallow clouds; instead, she had flown to Paris for a holiday and ended up staying (she sent a postcard to explain herself). Paris is heaven in a way, as I said to Andy, crossing my fingers that Noah wouldn't think to ask for a rendezvous when we finally made it to Bluey's new home. Fortunately, he had forgotten poor old Bluey by then.

Notre-Dame was built at a time — from the 1160s to 1340s — when Parisians feared the afterlife. Its Gothic style — as it was dismissively named in the modernity-minded Renaissance, in reference to the savage tribes of the Dark Ages — perfectly suited the heavenly aspirations of the era, with pointed arches and spindly spires straining skywards, as though in perpetual prayer. Paris is the birthplace of Gothic, and Notre-Dame one of its finest examples. The cathedral has come to dominate this city physically, but it also soars over the country spiritually, because it's the official heart of France, from where all distances are measured. As my father had pointed out, France remains an intrinsically Catholic country, where clans still ritualistically gather on a Sunday to celebrate life, if not actual Mass, as we ourselves had just done.

But no religion exists in a vacuum in the modern world. Even when the framework of Gothic architecture was being forged, the inspiration came from the East, after the First Crusade opened up trade routes that brought back not just exquisite wares of glass and gold, but also new ways of scientific and mathematical thinking. Have a look at the pointed arches and rib vaulting throughout Notre-Dame. They echo profoundly with Islamic influence, which surely shines a new, bright light on religion in a multicultural society and interconnected world.

'It almost doesn't look real,' commented Andy, as we stood staring at the frontispiece, with its ornamental tiers and towers. 'Like something designed for Disneyland.' It's true. Preservation efforts have spruced up Notre-Dame, scrubbing its stones of dirt and the patina of history. Some authenticity seems to have disappeared in the freshening process, but then again the past in Paris is often not what it appears, being constantly reimagined for a new audience.

Notre-Dame, so scorned and scarred in Revolutionary times, was once a symbol of an autocratic age when royalty and religion ruled in cahoots. Then along came its saviour, in the form of writer Victor Hugo, one of the first French nostalgics and a lover of all things Gothic. His 1831 book *The Hunchback of Notre-Dame* had all the ingredients for a Romantic blockbuster: a character with a dark past, oodles of heart-stirring sentiment and a strong underlying social message — not to mention the beautiful gypsy dancer Esmerelda and a misunderstood freak. Parisians swooned, falling in love with the modern fairy tale, along with their city's past. But Notre-Dame was the real damsel in distress, and she was promptly placed at the top of the restoration list. Architect Eugène Viollet-le-Duc didn't so much resuscitate as reinterpret Notre-Dame, ramping up the Gothic drama with faux medieval masonry, an ornate new spire, and a motley crew of ghoulish beings who lurk up top, along with the old gargoyles, like evil beings from foreboding fairy tales themselves. Viollet-le-Duc has been accused of Disneyfying Notre-Dame and so it's little surprise that the cathedral has actually become a legitimate Disney movie star. 'Quasimodo's house', as Noah calls it.

A few days later, we returned to march the boys' little legs up to Quasimodo's old haunt, around a seemingly endless twirl of time-worn stone steps that resonate with the thud of thought written in stone, as Hugo described Gothic architecture. Noah and Otto, having not yet developed a love for olde-worlde ways, were most unimpressed by the absence of a lift. By the time we reached the parapet connecting the two towers, they were practically as moody as the brooding cluster of horned, winged and hooked creatures that call Notre-Dame home. Perched upon the ledge of the balustrade, these chimeras stare stonily over the mere mortals below, in disdain for the square that was once a bustling medieval quarter before Haussmann razed it in the name of modernisation.

Parisians — like the Gothic guardian sculptures of Notre-Dame — might seem to fear the future, to yearn for the golden days of the past, yet the Eiffel Tower proves that they can also set their minds to forward thinking. Erected in 1889 as the gateway to the Exposition Universelle, which celebrated a new technological age, the tower immediately stood out in a city of classic stone. Gustave Eiffel, a cutting-edge engineer, believed that iron was the future of building, and that medieval cathedrals had taken their medium of stone as far as it could go. His tower was nothing short of a sky-high icon for the industrial age, with its mass-produced prefabricated metal parts assembled on site and secured by 2.5 million hand-hammered rivets. Therein lies the real allure of the tower, because it was a work of the machine but also the hand, melding technological mastery and artisanal elegance. No wonder the effect is both weighty and ethereal, masculine yet feminine.

The tower was intended to stand for only twenty years but wily Monsieur Eiffel proved his creation's long-term value as a communications instrument. To this day, the tower beams radio and television across the city and is still a steeple and shrine to technology. And perhaps that's why children intuitively love it so much, because it's a tower that is open to the world, that shoots for the sky — and, of course, that has lifts. 'Whoah,' cried Noah, as we whizzed by the lattice girders and trusses. 'How cool — another big Meccano building.'

I hadn't bothered with the Eiffel Tower for years — it felt too done, too touristy. But the joy of travelling with children is that you get to polish up memories dulled by time, and see things shiny and fresh once more, as the jaded filter comes off and the rosy glasses go back on. And you can't help but regress to a state of childlike amazement as you step onto the top level of the Eiffel Tower, into a near mystical realm. There are no sullen kids or gloomy chimeras, only communal wide-eyed wonder at the city spread like a map below. As I sipped a glass of champagne (rose-tinted, of course), I watched my boys watch the world with awe, and tried to recall what it was like, when I went up there as a young girl, looking down and seeing how small we are, and yet how collective, how we cross one another's paths like the metal parts in the Eiffel Tower, yet how we also interconnect, riveted by the glue of humanity. It's when you step away and look at the big picture that you can get the best perspective on life. When you zoom out — so that the clothes you wear or the colour of your skin blurs to insignificance — you see that we're all just human beings, trying to make our way in this world as best we can.

&

I finally had a day to myself, which I wholeheartedly devoted to fashion, and searching for something to wear to my father's birthday dinner. Clothes shopping in Paris can be an overwhelming experience and the only way to stay sane, and solvent, is to shop within very clear boundaries. I usually only look for dresses, and even then there are set guidelines: there must be some kind of a sleeve, for instance, and the hemline can never, ever drift north of the knee.

I'm sometimes told I'm small, but I'm actually not. I can always do with losing five kilograms. My trick is to wear dresses that play down any of those bits that would otherwise take a few months of gastronomic deprivation or yogic exertion to deal with, dresses cut to allow for the occasional pastry or chocolate. I don't wear short bandage frocks, in other words, even at the risk of looking unfashionable some seasons. But it's not only the lazy girl's way to keep in shape. I'm just not cut from sheer or tight fabric. It's like I have an in-built modesty rating monitor that lets me size up, at first glance, what will suit me not only physically but psychologically. Like the dress I ended up buying that day: a button-through maxi shirt-style design, with long sleeves, and nifty vertical stripes to create a leaner look, along with a ribbon-belt to cinch in the illusion of a smaller waist.

I've always found my favourite dresses in France, where the word for fashion, *la mode*, is derived from the Latin word *modus* (manner) — just as is *la modestie*. Which means that fashion here is historically and intrinsically modest. French women, you might interject, have a reputation for flirty dressing, along with behaviour — but I've always seen this as mostly a clever marketing ploy to make the world fall in love with *les françaises* (and buy their perfumes and lipsticks while they do). In reality, most French women dress themselves as discreetly and demurely as they do their daughters.

At the time of our holiday, *la mode pudique* was the hot fashion topic. *Pudeur* is a nuanced synonym for modesty in France, defined in the eighteenth century as a fusing of purity and shame. It was all shiny on the surface in its virtuousness, yet had a dark underlining because it suggested that every woman had the potential to come morally undone. You'd think *pudeur* might have gone the way of corsets and chastity belts, but a 2009 poll had 88 per cent of French women calling themselves *pudiques*. But I get this, because the term *pudeur* isn't as loaded anymore, having morphed from a quality of virtue to one of conservative comfort. I'd describe myself as *pudique*, but I make no judgement against women who wear mini skirts — in fact I'm rather envious of their ease in such clothes. And most Parisiennes still cherish having the right to bare skin, even if they don't flaunt it; after all, they live in a city populated with statues and paintings of near-nude nymphs. They believe in retaining a little mystery (remember those secret gardens of theirs — which probably contain a few sexy nymphs, too), but try to take away their right to wear less, and they'd surely take to the streets in indignation.

La mode pudique, however, is getting political. An increasing number of fashion brands have released modesty collections to appeal to Muslim customers, prompting some French identities and intellectuals to accuse this fashion sector of social control and misogyny. So that means I can assert my freedom of sartorial expression by walking down a boulevard in my modest new dress — but a Muslim woman beside me, in her designer *abaya*, will be death-stared for her supposedly demeaning submissiveness.

She would, in fact, be considered more socially provocative than the Parisienne strutting by in a tiny bandage frock. Similarly, I can wrap on an old scarf to hide a bad hair day, but a Muslim Parisienne in a head veil, no matter how gorgeously coloured or patterned it might be, will be scorned.

I get it: the *laïcité* factor. Fashion, in France, is meant to be secular. And don't forget, fashion was originally a tool of conformity there. The Sun King well knew this when he established the industry in the first place, using fashion to bring his rebellious subjects to heel. And yes, on the whole there remains a distinctive French look: the dark jeans, the striped top, the white shirt, the beige trench and so on. If you wanted to assimilate seamlessly, this would be how you'd do it (along with perfecting your subjunctive and learning to love snails). And it's a great look, but the problem is that fashion is no longer a uniform in our globalised society, only altering by the season. It's an ever-changing mode of expression and one of the ways we find our place and personality in that world. That's why some of us dress modestly, and others not, for whatever reason: cultural, religious, psychological, perhaps all of the above. And at any one time, in any one shop, you will find everything from mini skirts to maxi dresses; that's what keeps the fashion industry ticking and the world evolving and us experimenting. After all, we want our kids to have the freedom to dress up when they're little, to try on different costumes and personas — and then surely to grow up with choice to be whoever they want to be. Even Parisians, who know the value of conforming, are also well aware that we're all individualistic rebels at heart.

&

Our celebratory dinner was at La Tour d'Argent, where I had marked my twenty-first birthday half-a-life before. In some ways, it was like stepping back in time: again, we were greeted by a dapper doorman and escorted into a lavish waiting salon, before being whisked up to the top-level dining room, with its mirrored ceiling that creates the impression you're floating beneath a shimmering sky; and once more, we were led to the corner window table, looking out towards the elaborately trussed-up and buttressed Notre-Dame, that eternal symbol of a timeless city; and Dad spent twenty minutes perusing the wine list, which is about as thick as a bible, and as revered; and I ordered a plate of vegetables in a restaurant world-renowned for its duck (they were, needless to say, not your garden-variety steamed veggies).

'*Plus ça change …*' said Mum with a smile.

'Well, I've collected a few wrinkles and grey hairs since then,' remarked Dad.

'Kat has collected a few boys since then,' said Andy. Fortunately, the two littlest ones were back at the apartment with a babysitter, safely out of embarrassment's way.

'My French is nowhere near what it was then,' I said, sighing.

'It's so hard to practise it anymore,' noted Mum. 'Everyone wants to speak English.'

'Maybe they're more open to globalisation than we think,' suggested Dad.

'Or maybe they don't need Anglo-Saxons to be the enemy anymore,' countered Mum.

We all fell silent for a while.

'It's definitely a fraught time for France,' said Dad. 'But you have to remember that this city, more than most, has had its tough times and got through them. It needs to work out how to adapt to globalisation but keep its French way of life, and how to integrate subcultures into that way of life. I think what the French are really good at is thinking something through, philosophising it, finding the right language to move forwards. Just think of the Enlightenment.'

'There's a definite malaise that you feel at the moment, more than the usual French style of pessimism,' said Mum. 'But they're also great at *joie de vivre*, and you have to hope this will win out in the end.'

'For years after you first brought me here, Paris was a fairyland to me,' I said to my parents. 'As I've got to know it over the years, I've realised that it has its faults, like any big city, but I still don't think there's anywhere like it on earth. I love its commitment to a good life even in the face of adversity. It's like a reality check for me. It reminds me to live in the moment, as well as to live for moments just like this.'

Our last day in Paris was Bastille Day, France's official Fête de la Fédération. Andy and I had stayed on so the boys could see the French soldiers in all their regalia. They are, as you can imagine, some of the most fancily dressed troops on the planet, proud descendants of those spiffy medieval knights. The morning's military parade marches down the Champs-Élysées and, rookies as we were, we arrived too late to secure a spot, so ended up back in our apartment, in front of the television with champagne, cheese and *macarons*.

Une parade was originally an assembly of troops for inspection, and as much as there is the grand procession down from the Arc de Triomphe, the Bastille Day ceremony is ultimately one big show-off to the president, who sits front and centre on a stand on Place de la Concorde. 'He's the boss of France?' asked Noah, as we watched François Hollande take his seat. 'I thought he'd wear something a bit more exciting.' To Noah's relief, the following procession of uniforms made up for the president's rather dull dark suit and tie. First came the Republican Guards, dressed in gold-embellished navy liveries and red-feathered hats, like the little wooden soldiers we'd bought in Les Drapeaux de France, the old Palais-Royal store famous for its miniature military figures. The guards performed a choreographed drill show as intricate and graceful as any ballet, criss-crossing one another with the same immaculate neatness and precision as their expertly cut tailoring; 'Only in France could soldiers practically break out into a dance show and not look ridiculous,' observed Andy.

Next came a succession of infantries, marching down the avenue in foot-stomping, arm-swinging synergy, tall and upright like the clipped plane trees that line the sides of the famous street, and the poles bearing tricolour flags. Today marks the day that triggered the beginning of the French Revolution, when Parisians took to the streets in anger and hunger, and stormed the Bastille prison, a symbol of autocracy and injustice. So how ironic that it's now the day when the boulevards and avenues are the domain of the officers of law and order, those figures the Parisians love to hate, perhaps because they remind them of the city's shadowy flipside. Because, as any French parent knows, without order there's chaos.

'I think I want to be a French officer when I grow up,' declared Noah, who has long loved the trappings of formal uniforms, requesting jackets with brass buttons and braided trim. We proceeded to ooh, and sometimes chuckle, over what doubled as an hour-long fashion parade: the tasselled red and yellow epaulettes, the brightly hued bursts of neckerchiefs, an array of hats from slanted berets to metallic helmets to Napoleonic bicorns, the shiny shoes worn with white spats (spats!), the hipster-like leather aprons and long fuzzy beards of the Foreign Legion.

After the parade, we headed outside and back to the Champs-Élysées, the arc up top fluttering an enormous tricolour flag. 'It's funny how Parisians don't seem to wear their national colours, or drape themselves in flags like you see back home,' Andy observed. He was right; perhaps nationalism was taking hold more slowly in the capital. It certainly didn't feel like the moment for a political statement. For many, it was the first day of summer holidays, and there was a lovely light-hearted feel to the atmosphere, as though the air had been diffused with lavender. Parisians, usually so contained and orderly in the way they walk around their city, had softened into relaxed mode, even smiling at strangers. They could be found drinking wine with friends on chequered picnic rugs, playing *pétanque* with family in the city's parks and squares, slouching on rattan chairs *en terrasse* and turning life into playful satire.

The Eiffel Tower lit up with its famous Bastille Day show of fireworks long after the boys' bedtime, so Andy and I were again by the television, champagne in hand. We soon drifted off to dreamland, too, after a holiday that itself seemed a reverie. And then, the nightmare news of the morning jolted us back to the reality of the world: in Nice, a disaffected delivery man had run his lorry through a crowd of beachside revellers, killing scores of people, including children. In this new war of terrorism, not only have the uniforms changed, so have the weapons and the rules.

We left Paris with heavy hearts. The city felt changed, but so did the world. It's far, far from Disneyland, but even there the beloved ride, It's a Small World, acknowledges a planet of laughter as well as tears, hope along with fears. And that's especially so in a world that's getting even smaller, more crowded, making life on earth even more complex.

We have to learn to live with different sensibilities, to respect various opinions, but also realise that words are simply a sometimes-random succession of letters. And yet, conversation matters, because it's how we come to comprehend one another and the universe. And if anyone can create a new lingua franca of understanding, it should surely be the eloquent French, the people who gave the world the official language of diplomacy, after all. We need their intellectuals to speak up and out against hatred, to remind us why we once fell in love with the minds of France, as much as the fashions and fragrances. Few nationalities know how to build such a grand framework for life, how to establish and buttress the big ideas. Because as the French well appreciate, the grandiose notions aren't important in themselves — they're there to shield and protect the little things, the small pleasures. With order, for instance, come the simple delights of sailing old boats in park ponds, or eating Nutella crêpes while sitting by the Seine. France has long been adept at building a world within which its citizens can live calm, contented lives. Their children have *le cadre*, the frame in which to grow; as adults, there are also boundaries, guidelines for a civilised existence. Rules might be made to be broken from time to time, but mostly Parisians prefer harmony — lounging in parks eating pastel *macarons* rather than chanting angrily in the streets.

And maybe, as with Notre-Dame, the foundation structure of France, the *liberté, égalité, fraternité*, is one that needs to be restored or reformed from time to time. Is that really a big deal? The history of Paris demonstrates that cities, as much as citizens, continually evolve for the times. And never have we needed the French to do that more than now. 'Does the latest attack make you want to come back a little less?' asked Andy later that day. 'Are you crazy?' I responded. This is precisely the time we need to remember the importance of the little moments, the simple joys. So no, nothing will keep me away from Paris, keep me from sharing my love of this city with anyone who will listen to me — and, most of all, with my sons. When my parents introduced me to Paris, my world suddenly became all the more wonderful for it. It's only fair that I should pass on the emotional heirloom.

&

'I'd actually rather be a French chef than a French soldier,' Noah informed me soon after we arrived home, dressed in a white apron and *toque* he'd bought from a souvenir stand; this from a child who until recently only ate nine items of food. 'I'm not going to cook snails though,' he added, nose screwed up.

'I want to build huge towers right up to the sky,' declared Otto.

'Then maybe Daddy and I will have to move to Paris with you one day so you can study,' I said, adding hopefully: 'And perhaps you'll end up marrying nice French girls.'

'Eww, girl germs!' they both shrieked, with a grimace.

Hélas … it might be a while before we make it to that particular Parisian chapter.

EPILOGUE

GRANDE DAME

[gRɑ̃d] *adj* great [dam] *nf* lady; respected, usually elderly woman

What's the opposite of déjà vu? As in, something you can picture even though you know it has yet to play out in reality. *Presque vu* means 'almost seen' although it's usually defined as an unfulfilled experience, an ephemeral mental picture that frustratingly, teasingly evaporates in the harsh glare of reality. A vision, perhaps? No, that has the chimerical about it, too. Premonition? No again: too foreboding. Perhaps there's no true antithesis of the relived sensation. Maybe all we have when it comes to the future is, simply, wishful thinking.

I sometimes see a flash of myself as I hope to be one day. I'm in my sixties, maybe seventies. My hair is a halo of silvery strands, which I wear twirled into a French twist, at the risk of exposing the love heart inked on my nape, a mark of both youthful frivolity and artlessness. I've finally bought my own Chanel jacket: collarless, cream bouclé, with black trim. And I've convincingly mastered the art of scarf tying (it's Hermès, by the way — vintage), which conveniently camouflages my tattoo transgression of the past.

Now, let's set the scene: Paris (I know, *quelle surprise*). We're living there several months of the year. Andy has softened his sharp, minimalist interior stance and our apartment is a treasure-trove of gilt-trimmed chairs, twinkling chandeliers and floral rugs, sourced from the city's flea markets. The boys come and go, with their Parisian girlfriends (I can dream, okay). We often have long Sunday lunches, complete with Poilâne bread, an array of pungently perfumed cheese, and a rainbow of *macarons*. Needless to say, I'm still relying on cleverly tailored dresses to keep various gastronomic indulgences in fashionable check.

It's springtime, and I've just spent a couple of midday hours in the Tuileries, reading in the shade of a budding grove of horse chestnut trees. I'm finally close to finishing the epic that is Marcel Proust's *In Search of Lost Time*, an exercise that has indeed lost me months of my life. One of the most linguistically intricate works of literary art, it's the kind of book that reveals its full glory seductively slowly. Tackling Proust requires a concentration we're not used to exercising in this fast-paced age, a total commitment to living in the moment. You often find yourself reading Proust's sentences twice, maybe three or four times, to fully immerse yourself in their mesmerising flow, to appreciate the masterful metaphors and evocative adjectives, or to simply make sense of all the words. This is, after all, the book that boasts the longest sentence in French literature: a whopping 847 words. That's practically a novella in itself.

I look up at the chestnut trees, the white floral cones incandescent against the lush leaves, like candles dotted around a chandelier. Somehow, I find myself noticing the latest burst of flowers more with each season, which is curious, as I theoretically have less time than ever for the proverbial roses. But then, I think, that's what Paris has taught me: to stop and look, smell and taste, live with all senses. Friends sometimes ask why I never tire of this city; the answer is that the experience has been richer each time. Paris, like Proust, teaches you to slow down and savour life. The author wrote that a true journey is not about travelling to new places, but about looking at life with new eyes. You can be anywhere on earth — you might have never left home — but you still have the power to see the world afresh, by searching for new details.

After tossing the almost-finished brick of a book into my Vanessa Bruno tote, I amble along Rue de Castiglione towards Place Vendôme, guided by Napoléon atop his verdigris column. I swerve left, and head into the Ritz, which was beautifully renovated back in 2016, following in the footsteps of Marcel (I'm going to switch to a first-name basis, okay? — him being basically family and all). Here, I take a seat in Salon Proust, a cosy wood-panelled alcove where the author himself once whiled away many hours in thoughtful observation of society life, and order afternoon tea. The feast served up is inspired by the madeleine, the cake that Marcel made famous for the way that it, when dipped in lime-blossom tisane, sent him whirling back into a world of childhood memories.

The petite shell-shaped delicacy, for me, is little more than a pretty treat, but I have many figurative madeleines in Paris. There's the aroma of roasted chestnuts that ignites a vision of fairy-lit Christmas markets. The flavour of salted cocoa is bittersweet, recalling the time I cried heartbroken tears into chocolate ice cream, newly single and alone in a romantic floral-wallpapered hotel room. On my first sip of a pale, dry rosé, I'm once again celebrating my third-of-a-century, dancing under a pastel-*ombré* Parisian sky as the light summer rain shimmers down. And the thick hot chocolate at Angelina smells and tastes like glorious freedom; it was what I gorged myself on in celebration of finishing high school, and in liberation from a period of starving and striving for perfection.

I order a flute of champagne to accompany my tea and tiered trays of cakes. It doesn't, however, send any particular bubble of memory to the surface of my mind. I've evidently drunk too much sparkling wine in my lifetime for it to have fermented into any specific significance.

Marcel loved his champagne, too. Before breaking out as one of history's greatest authors, he was a committed party boy, a regular of the city's aristocratic salons and swankiest soirées, such as the 1898 grand opening of this very hotel, which would quickly become a favourite hang. But Marcel tired of high society, the frothy Belle Époque that was dissolving into gossamer memory as a bold, brash modernity loomed. Not that this nervous old-fashioned soul was excited by the prospect of the new century. Writing was, in large part, his mechanism for coping with an uncertain reality, of slowing down the relentless pace of the march of time, and exerting some measure of control over his own storyline. *In Search of Lost Time* helped him to confront his future — and he did so by looking at how his past fused with his present, which is why his sentences often weave together tenses and times, acknowledging the fluid, interconnected nature of a life we try to neatly segment and order, like chronological chapters in a biography.

Marcel was perhaps also searching for his lost happiness. When you're young, you gleefully exist in the present, with its parties and its shopping and its here-and-now hedonism. But comes a time when you realise that's a very one-dimensional definition of pleasure. You sense that real joy — the kind that makes you want to get up every morning — is about having a purpose to life, something that links your past with your future.

So Marcel, tiring of the shallow glamour of society life, got to work on his thinly veiled autobiography, taking on the future by looking to the past. He no longer lived just day-to-day, but in all dimensions of tense, just like his book. The long nights holed up in that cork-lined room, scrawling feverishly, were most likely not fun in the usual sense — they doubtless triggered hours of angst amid the soul-searching and memory-mining — but these were surely also some of the most satisfying moments of the author's life.

The French, obviously, love their pleasures. This is the country, after all, that invented high fashion and fine dining. It was their Age of Enlightenment that taught the world we all have the right to happiness — and in *this* life, not just the one after. The French constitution, originally inked out in the years of the Revolution, even proclaims the concept of '*bonheur de tous*'. But the French also know that happiness is complex. Often derided for their reticence to smile, they simply shrug their Gallic shoulders and say, *bah*, why grin like an idiot for no reason? For them, happiness is elusive in nature, and most sweetly, satisfyingly enjoyed when attained and earned by a certain struggle. I mean, it took a bloody revolution for happiness to become a universal entitlement in the first place. French history shows that life has its ups and downs, which is perhaps why the French accept the melancholy sorrows and turbulent angsts of life, and put happiness in perspective, just as Realism counterbalances Romanticism.

In this land of contradictions and opposites — a hexagon of a country that encompasses all extremes of climate — it is arguably the continual tension between contrasts that keeps things balanced, ordered and harmonious. It's that taking of the serious things lightly, as much as the light things seriously. It's being as hard on yourself as you are good to yourself. It's the constant questioning of self, the looking at things from all angles, the relentless search for meaning, that keeps the spirits striving high. (Even those black-garbed furrowed-brow Existentialists were blissful in their own perverse way.) It's the fact that everyone is an aesthete, but also a philosopher; it's the importance of a groomed appearance as much as a beautiful mind. It's that beauty belongs to the young, as well as to the old, to the past, but also the present and future.

Paris is where I've grown up, I reflect, as I sit in Salon Proust sipping my tisane and savouring a lemon-iced madeleine. I watch little girls in floral smocks and long plaits skip by with their parents, their world still a wonderland in a snowdome. Then skulk past the sulky, sooty-eyed teenagers, clad in black and shrouded in confused rebellion. I can't help but sigh nostalgically over a gaggle of trussed-up twenty-somethings, as sparkly and bubbly as Bollinger. At the table next to me, a woman in her thirties with a diamond flashing from her ring finger nibbles cake while her paramour whispers sweet nothings. Over in the corner, a mother tries to beg then bribe then blackmail her young children to behave appropriately.

I've played all of these roles during my various times in Paris, this quintessentially feminine realm that has been the domain of so many strong females, and that so naturally welcomes women — especially those in search of their inner Parisienne. Australia might be my country, but Paris is my hometown (to paraphrase Gertrude Stein, the American novelist and honorary Parisienne). I've come here at every life stage, and have never not felt at home in this city that celebrates all ages, this city that is as delightful in the fresh bloom of spring as she is breathtaking in the sparse elegance of winter. A city for all seasons, she's also one for all emotions. There's no better place on earth to either fall in love or mend a heartache, to dance the night away or hunker down with existential angst. I've certainly had some miserable moments here, although mostly elated ones, because Paris has given me my purpose to life. She's my own madeleine, where the past, present and future all suddenly make sense.

Some people find their place in the world at home, others in an ashram in India or on the sun-bleached coasts of Italy or amid the madness of Manhattan. It was Paris that spoke to me, and taught me the most about how to see the world around me — and myself in it. I'm often lulled into an enchanted calmness when I lose myself in Paris, winding around streets steeped in history, and it's like my sense of self sharpens into focus, my place in the world falling into perspective. I think about the countless feet that have walked over the same time-smoothed stones, steps heavy with worries about long-gone everyday lives, and I realise we're but a blip in this universe. It reminds me to enjoy every little second of this precious life. It's little surprise that the French came up with *joie de vivre*, the joy of living. *Joie de vivre* is about indulging not just in beauty and luxury, but also in pure and simple pleasures, such as crunching into a fresh baguette, or chatting about anything and everything over a carafe of house wine as the world rushes by, or strolling for hours on end.

With each visit, as the layers of history revealed themselves a little more, I delved deeper into the city's story, ventured further on the city's streets. The French prize their *lieux de mémoire*, those monuments and museums infused with historical gravity. But we all have our own personal sites of memory that, like Marcel's madeleine, are portals to our past. Many of mine are in Paris, of course, like the café in which I agonised over the meaning of life in my university years. From time to time, as I retrace old steps, I notice that a beloved old shop or restaurant has been shuttered up, and a pang twists my heart, but then I realise that the new lick of paint has not erased my recollections — they're only a pastry-thin layer away. You might not be able to completely re-create a memory, as Marcel lamented, but you can still keep it alive. All you need to do is remember.

The world might change — and you, too, might continually transform yourself, as you grow into new life stages. You can let the past run away from you, or you can run away from the past. Or you can simply run away. But the past is always there, ready for recall at the click of a button or dunk of a cake or close of the eyes.

Paris has taught me to revere, not regret, the past, but not at the expense of enjoying the present. She has shown me how to love the good things in life, but also the simple ones; to worship family and friends above all, but never forget my place in wider society; to live to eat; to work to live, and to live within my means; to fight the dreaded groundhog-day life known as *boulot-métro-dodo* (job, train, sleep) by never being too busy to stop and just be. Because when you exist in the moment, or even a past moment, this is when you have time to reflect, to recalibrate your perspective, to reconnect with yourself, or who you really want to be.

I've always loved that the French don't slavishly follow trends, even though their fashion industry sets most of them. In the same way, their style of beauty is not prescriptive, but vague enough to be personalised. Abstract in nature, French beauty isn't weighed down by the concrete. It's not set in stone, in other words, although sometimes it literally is: in the sculptures, the bridges, the buildings. It's this all-encompassing, often overwhelming nature of beauty in Paris — at once humbling and heart-soaring — that keeps many women going back, and back to the city. But this multifaceted definition of beauty has also shone a new light on beauty for me, as a writer who specialises in the subject, as well as a woman who is ageing. Perspective, it turns out, is a pretty effective beauty treatment — especially when that viewpoint is Parisian.

I order another glass of champagne, and salute Paris, the City of Light, of love, of lipstick — and, above all, of life.

~ FIN ~

A NOTE FROM THE AUTHOR ABOUT THE FONT

This book has been set in Adobe Garamond, a beautifully clean and elegant font that was inspired by the work of the early-sixteenth-century Parisian punchcutter, Claude Garamond. Toiling away in the era of the French Renaissance, Monsieur Garamond was also a star of the so-called Golden Age of French Typography. Back when scribes were artists and printers were goldsmiths, Garamond's exquisite hand-cut metalwork helped to move the written word from Blackletter (a.k.a. the fierce barbaric font known as Gothic) towards Roman, encouraging the French language to make itself over in time for the *grand siècle* of the 1600s. In this way, Garamond gave form to the modern French language, and remains to this day timelessly chic. You could, in fact, say that it is the Parisienne of fonts: slim and neat, but with a touch of panache, just as a local might set off her sleek jeans and Chanel jacket with a nonchalant beret. And as for the exuberant flourish that is the italicised Garamond ampersand — *&* — surely that's the font equivalent of a Parisienne's swirled-on scarf?

ACKNOWLEDGEMENTS

They say it takes a village to raise a child. The French say it, too. *Il faut tout un village* … A book being basically a baby (albeit with a sometimes elephantine gestation period), I was blessed to have a particularly brilliant town around me — my own little literary City of Light. So I cannot truly sign off without sending a big *bisou* and *merci* to …

Selwa Anthony, my wonderful, kind-hearted, glamorous agent, for taking a chance on me, for holding my hand throughout this epic journey of ups and downs (but mostly ups), and for always having the door open for tea, cheesecake and chats (thanks, too, of course, to Brian and Linda for always being there).

Drew Keys, for giving me the confidence to push through in those early, slightly befuddled days, when my manuscript meandered around like a first-time visitor to Paris without a map or sunglasses.

The various publishers and editors I saw early on, who happily gave me their time and constructive advice, with no strings attached.

HarperCollins. I'm still pinching myself to have such a dream publishing team. I am forever indebted to Catherine Milne, my publisher, for her warmth and wisdom; and to Nicola Robinson, my editor, for her unfailing encouragement, awesome organisational skills, and shared enthusiasm for Emmanuel Macron's victory (oh, and for letting me squeeze in a few thousand more words). It has been beyond inspiring to work with such lovers of fonts, facts and em dashes.

Virginia Lloyd, for such gentle and generous guidance at the structural stage of things — for prodding me where I needed to be prodded, and also pulling me back from where I didn't need to go. This book is immeasurably better for her involvement. Julia Cain, for taking a gilded fine-tooth comb to the almost-completed manuscript, and pushing me to polish things up even more — while helping to control the excess of adjectives like 'twinkling' and 'glittering' (it's the beauty writer in me!). Nicola Young, our proofreader, for her awe-inspiring mastery of grammar as much as her appreciation of French culture, and for keeping me on point — as well as *en pointe.* I could not have wished for a more formidable squad of editors and readers.

Josephine Pennicott, who first encouraged me to write a book, so many years ago, and who graciously passed on my early manuscript to Selwa, also her agent.

Sarah Ayoub, for her belief in and excitement for the book from the get-go.

Clémentine Campardou, for her soul-satisfyingly beautiful illustrations, and for casting her stylish eye over my French vocabulary. I'm so thrilled that her inner *australienne* got to work with my inner *parisienne.*

Yasemin Trollope and Jocelyn Petroni, for sparking the idea for the book in the first place. It is to date my all-time favourite Café de Flore session.

Kirsten Carriol, Elsa Morgan and Yasmin Boland, my three Parisian graces as much as muses.

Mija Crasnich, Anna Hamilton and Carolyn Cliffe, for keeping the pompoms fluttering.

Mum and Dad, for introducing me to Paris, and for always believing that I would eventually reach my ideal destination, despite all the day-dreamy strolling and scenic detours along the way. I could not possibly have better Paris travel partners, nor life guides.

Andy, for giving me his home office (complete with rose-tinted windows and angel on ceiling), putting up with the various bouts of hysteria and plagues of post-it notes, and for coming to accept that I will never get over my Paris obsession. But, most of all, for his unerring faith in me.

Noah and Otto, for giving me the ultimate reason to continue to relive the wonders of Paris, that City of Light and life.

BIBLIOGRAPHY

Thomas Asbridge, *The Crusades: The Authoritative History of the War for the Holy Land*, Simon & Schuster, London, 2010.

Andrew Ayers, *The Architecture of Paris*, Edition Axel Menges, Stuttgart & London, 2004.

Elisabeth Badinter, *The Conflict: Woman and Mother*, Text Publishing, Melbourne, 2011.

Sarah Bakewell, *At the Existentialist Café: Freedom, Being and Apricot Cocktails*, Chatto & Windus, London, 2016.

Muriel Barbery, *The Elegance of the Hedgehog*, Gallic Books, London, 2008.

Julie Barlow & Jean-Benoît Nadeau, *The Bonjour Effect: The Secret Codes of French Conversation Revealed*, St Martin's Press, New York, 2016.

Anne Berest, *Sagan: Paris 1954*, trans. Heather Lloyd, Gallic Books, London, 2014.

Philipp Blom, *Wicked Company: Freethinkers and Friendship in Pre-Revolutionary Paris*, Phoenix, London, 2011.

Noelene Bloomfield, *Almost a French Australia: French-British Rivalry in the Southern Ocean,* Halstead Press, Sydney, 2012.

Julia Child & Alex Prud'homme, *My Life in France,* Anchor Books, New York, 2007.

Colette, *The Claudine Novels,* trans. Antonia White, Penguin Books, London, 1956.

Jonathan Conlin, *Tales of Two Cities: Paris, London and the Birth of the Modern City*, Atlantic Books, London, 2013.

Benedetta Craveri, *The Age of Conversation,* trans. Teresa Waugh, New York Review Books, New York, 2005.

Alain de Botton, *How Proust Can Change your Life*, Picador, London, 1997.

Joan DeJean, *How Paris Became Paris: The Invention of the Modern City*, Bloomsbury, New York, 2014.

Joan DeJean, *Tender Geographies: Women and the Origins of the Novel in France,* Columbia University Press, New York, 1991.

Joan DeJean, *The Age of Comfort: When Paris Discovered Casual — and the Modern Home Began*, Bloomsbury, New York, 2009.

Joan DeJean, *The Essence of Style: How the French Invented High Fashion, Fine Food, Chic Cafés, Style, Sophistication, and Glamour*, Free Press, New York, 2005.

Madame de Lafayette, *The Princess of Cleves*, trans. Nancy Mitford, New Directions, New York, 1951.

Christophe Destournelles, *Old-Fashioned Corners of Paris*, The Little Bookroom, New York, 2013.

David Downie, *A Passion for Paris: Romanticism and Romance in the City of Light*, St Martin's Press, New York, 2015.

David Downie, *Paris, Paris: Journey into the City of Light*, Broadway Books, New York, 2005.

Pamela Druckerman, *French Children Don't Throw Food: Parenting Secrets from Paris*, Doubleday, London, 2012.

Alexandre Dumas fils, *Camille*, Signet Classics, New York, 1984.

Francine Du Plessix Gray, *Madame de Staël: The First Modern Woman*, Atlas & Co., New York, 2008.

Henry Dwight Sedgwick, *Madame Récamier: The Biography of a Flirt*, The Bobbs-Merrill Company, Indianapolis & New York, 1940.

Piu Marie Eatwell, *They Eat Horses, Don't They?: The Truth About the French*, Head of Zeus, London, 2013.

Gustave Flaubert, *Madame Bovary*, trans. Alan Russell, Penguin Books, London, 1950.

Antonia Fraser, *Marie Antoinette: The Journey*, Weidenfeld & Nicolson, London, 2001.

Leonie Frieda, *Catherine de Medici: Renaissance Queen of France*, Weidenfeld & Nicolson, London, 2003.

Marc Fumaroli, *When the World Spoke French*, trans. Richard Howard, New York Review Books, New York, 2001.

Nancy Goldstone, *The Rival Queens: Catherine de' Medici, Her Daughter Marguerite de Valois, and the Betrayal That Ignited a Kingdom*, Little, Brown and Company, New York, 2015.

Adam Gopnik, *Paris to the Moon*, Random House, New York, 2008.

Sudhir Hazareesingh, *How the French Think: An Affectionate Portrait of an Intellectual People*, Basic Books, New York, 2015.

Ernest Hemingway, *A Moveable Feast*, Charles Scribner's Sons, New York, 1964.

Jacques Hillairet, *Connaissance du Vieux Paris*, Editions de Minuit, Paris, 1951.

Lisa Hilton, *The Real Queen of France: Athénaïs & Louis XIV*, Little, Brown, London, 2002.

Lucinda Holdforth, *True Pleasures: A Memoir of Women in Paris*, Vintage Books, Sydney, 2004.

Alistair Horne, *Seven Ages of Paris*, Macmillan, New York, 2002.

Andrew Hussey, *Paris: The Secret History*, Bloomsbury, New York, 2006.

Diane Johnson, *Into a Paris Quartier: Reine Margot's Chapel and Other Haunts of St.-Germain*, National Geographic Society, Washington DC, 2005.

Colin Jones, *Paris: Biography of a City*, Allen Lane, London, 2004.

Julie Kavanagh, *The Girl Who Loved Camellias: The Life and Legend of Marie Duplessis*, Vintage Books, New York, 2014.

Marie-Morgane Le Moël, *The Truth About French Women*, Random House, Sydney, 2015.

Antoine Lilti, *The World of the Salons: Sociability and Worldliness in Eighteenth-Century Paris*, trans. Lydia G. Cochrane, Oxford University Press, New York, 2005.

Herbert Lottman, *Colette: A Life*, Minerva, London, 1991.

Paula J. Martin, *Suzanne Noël: Cosmetic Surgery, Feminism and Beauty in Early Twentieth-Century France*, Ashgate, Farnham, Surrey, 2014.

Tilar J. Mazzeo, *The Hotel on Place Vendôme: Life, Death, and Betrayal at the Hôtel Ritz in Paris*, HarperCollins, New York, 2014.

Mary McAuliffe, *Dawn of the Belle Epoque: The Paris of Monet, Zola, Bernhardt, Eiffel, Debussy, Clemenceau, and Their Friends*, Rowman & Littlefield, Lanham, Maryland, 2011.

Mary McAuliffe, *Twilight of the Belle Epoque: The Paris of Picasso, Stravinsky, Proust, Renault, Marie Curie, Gertrude Stein, and Their Friends through the Great War*, Rowman & Littlefield, Lanham, Maryland, 2014.

Nancy Mitford, *Madame de Pompadour*, Penguin Books, London, 1954.

Nancy Mitford, *Voltaire in Love*, Hamish Hamilton, London, 1957.

Jean-Benoît Nadeau & Julie Barlow, *Sixty Million Frenchmen Can't Be Wrong (Why We Love France But Not the French)*, Sourcebooks, Naperville, Illinois, 2003.

Jean-Benoît Nadeau & Julie Barlow, *The Story of French: The Language that Travelled the World*, Portico, London, 2006.

Marcel Proust, *Remembrance of Things Past: 1*, trans. C.K. Scott Moncrieff & Terence Kilmartin. Chatto & Windus, London, 1981 (first published 1913).

Elaine Sciolino, *La Seduction: How the French Play the Game of Life*, St Martin's Griffin, New York, 2011.

Valerie Steele, *Paris Fashion: A Cultural History*, Oxford University Press, New York, 1988.

Anthony Sutcliffe, *Paris: An Architectural History*, Yale University Press, New Haven & London, 1993.

Lucy Wadham, *The Secret Life of France*, Faber & Faber, London, 2009.

Alison Weir, *Eleanor of Aquitaine: By the Wrath of God, Queen of England*, Pimlico, London, 2000.

Edith Wharton, *French Ways and Their Meaning*, Berkshire House Publishers, Lee, Massachusetts, 1997 (first published 1919).

Edmund White, *The Flâneur: A Stroll Through the Paradoxes of Paris*, Bloomsbury, London, 2001.

Kate Williams, *Josephine: Desire, Ambition, Napoleon*, Arrow Books, London, 2013.

Marilyn Yalom, *How the French Invented Love: Nine Hundred Years of Passion and Romance*, Harper Perennial, New York, 2012.

~ for the complete bibliography, visit www.theparisdreamer.com ~